THREADS OF TIME

BOOKS BY PETER BROOK

THE EMPTY SPACE
A Book About the Theatre:
Deadly, Holy, Rough, Immediate

THE SHIFTING POINT
Theatre, Film, Opera 1946–1987

THE OPEN DOOR
Thoughts on Acting and Theatre

PETER BROOK

THREADS OF TIME

RECOLLECTIONS

A CORNELIA & MICHAEL BESSIE BOOK

COUNTERPOINT
WASHINGTON, D.C.

Library of Congress Cataloging-in-Publication Data
Brook Peter.
    Threads of time: recollections / Peter Brook.
    "A Cornelia & Michael Bessie book."
    Includes index.
    1. Brook, Peter. 2. Theatrical producers and directors — Great Britain —
Biography. 3. Motion picture producers and directors — Great Britain —
Biography. I. Title.
    PN2598.B69A3   1998
    792'.0233'092 — dc21
    [B]   97-52007

ISBN 1-887178-35-X (hardcover: alk. paper)

Book and jacket design by Caroline McEver
Composition by Graphic Composition, Inc.

Printed in the United States of America on acid-free paper that meets the American
National Standards Institute Z39-48 Standard.

A Cornelia and Michael Bessie Book
COUNTERPOINT
P.O. Box 65793
Washington, D.C. 20035-5793

10 9 8 7 6 5 4 3

For Natasha

WITHOUT CORNELIA BESSIE, THIS BOOK
WOULD NEVER HAVE BEEN WRITTEN.
AND WITHOUT CORNELIA IT
WOULD NEVER HAVE BEEN REWRITTEN,
AGAIN AND AGAIN, IN THE LIGHT
OF HER SYMPATHETIC, PENETRATING,
AND ALWAYS INVALUABLE CRITICISM.

I

I could have called this book *False Memories*. Not because I want consciously to tell a lie but because the act of writing proves that there is no deep freeze in the brain where memories are stored intact. On the contrary, the brain seems to hold a reservoir of fragmentary signals that have neither color, sound, nor taste, waiting for the power of imagination to bring them to life. In a way, this is a blessing.

At this moment, somewhere in Scandinavia, a man with a prodigious capacity for total recall is also recording his life. I am told that as he puts down every detail that his memory provides, it is taking him a year to write a year, and as he started late he can never catch up. His predicament makes it clear that autobiography has another aim. It is to peer into a bewildering confusion of indiscriminate, incomplete impressions, never quite this, never quite that, in an attempt to see whether, with hindsight, a pattern can emerge.

As I write, I do not feel a compulsion to tell the whole truth. It is impossible, however hard one tries, to penetrate into the obscure areas of one's own hidden motivations. Indeed, there are taboos, hang-ups, and areas of obscurity behind this story that I am not exploring, and I certainly do not feel that personal relationships, indiscretions, indulgences, excesses, names of close friends, private angers, family adventures, or debts of gratitude — which alone could fill a ledger — can have a place here, any more than the well-known splendors and miseries of first nights. I have no respect at all for the school of biography that believes if every social, historical, and psychological detail is added together, a true portrait of a life appears. Rather, I side with Hamlet when he calls for a flute and cries out against the attempt to sound the mystery of a human being, as though one could know all its holes and stops. What I am trying to weave together as best I can are the threads that have helped to develop my own practical understanding, in the hope that somewhere they may contribute usefully to someone else's experience.

The nurse tries to be kind to the five-year-old boy, who is puzzled at finding himself in a hospital bed in the middle of the night. "Do you like oranges?" she asks. "No," I answer stubbornly. Irritated that her customary trick has failed, she loses her patience. "You're going to have them anyway," she snaps, and I'm wheeled to the operating theater. "Here, smell these oranges," she says, as a mask is clamped over my nostrils. Immediately, there is a roaring and a bitter smell, a wild plunging and a surging swing upward. I try to hold on, but I lose; noise and fear merge into pure horror, then oblivion. It was a first disillusion, and it taught me how hard it is to let go.

Years go by. I am dressed for war. It's a disguise; this anonymous figure can't be me. But there's a war on and a student at Oxford has to pay for his privileges once a week by training to be an officer, because an undergraduate is officer material. Since childhood, the thought of war has terrified me, but because it seemed to take place far outside normal time, I always believed that if it came, I could escape by hiding under my bed for the duration. Now I see that I can't get out of it so easily and, all excuses and evasions having failed, I'm on parade, in heavy boots and a scratchy tunic.

Today is our first experience of the Obstacle Course. When the whistle blows, we set off, the sergeants shouting encouragement and all the enthusiasts charging forward, with leaps at the ropes, vaulting over the barriers, eagerly scaling the scaffolding. I come last, from school days a professional shirker, ignoring the sergeant's jeers, dragging myself laboriously over the mock-up walls and instead of jumping, sliding down until I hang by one hand, before dropping cautiously to the ground. By the time it comes to crossing the river on a log, the others have long since reached the other bank and are vanishing with joyful shouts into the distance. The sergeant waits for me. "Come on, sir!" he roars.

The tone is insulting, but I am a budding officer, so the "sir" is mandatory.

I put my great boot on the log and grab a branch from an overhanging tree. Now both feet are on the log. "Come on, sir!" I advance. "Let go of the branch!" I do so. Two more steps, I reach up to steady myself and catch hold of a leaf. The leaf gives me courage, I walk forward, my balance is good, I can manage. The log stretches ahead of me across the water, the sergeant beckons encouragingly. Another step. The hand holding the leaf is even with my shoulder; another step and it's behind me. I'm balanced, confident, but my arm's fully extended. I can't take another step unless I let go of the leaf, and I can't let go. "Let go of the leaf!" the sergeant bellows. "Damn it, let go of that bloody leaf!" I resist. He roars. I call on all my willpower to force my fingers to let go, but they refuse. With my arm way behind me, I try to go forward. The leaf still gives me confidence, my arm is stretched to its full limit, it pulls me one way, my feet go the other. For a moment, I lean like the Tower of Pisa, then at long last I let go of the leaf and fall splashing into the stream below.

Again and again I return to this picture: the log and the leaf have become part of my private mythology; in a way they contain the essential conflict that I have tried all my life to resolve — when to cling to a conviction, and when to see through it and let go.

When I was a child, I had an idol. It wasn't a protective deity, it was a film projector. For a long while, I was never allowed to touch it, as only my father and my brother could understand its intricacies. Then the time came when I was considered old enough to attach and thread the little reels of nine-and-a-half-millimeter Pathé film, to set up a tiny cardboard screen within the proscenium of my toy theater and to watch with ever-repeated fascination the scratched gray images. Despite my love for the pictures it produced, the projector itself was a dour and charmless machine. There was, however, a shop I would pass every day on my way back from school, and in the window stood a cheap toy projector, made of red and gold tin. I coveted it. Again and again, my father and my brother would explain to me that this object of my desires was nothing compared with the serious grown-up instrument we had at home, but I refused to be convinced; the lure of the trashy redness was stronger than any persuasion they could offer. Then my father would ask me, "What would you prefer, a shining golden penny or a dirty gray sixpence?" I was tormented by the question, I could feel it had a catch to it, but I would always settle for the gleaming penny.

One afternoon, I was taken to Bumpus, a bookshop in Oxford Street, to see a performance for children on a nineteenth-century toy theater. This was my first theatrical experience, and to this day it remains not only the most vivid but also the most real. Everything was made of cardboard: on the cardboard proscenium, Victorian notables leaned stiffly forward in their painted boxes; under the footlights in the orchestra pit a conductor, baton in hand, was suspended for eternity preparing to attack the first note. Nothing moved; then all of a sudden the red and yellow picture of a tasseled curtain slid upward and *The Miller and His Men* was under way. I saw a lake made of parallel rows of blue cardboard with wavy lines and wavy edges; in the far distance the tiny cardboard figure of a man in a boat, rocking slightly, passed through the painted water from one side to another, and when he returned in the opposite direction he seemed closer and bigger, for each time he was pushed into the wings by a long wire, he was invisibly replaced by a larger version of himself, until in the final entrance, the same figure was fully two inches tall. Now he was out of the boat with a menacing pistol in hand, and he slid magnificently to center stage. This grand entrance, worthy of a leading man, was absolute reality, as was the moment when hidden hands whipped away a mill with sails that really turned and a summer sky, blue with fleecy white clouds, and in their place dropped a lurid picture of the same mill in apocalyptic explosion, with fragments bursting from its orange core. Here was a world far more convincing than the one I knew outside.

Childhood is happily literal; thinking in metaphors has not yet begun to complicate the world. Even if one never asks oneself, "What is real?," childhood is a constant wandering back and forth across the borders of reality. Then, as one grows up, one either learns to distrust the imagination or else one comes to dislike the everyday and seek refuge in the unreal. I was to discover that the imaginary is both positive and negative — it opens on to a treacherous field, where truths are often hard to distinguish from

illusions and where both throw shadows. I had to learn that what
we call living is an attempt to read the shadows, betrayed at every
turn by what we so easily assume to be real.

Lying in my bed with the sort of fever that makes the sheets rough
and the day interminable, I would hear noises from the floor below and interpret them as the grinding of the Earth Submarine,
from the comic I read every week. I was convinced that at any
moment it would bore its way through the floor, and its rakish
captain would invite me to join him in a new and perilous underground adventure. My dialogue was all ready, but he never came,
so I would return to my true fetish, two precious rolls of professional cinema film that I had found in some dump. I would hold
them up to the light, framed between two fingers, making them
come to life with tiny jerks of the wrist. One was tinted green,
and it showed two men in silhouette on a roof, while the other
in pinkish red showed a figure slowly opening a door. Each time
a new story would emerge from these fragments of action, and I
happily discovered that the possibilities were inexhaustible. Cinema and theater seemed made to help one to go "somewhere
else."

At the big radio exhibition, a crowd had gathered around a box,
watching a gray and grainy image on a tiny glass screen. I pushed
my way to the front to see this great new invention called television. The miniature picture showed a man drawing a gun. At
once I was swept inside the screen; the crowds, the exhibition
hall, all vanished, and nothing mattered anymore. I was part of
the story, only interested to know what happened next, experienc-
ing for the first time how quickly an illusion can grab hold of us,
how easily our substance dissolves and we disappear into the
unreal.

Another time, my mother and I slipped to our seats in a little
Swiss mountain cinema at the moment when the trailer for the
next week's film was on the screen. Here, too, the picture showed
a man with a gun, but this time it was pressed against a girl's
head, just visible on a pillow in the dark. "Wo ist der Schlüssel

der Garage?" he was murmuring. To this day, I hear this phrase and it gives me the same shudder. "Where is the key to the garage?" A quarter of a century later Brecht explained to me how important it was for him to prevent an audience from identifying with what happens on the stage. For this he had invented a whole series of devices such as placards, slogans, and very bright lights to keep the spectator at a safe distance. I listened to him politely but remained unconvinced. Identification is far more subtle and subversive than he seemed to imply. A television screen is bright, and while we know in our bones that it is a box and we are in our own room, nonetheless if a finger is rightly raised we identify with it. A gun, a clenched fist, and the illusion is complete. Where is the key to the garage?

The movies were my real windows on another world. I rarely went to a play and if I did so, it was reluctantly, dragged off by my artistically minded mother while my father would say with a wink, "We're not highbrow, you and me, we like films." Once inside the theater, I was usually fascinated, but it was neither the story nor the acting but the doors and the wings that captured my imagination. Where did they lead? What lay behind? One day, the curtain rose and the set was not just the three walls of a drawing room. It was the deck of a ship, of a real ocean liner, and it was inconceivable that such a splendid vessel could end abruptly in the wings. I had to know what corridors led away from those thick iron doors and what was out there beyond the portholes. If it was not the sea, it had to be the unknown.

Every day, to go to school, I would take the London Underground; the Tube, a train as cylindrical as its name, would nose its way through round tunnels and in each station, on every platform, there were doors marked NO ENTRY. I evolved wild fantasies round these entrances, convinced they hid obscure labyrinths that led to a world below the city, and I longed to turn the handle of the forbidden iron doors, just to peer within. I could never pluck up the courage to do so, but I always had the intimation that just behind the wall lay another world, accessible, rich with mystery, full of wonder — which could lead to another and still another until it reached a last one that was completely invisible. On half-days from school, I bicycled into the country and would lie on the ground, trying to hear the breathing of the earth. I wanted to thrust myself into nature, so I pressed on the rocks as though they were doorbells, in the hope that some primitive power, some unheard-of creature would answer my call. One day, as I lay contented in the long grass, a sudden question arose from nowhere and grasped me by the throat. "What if at this moment you are as close as you will ever be to the truth? What if the rest of life will be a gradual moving away from what you are now?"

Attractive girls, podgy girls sweating and unappetizing, young men in bowler hats and striped trousers reading the financial pages of their newspapers — my eye as a fascinated sixteen-year-old would pass to and fro across the row of figures in the Underground train. Each time it came to rest on an older person looking vacantly into nowhere, an intimate voice would murmur in my ear a line of T. S. Eliot's that I had learned at school: "In the halt between stations, the mental emptiness deepens," and the same questions would recur: "Why is growing up a decline? Do the shoulders have to stoop with passing time, does the excitement have to wane? Is this part of nature's plan, this slow slipping-down toward the grave?"

I would walk along the street looking at my fellow humans with a sense of wonder I have never lost, asking myself, "What are these creatures? How odd they look!" I would see the faces without recognition, as we imagine Martians, just balls of flesh, slitted and potted with curious bumps and holes, and I would stare, as though momentarily endowed with the eyes of the future, at the absurdity and ugliness of the motorized boxes of armor wheeling these people up and down the street.

I read books of science, not so much because I liked facts and measurements but because I was captivated by the ideas they aroused. In those days, a writer called James Dunne was making a great stir with books on Time, and as I devoured them, it seemed to me that all life's questions were finally resolved. Eternity, he wrote, is the keyboard of a piano, and Time is the hand that strikes the notes. The explanation seemed flawless, both elegant and complete.

Walking along Charing Cross Road one day, peering into the windows of the bookshops, my eye had been caught by a fat volume on display. On its cover in large letters was printed the magic word *Magick*. At first I was ashamed at my interest and several times would enter the shop and pretend to rummage on other shelves before furtively turning its pages. Suddenly, a footnote caught my attention: "A pupil who reaches the grade of Magister Primus can produce wealth and beautiful women. He can also call up armed men at will." This was irresistible, and although the book was far too expensive for me, I bought it and at once set out to trace the author, whose very name, Aleister Crowley, was notorious enough to produce a thrill of excitement and fear. A letter to the publisher produced a phone number, which led to an appointment at an address in Piccadilly, where gentlemen-about-town lived in expensive service flats. The great magician was elderly, green-tweeded, and courteous. He had been known in the twenties as "The Wickedest Man in the World," but I think he was down on his luck. He seemed touched by my interest, and we met a few times, strolling along Piccadilly together where to my great embarrassment he would stand in the middle of the traffic at noon to raise his elaborately carved walking stick and chant an invocation to the sun. Once he took me into the Piccadilly Hotel for lunch, and again in the crowded and startled dining room, he roared out a conjuration across the soup. Later he allowed me to hide him in my bedroom in Oxford so that I could make a sensation by producing him at the height of a college party, and on the same occasion he outraged a waiter at the Randolph Hotel who asked him for his room number by bellowing, "The number of the Great Beast, of course — 666!"

When I did my first production in London, *Doctor Faustus*, he agreed to be magical adviser and came to a rehearsal, having first made me promise that no one should know who he was, as he just wanted to watch unseen from the back of the stalls. But when Faustus began his incantation, it was too much for him and he was on his feet, roaring impressively, "No! No, no! You need a bowl of bull's blood. That'll bring real spirits, I promise you!" Then he added with a broad wink, "Even at a matinee." He had demystified himself, and we laughed together.

What dominated my early years was alternately a natural skepticism and a delight in mockery, and on another level, a longing for belief. At school, Scripture had been taught by a Mr. Habershon. He wore a clerical collar and had a trick of rubbing his face with both hands so that it looked as though he had scraped away a layer of skin, leaving the whole face corrugated and red. I had learned as a child that I was Jewish and Russian, but these words were abstract concepts to me; my impressions were deeply conditioned by England: a house was an English house, a tree was an English tree, a river was an English river. Our school chapel was a place where we sniggered from boredom, yet at times it glowed with secret ardor, so when the age came for us all to be candidates for confirmation, I went to Mr. Habershon, confused, shamefaced, wanting so much to be taken by him on his special religious journey yet painfully embarrassed at the thought that I was opening my heart to the butt of our jokes and fearful that I might be forced to mention God in our liberal, scientifically minded home. Mr. Habershon sat there, rubbing his face: "There's a time in life when you know without question 'This is the moment.' If you let it pass, it will never come again." He rubbed his face again, as if it were a crystal ball in which he could read the truth. I wasn't quite clear which moment he was referring to, but I went through with the ceremony of confirmation. His phrase has haunted me ever since. Can one ever know "This is the moment"? I still wonder and shudder at the thought that I might have let it pass, that I am letting it pass again.

At Oxford each morning, there was a very precious moment of solitude when I would pass through a gate that led to a private path which ran beside the river. It was thickly overgrown, but the sun, when it shone, illuminated every twig, bringing into sharp relief each complex tangle of branch, stem, and leaf. When I walked there, I would revel in these inexhaustible patterns, for the details moved and rearranged themselves with every step I took, and I would go slower and slower, even rocking forward, then backward, to shake the details of the kaleidoscope and enjoy more and more intense glimpses into the ever-changing atoms of perception. I would become aware that a sigh was arising in me from some deep unknown source and that the sense of beauty was inseparable from a special sadness, as though the aesthetic experience was a reminder of a paradise lost, creating an aspiration — but toward what I could not say.

Many years later, experimenting with hallucinogenic drugs, I swallowed a pill made from the Mexican mushroom and at first was disappointed not to enter into a world of extraordinary visions. Then to my surprise, it awoke an infinite sensibility just in the point of my index finger. This time, my perception of detail through touch was so rich and full that I felt I would willingly surrender all my other senses, accepting to be both deaf and blind, if only touch were left, for that tiny point was universe enough. Had I penetrated to the heart of the fleeting moment?

It has often been said that the Elizabethan theater was the image of the world. The open stage was a busy marketplace, its trapdoor led down to hell, the curtained inner stage exposed the confidences of private life that four walls hide, the balcony was that higher level from which some may look down so that others can look up, and the highest gallery was a reminder that the order of the world is maintained by gods, goddesses, kings, and queens.

In the same way, the house where I grew up was the image of a complete universe — a universe located at 27 Fairfax Road, London, W.4, telephone Chiswick 0575.

As you came through the gate, behind the box hedge was a tiny front garden with a step that led to a green front door, with a brass knocker and the number in shining brass, which when summer came was concealed by a striped but faded cotton awning. To one side and at the lower level was the back door, called the tradesman's entrance. This meant that unimportant persons had access to a narrow passage, full of bicycles, with a door through which at some early age I had toddled, only to fall crying in terror, bumping down wooden stairs into the darkness of our cellar. Here was a complete underworld of coal and cobwebs and grime, where a dim yellow lamp threw fearful shadows, where strange square airholes, too small to crawl through, led to nowhere. Yet this was a place of blackness that had its own light, its own warmth, its own security, and when the war came, the underworld became our shelter from the bombs. My perfectionist father furnished it with beds and little decorations, and my mother later swore that the happiest time of her life was holding her family close to her in this deep womb. In the passage next to the cellar door was a yellow old-fashioned kitchen, where beside a black Aga stove an underpaid cook made pastry with a rolling pin. She was also the maid. It was she who drew the curtains, carried coal to the fire, and sullenly bore my mother's reproaches. She was often accused of theft, regularly dismissed, and always reinstated. Three steps led up to the hall through a door, which to my shame

I once trained our dog to slam in the maid's face as she came through it bearing some heavily laden tray. On the right was the dining room, which gave out onto the street, and on Sundays my father would draw the heavy curtains so that the people in the houses opposite wouldn't see us eating chicken with our fingers. The dining room was separated from the drawing room by more thick red curtains, which were an endless joy as they alone made a theater: they could part, they could close, they could be swept up and festooned, and when we had parties my father would do conjuring here, with Alexis, my brother, as his assistant. My father was very accomplished and had an intriguing wooden case that was full of wands, collapsible top hats, trick decks of cards, and other devices. He would read off cards at a distance with a thin ivory telescope, one by one from the top of the pack, and at the end of the trick, he would innocently say, "It's very easy," inviting anyone who wished to try for themselves. His unsuspecting victims would peer through the telescope, and when asked what they saw, they would invariably answer, "Nothing." He would at once cross the room to where the pack stood on an occasional table, turn up a specially prepared card that had nothing on it, and say triumphantly, "You're right!" Then he would make an omelette in the top hat, and the evenings came to a joyful end when a fat Russian lady with dyed jet black hair and gypsy earrings would sit at the piano and sing.

Our piano was upright, a shape I found very unromantic, and it was the cause of much scolding from irritated ladies in hats trying to teach me scales. But the piano was also the instrument I link to my mother and her special sadness, for there was a particular movement from a Beethoven sonata that she would play badly but with deep feeling, while sighing in Russian, *"Dusha bolit . . . dusha bolit"* — the soul hurts! And the same piano became the tool with which I learned to distinguish my right hand from the left. Even now as a grown-up, at moments of doubt I still flash a glimpse of the keyboard into the space before me and know my right from my left by its two ends.

Up the stairs from the hall was a half-landing with the lavatory. This was a place of excitement because of an electric fan, invented by my father, that automatically began to turn when there was pressure on the seat. Hours would be spent with fellow school-boys pretending we were in an airplane, dropping balls of toilet paper through the hole onto enemy submarines in the water below. Opposite this room was my father's study, a masculine place with a mahogany desk, the telephone, a well-worn leather armchair, and a clock made from the propeller of a German bomber of the First World War. Hidden behind the large volumes of the *Encyclopaedia Britannica* were books brought back from trips to Paris and Ostend that my brother and I were not supposed to find. Our favorite was called *Wagon de Fumeurs*, with a cover showing a compartment of red-faced Frenchmen filling the air with smoke and slapping their thighs with laughter; inside were jokes that we would giggle over without understanding a word.

Here also I first encountered Shakespeare, not through books but directly, as I lay on the floor with earphones and what was oddly called a "wireless," scraping at a crystal with a thin springy wire called a cat's whisker and hearing a new world open up as the crackle suddenly ceased and BBC voices could be heard, crying enthusiastically, "Hail, Caesar! Caesar, hail!"

On the landing above there was the bathroom and the nursery, where Alexis and I would lie at night, hearing our parents quarrel in Russian in their bedroom on the other side of the communicating door. I didn't learn much Russian — when my mother tried to teach me, I would throw the books on the floor — but today when I hear Russian spoken, even when I have no idea of what is being said, I have a deep feeling of understanding through layers of sound far deeper than sense.

The house went still higher: another flight of steps with banisters for sliding on, leading to a vast all-purpose attic that once had been an artist's studio and that was flooded with light from a great glass roof.

Even though this was just a small suburban house in an ordinary street attached to other similar houses on both sides, it gave me my first sense of fullness. From its dark underworld, that place of mystery and fear, to its luminous summit, it was a universe, it was complete.

My childhood stability in the world was rooted in the house, in the tiny circle of family, and above all in the unshakable presence of my father — in my subconscious, I am sure that they make a whole. One of my earliest memories is of sitting on my father's lap and kneading his face with my fingers. Suddenly a shaving cut opened and a pinpoint of blood appeared. Even today I can relive the moment of shock that this tiny dot aroused. I adored my father and miraculously never knew the tragic rejection of the father figure that is so much a part of our time. The only thing that could irritate me was the knowledge that when he gave me advice he was always maddeningly right. He was never wealthy; he lived through the Depression, changing from an electrical engineer into a manufacturing chemist, and his constant care was never to let his family feel any shortage — this for him was what being a father meant. So my brother and I were encouraged to believe that life was a cornucopia, our home a land of security and abundance where if the need arose, anything could be found. It was a dangerous illusion, yet one that helped to create a basis of inner security for later life.

At the beginning of this troubled century, in a small backward village in Latvia, my father had been a childhood revolutionary. His parents had kept the general store, and like their neighbors they had been appalled when at the age of sixteen he had made a fiery speech to the local peasants about plunging a knife into the fat bellies of the bourgeoisie. This earned him an invitation to Moscow as the youngest delegate at a clandestine All-Russia agitators' meeting, which within the first few hours was denounced to the police. After a few weeks, his father managed to buy him out of prison on condition he leave the country, so in 1907 he went to Paris to study science at the Sorbonne, followed by a girl with apple-red cheeks whom he had met by a bandstand one Baltic summer's evening and whom he then married. His studies took him to Liège, and when the First World War began, he and my mother retreated from the advancing army as far as Ostend, then as the shelling grew closer, on to a boat bound for England.

The family name had always been Bryk and as the Russian *y* has a *u* sound, in France this became Brouck. But the passport officer at Dover said, "That's not how you spell it" and wrote down Brook. So it has remained. Both my parents worked for the war, my father inventing field telephones and at the same time writing revolutionary articles for émigré journals, my mother putting her doctorate of science into practice by manufacturing antidotes to poisonous gas. When the war ended, my father, a Menshevik, was appalled by Bolshevik violence, so he decided not to return to Russia, becoming a proud Englishman for the rest of his life.

He was convinced that a father needs to be a teacher to his

children and had a large repertoire of sayings and quotations, which remain pillars of wisdom for my brother and me to this day:

"The only way to have a friend is to be one."

"Wait a little longer till your little wings are stronger."

"Every phenomenon becomes clear when it is reduced to numbers."

"Nothing is created, nothing is destroyed."

"Se non è vero, è ben trovato."

"Qui prouve trop ne prouve rien."

"When you're in heaven, you have to dance."

As a reaction against the cramped and poorly lit conditions of his childhood, he loved to stay in grand hotels and at home pressed every switch so that the house was always blazing with light. He would say that all he needed in life was a sheet of paper and a pencil, then he would be happy all day long, making inventions, thinking up new ideas, as everything can always be improved. If he had no other work, he would tell us, he would become an attendant in a public lavatory, because he would immediately find ways of making it the most astonishing and unique public convenience in the world. Above all, he treasured the mind, and the few attempts he made at healthy physical exercise were soon abandoned. He wrote notes using several colored pencils and underlined everything with a ruler. He never moved without rubber bands and a box of drawing pins, and he taught me always to put a date on every document and never write in a letter, "I personally believe" as no belief could be anything but personal. He voted alternately right and left, counting off on his fingers the basic necessities that he insisted a state was there to provide. When my brother studied to be a psychiatrist, he delighted my father by showing him a textbook that cited perfectionism as a psychological disease. After this, my father would tap his forehead and say proudly, "I am a perfectionist."

"You are like the Mona Lisa," my father would often say to my mother, so on one trip to Paris he took us to the Louvre to admire the likeness. Indeed, my mother had the same tiny suggestion in the lips of a smile that is never complete. However, when I conjure up her face and see her smile, I now know that it contains no mockery, only an infinite, half-hidden sadness.

She was hypersensitive, unhappy, artistic, both stubborn and afraid. She had given up her deepest ambition — to become a doctor — in order to follow my father to a university that had no medical course. Out of devotion to him, she studied chemistry instead, but although she succeeded, she never lost a sense of deep disappointment with herself and life. When guests came to the house, my mother would panic and hide in the bathroom, leaving my father to organize every detail of the evening.

My father saw in her need for concealment a rigidity that he attributed to the fact that she came from a German region of the Baltic and had a Prussian nature. When he came home from a very hard day at the office, expecting to be greeted by a pretty wife, well dressed, with a comforting meal waiting for him, this was never what he found. Instead, my mother would emerge surprised from her little laboratory where she had been pursuing her own work, experimenting with hydrochloric and hydrofluoric acids, her nose red, wiping her streaming face with the sleeve of her overall, saying agitatedly that she had not had time to buy the meal.

Inevitably they quarreled a lot and there must have been many tensions, but they never reached my brother or me in a destructive way. I always took both their sides, and today I can find both my parents in me. If I try to understand the sources of my own impulses and my contradictions, they are to be found in the unremitting struggle between energy, impulsiveness, and determination opposed by a need for yielding, for balance, for reconciliation, reflecting the undying presence of both father and mother.

For a bold yet timid child, the house was a rock and my parents and elder brother strong protectors; the outer world was fascinating, but it was uncertain and obscure. Still, it was there to be explored. My father was a great believer in journeys and languages so we traveled together a great deal, and this planted in me very early a restlessness that has never gone away.

When the protection of the family was removed, however, the real world became very ugly. I hated school and was persecuted a lot of the time for not being, either in body or in mind, one of the team. It took some thirty years for me to begin to discover that a certain quality of experience can only be found through the shared life of a group, but when that came about, it was in conditions very far from those of the typical British school.

School was the smell of latrines, sweat, unkindness, and boredom; it was boxing, with blood streaming down the face; it was never being left alone; it was being bullied. School was thick slices of white bread called "doorsteps" with butter shining a particularly vivid yellow in the electric light, while the masters ate neatly trimmed triangles of brown toast that they would butter elegantly, mouthful by mouthful. Once, in a fury, I flung a plate of porridge in another boy's face and the lumps flew upward until they joined the molding of the ceiling. When I revisited my school many years later, the hardened remains were still there, almost completely integrated into the plaster.

At the same time, there were many compensations, and these were the opium of rebellious small boys. There were books and music, the pleasure of avoiding cold showers, exalted moments evoked by the scent of clear, polished wood in the school chapel, the magic of the darkroom, watching an enlargement slowly appear, an image constructing itself fragment by fragment under a dim red light. There were two merciful years of idleness, thanks to illness, first in a long basket on wheels called a spinal chair and later in the Swiss mountains with my anxious mother all to myself, talking to grown-ups, wondering why the shadows in the snow were a luminous blue, devouring Edwardian housemaids' novelettes left on the bookshelves of *pensions de famille,* or else unmentionably wicked books forbidden in England and available at railway bookstalls in what were called Tauschnitz editions. There was the first shock of the Italian lakes, the whiteness of light in heat, the coolness of shuttered rooms, the cascades of purple bougainvilleas, the crumbling wonder of decrepitude, the colonnaded villas and their dark cypresses reflected in the water, the lurid ends of day and the wild sickness of love, born of one glimpse of a dark-haired Italian schoolgirl, looking down at me from the top of a flight of steps.

This arousal of yearning, this opening onto an adult world could not last. War came and I was back in my boarding school, but I was older and cockier and my teachers found that I asked too many questions. The school doctor, a pompous red-faced man, reported me to my housemaster for insolence because I had come to him with a rash and had asked, "Do you know what this is?" No doubt I said it in a man-to-man way, unsuitable to a small boy; still, for a long time I was baffled that anyone could be hurt by the assumption that there was something he did not know.

In fact, the grown-up world was full of disappointments. I rapidly learned that teaching was the last option for university graduates who had failed to find their place in journalism or publishing. Drawing teachers frightened the eye and made the hand clumsy, singing teachers blocked the voice, geography teachers made the world uniform and arid, Scripture teachers closed the spirit to wonder, games teachers made movement of the body a punishment rather than a joy. The only exception was Mr. Taylor, who taught music with no great enthusiasm, for his real interest was in producing the school plays. He was young, dark, and dashing, an exciting outsider who could be wickedly indiscreet about the other members of the staff. The greatest privilege was to be invited by him to tea, when he would gossip freely about masters and boys. One day when he was chatting to a group of us about the subjects we would choose for our holiday essays, he suddenly turned to me and asked, "Why is rhythm the common factor in all the arts?" I now realize of all the thousands of words of criticism, exhortation, and moral guidance that my teachers uttered, I can retain just this one single phrase. It still nags at my understanding, and if it is all that my many schools provided, I am well repaid. It made me aware that the movement of the eye as it passes across a painting or across the vaults and arches of a great cathedral is related to a dancer's leaps and turns and to the pulse of music. The question then is inexhaustible: what gives a work of art its true tempo, and what in life can bring to the shapeless succession of moments their true beat and flow?

My other music teachers were mostly ladies, either soporifically repeating, "Take it ever so slowly, careful, now stretch the little finger," or crushingly impatient, blocking the mind and muscles with cries of "No, for the last time, it's F-sharp, not G!" Neither method produced any results, leaving me convinced that if one wanted to learn, a teacher was the last person to trust.

Miraculously, everything changed and a new possibility of understanding was born when I met Mrs. Biek. Her husband, a warm Russian bear of a man, was an arranger of light music, and she was a pianist and composer from the Moscow Conservatoire. The war was at its height, my parents had met them somewhere, and as Mrs. Biek gave music lessons, my parents suggested that she take me in hand. The first lesson was in our drawing room, in front of the black upright piano. She took the customary chair, and I perched on the stool. Placing a simple Mozart sonata on the rack she said, "Play!," but before my hand could touch the first note, she had already stopped me. "No! You must be prepared! Do you know what that means?" In that instant I discovered what it is to be challenged and began to learn the fundamental elements out of which all my future work was to grow. Her expectation was quite simple: she wished for every condition of a fully prepared concert performance to be observed at the first lesson. Without any indulgence, she swept away the notion that progress comes gently, step by step; it was now or never. At once, everything I had taken for granted was in question: how to sit, how to poise the body, what muscle to tense before the first note was struck, how to conceive the note in the mind so as to be able to listen for it, how to listen and how to relax the instant the note sounded so that one could hear it continue to sing. Immediately came the demand to play with both hands together, in tempo, with correct pedaling, for a phrase of music cannot be analyzed nor can the body of the player be dissected; finger and toe must be as one. Music, she would insist, is a whole, it must evolve with its own dynamic thrust; its natural urge forward must be served with passion so that each phrase can lead to the next and then beyond and even further still, through to the end of the piece. And when the last note is reached, it must not be cut short; the sound is there to be lived within a moment of suspension, feeling the fingers deep in the keys while the whole body listens, until the last vibrations die away. Only then can the hands be slowly withdrawn and another vital moment of stillness experienced, hands on lap, in a silence that is part of sound.

Her demand on her pupils to understand the reality of music made performance essential. Music, she insisted, must be shared, so all shyness and timidity were swept away. "I'm not ready" was not allowed, for as soon as a piece was learned, it had to be played in public. Every month she would hire a room in the Wigmore Hall where her pupils would give a recital to their relatives and friends. This magnet of performance gave an aim and a sense to the whole process of learning. Although she was always kind and her tone quiet and amused, she was merciless. She demanded perfect public manners. At first I thought it effective to sway a bit with eyes shut and my head nodding to the rhythm, but no, one had to be upright, alert, self-effacing, and above all relaxed so that energy could flow lightly down the arms into the fingers. One's strength was to be kept in reserve for the moments when only the full impact of every muscle in the shoulders, supported by the weight of the whole trunk, could produce massive thundering chords, to be followed once again by relaxation, while the mind listened lightly and freely to the pattern of movement in the melodic lines.

I now know that these music lessons were my only dramatic academy, for although I never became a musician, all my work to this day is an attempt to put into practice what I learned during these extraordinary sessions. Mrs. Biek showed me the true meaning of what a teacher can be, she enabled me to discover that the same principles govern all the arts, and her approach to music became a way both into theater and into life.

Not long ago, a good friend in New York who was terminally ill asked, as I came and left between two appointments, "What are you running away from, what are you running toward?" Even if one can never reply to such a question, it remains uncomfortably in the mind. But when I was nineteen, there was no uncertainty; all my attention went toward this thrilling phenomenon called the world, and as I was sure I would die before I was forty, I became what a newspaper described as "a young man in a hurry."

My father was very attached to symmetry, and as my brother was studying medicine at Cambridge, he decided that I would go to Oxford to study law. Opening each hand in turn he would say to his friends, "One son a doctor, the other a barrister!" Luckily, one of his firm principles was never to impose his ideas on his children. My own schoolboy choices had wavered among becoming a diplomat, a foreign correspondent, and a secret agent, but at some point, the idea of being a director must have taken root in my mind. Maybe it started when at the age of ten I was sent for my health to stay as a paying guest with two spinster ladies by the sea. On the pier, there was what was called a "concert party" in which men in blazers, their faces blackened with soot, sang to ukuleles and tapped out soft-shoe routines. Armed with a banjo and a clipped-on ginger mustache, I bullied, cursed, and cajoled two little girls who were staying in the house into performing our own variety show, tasting for the first time the feverish excitement of being the boss. Even so, performing seemed a hobby, not a grown-up way of life. It was like the marionettes, the photography, and even the amateur filmmaking at school — there to make the daily miseries bearable.

Then all of a sudden it had become a career. "What are you going to be?" "A film director." It is hard to say how or why. For a child, whiskey is disgusting, then without knowing it one finds one has acquired the taste; it is the same with a career. Many things must have crystallized. I recognized that formal education was of no interest whatever, and at the age of sixteen I abruptly left school and returned home, announcing to my father that I was going to take classes in photography in London as a first step toward filmmaking. He listened patiently, then proposed a compromise. Through some business friends, he was sure he could get me a job in a documentary film studio on one condition: after a year, I was to go to university and be educated. I agreed and was admitted to Merton Park Studios in South London, astonished to discover that a studio was not, as I had fondly imagined, a new world of futuristic whiteness and silence but a scruffy area of piled-up debris, in which fragments of parlors and suburban kitchens would only shine and gleam when the cameraman switched on his lamps. My job in the studios was unglamorous and disappointing — it was mainly sitting around — so I had plenty of time and energy to spare and cajoled an eccentric Italian maker of ballet shoes to turn the cellar under his shop into a theater. Having persuaded a group of friends to join me, I began to rehearse a lurid Elizabethan play whose blood-drenched atmosphere had long fascinated me, *The Duchess of Malfi*. But within a few hours we managed to irritate the unpredictable shoemaker, and we were thrown into the street with a torrent of abuse. The project was abandoned, but my imagination refused to accept this, so I went around claiming that it had taken place, describing it, embellishing on the story, until I began to believe that the production had been received in triumph, bringing me both experience and glory. In 1942, when my apprenticeship in the studios ended and I eventually arrived at Oxford, I expected the university dramatic societies to welcome me with open arms, but I found that they were totally monopolized by possessive professors and well-entrenched third-year students who had no intention of yielding an inch of their territory to a newcomer. There was only one solution, which was to use the freedom of the summer vacation to work away from the university, where the powerful academics had no sway. So I dragged my friends into another scheme, *Doctor Faustus*, which we put on in a tiny theater near Hyde Park Corner. What did it actually mean to direct other people for the first time? Here the clouds of memory refuse to open, and I think this is because it all took place in an area of the subconscious that was filled with instinct, energy, and excitement.

We sold tickets to everyone we knew, even going from door to door in the suburbs and, as the war had still not come to an end, we said that we were raising money for an Aid to Russia Fund. Fortunately, this happened to be true, and it gave our enterprise a certain respectability. As we made a small profit, we could even feel we were playing our part in the war effort.

When the new term began, I started the University Film Society, partly so that we could see the old silent films whose names were legends to us, but above all so as to be able to produce a film of our own. At that time, the movie I admired the most was Sacha Guitry's *Le Roman d'un tricheur*, and I saw in Laurence Sterne's eighteenth-century adventures of an amorous clergyman, *A Sentimental Journey*, the possibility of telling a story in the same free and insolent manner. I called again on the enthusiasm of my little group of friends, and pooling all our resources, we put together £250. Even in those days this was a small enough sum; besides, in wartime amateur filmmaking was totally discouraged, and it was illegal to sell sixteen-millimeter film. But we discovered a loophole: the air force had the right to dispose of the film stock used in fighter planes to record the trace of bullets as they passed in between the propeller blades if part of the batch was dud. So we acquired, very cheaply, rolls of film on which each shot in the camera was like a shot fired in Russian roulette — the chances of hitting unusable emulsion were dangerously high. There was also a strict regulation that no film laboratory could accept work that was not directly connected with the war, but this obstacle was soon bypassed when I chanced on a maker of pornographic movies off Oxford Street who had his own private processing plant. He was a jovial, portly man with shining spectacles, very tickled at the idea of university students needing his help. Photography was his only passion, and I discovered that his real motivation was not libidinous but technical. "You must see *Wood Nymph* — it's lovely," he used to say to me, rolling the name on his tongue. "I'm using a different emulsion so the skin gradations are quite ex-quisite." Somehow, he never got round to showing me *Wood Nymph*—perhaps he was secretly shy—and the last time I called him, I was very sad to learn that his laboratory had been raided by the police and he had been taken to jail.

For my first attempt at film directing I was up before dawn, anxiously waiting to discover the state of the sky, as we needed sun for the opening scenes. Agonizingly, the darkness yielded to somber shades of gray that did not evaporate but stayed ominously menacing. Would it rain? I prayed and made promises to the clouds. When day finally broke, it was neither fine nor wet, and we pushed out into the street, a bunch of confused and overexcited amateurs, with large hampers of eighteenth-century clothes borrowed from London costumers, a garden cart with rubber wheels as a camera trolley, and a genuine, quite splendid eighteenth-century coach generously lent by an eccentric local duke. Crowds assembled, I ran in all directions trying to hold the unit together, until eventually some order came out of the chaos, and I could for the first time live the magical experience of shouting, "Shoot!"

At the end of our first day, we sent the film up to London for developing by the only route we could afford—hitchhiking—and three days later all the unit assembled in my rooms in Magdalen College, screen and projector ready, excitedly awaiting the return of our very first rushes. The long summer evening drew on, we listened to music, drank beer, and waited. We knew that getting a lift back from London was an unpredictable business, and everyone was prepared to stay all night if need be. Darkness fell. Suddenly the door was flung open and the beam of a flashlight lit up the crowd of figures sitting or lying on my floor. "Is everyone here a member of this college?" came the accusing voice of my archenemy, the ferocious opponent of film, theater, and other decadent activities, the junior dean. He only asked because he knew the answer and immediately ordered us to leave both the university and the town. We were far too excited to take these events and their possible consequences seriously; on the contrary, it gave an extra stimulus to our already well-developed sense of high adventure, so the actors defiantly put on their eighteenth-century costumes, and covering every surface of our stagecoach with noisy bewigged figures and whipping the reluctant horses, we made an anarchic demonstration as we rode out of town to Woodstock, a village just beyond the college's authority. We hastily improvised new locations, but in the excitement I overlooked the fact that I also had to pay a college fine, so I was formally expelled from Oxford. I did not care, but my father, who was on holiday in Scotland, had no intention of allowing my education, on which he had so insisted, to end in disgrace. Appalled, he found a seat on a plane — a considerable achievement in wartime — and arrived dramatically and unannounced to see the president, who reluctantly granted me a reprieve on condition that I sign a paper swearing to have nothing further to do with cinema or theater. I have a feeling there was no date limit to this restriction; however, when twenty years later the college wrote to ask for a fee for keeping my name on the books, I guessed that I had been forgiven for breaking my oath.

We made a big event out of the first screening of the film, which was at the Oxford Town Hall. Our quarrels with the university had become sufficiently notorious for the big auditorium to be packed with excited, expectant students. Although we had been shooting silent on the scraps of retrieved celluloid, we had pieced together an hourlong film and had invented a sound system of our own that was primitive but seemingly foolproof. It was possible in those days to make private recordings on large, soft-wax disks, so a couple of us had become quite expert at a synchronization system that consisted of keeping a finger on the speed control of the turntable in order to slow down the sound or catch up with the picture without anyone noticing. However, we hadn't tried out the projector in advance. It turned out to run above the normal speed, so to our horror the picture began to gallop away. When we pushed the speed control forward, the actors' voices rose in pitch. They got higher and higher as we vainly tried to catch up to the fleeing image, until all sound was drowned in the audience's laughter. We lost the race and the show ended in disaster. The shame and ridicule taught us a lesson. We carefully rehearsed for the next screening, which was in London in the same tiny theater where we had played *Doctor Faustus*, and the film was well enough received for confidence to be restored.

Five terms were all that was allowed for a wartime degree. I had studied French, German, and Russian, hating medieval German, loving Old Provençal and Church Slavonic, fascinated by the incredible peregrinations and transformations of words that we followed in compulsory philology. Nonetheless, after A *Sentimental Journey* there was no doubt in my mind that all I wanted to do was direct films. An effusive Italian producer, who was a great tycoon at the time, took me by the hand, pressed it to his chest, and said, "You come and work with me, you be assistant in every department, and I promise you, in ten years you can direct." In ten years, I thought, I would be nearly thirty; this seemed a ridiculous waste of my few remaining years, so I declined.

Instead, I spent every spare moment writing scripts — none of them was ever completed — and discussing wildly ambitious movie projects with shady men in Soho pubs. I wound and rewound film in dingy cutting rooms without getting paid. I had been rejected from the army at my medical, thanks to the ominous specter of TB raised by my years in the Swiss mountains, so I did what was considered war work in a company ostensibly making training films for the army. Behind this facade, the company carried on with its profitable peacetime business of producing forty-second commercials for toothpaste and tea, which were shown in every cinema before the main feature. I wrote about one hundred of these scripts for them, but all I wanted was to direct, and I plagued my bosses until, for the sake of peace, they allowed me to shoot an advertisement for Rinso, a washing powder that was a household name at the time. It showed how an inept conjuror needed Rinso to make a dirty shirt magically come clean. Carried away by excitement and artistic ambition, I forgot that a commercial is meant to be light and comic. I hired a professional magician and a fat lady, went on location to a gloomy Victorian variety theater called the Finsbury Empire, and as my idol at that time was Orson Welles, who had just made *Citizen Kane*, I filmed in his style, with the cameras on the floor and long ominous shadows on the back wall. When I proudly showed the result to the advertising agents, they were appalled. My disgrace was complete, my boss reshot the film in a straightforward way, and although for some unaccountable reason they forgot to fire me, I was never given another chance to direct.

It was the time of the flying bombs, when without warning pilotless planes packed with explosives would suddenly drop out of the sky. I would sit all day on a camera box in the middle of London, in front of a large plate-glass window, employed, paid, but idle, listening to the explosions and recognizing that in films I was getting nowhere. So I thought of the theater — without much enthusiasm. But it did seem that a possible detour through this old-fashioned province could eventually lead me back to the highway I wanted to take.

I was determined to start at the top. There was not much in the theater that thrilled me at the time. The Old Vic was the exception, and its finest moments were in the Olivier-Richardson wartime seasons of glory. An extraordinary Irish giant, Tyrone Guthrie, was in charge; he was the only stage director whose work I admired almost to idolatry. He had an extraordinary vitality, and his excitement pulsed through every detail, bringing the player of even the tiniest role into a state of passionate involvement. When I managed to see him, however, and asked to be given a production in his theater, to my great disappointment he simply said, "Come back when you've done something somewhere else." Luckily, common sense told me that none of us enters this world with any rights and that we thus have no cause to be put off by rejection, so I did not turn against Guthrie but went on persistently, from refusal to refusal, lower and lower down the scale until near the bottom I found a miniature theater in Kensington with a handful of seats where the production costs were infinitesimal. The lady in charge weighed my determination to direct, subtracted my lack of experience, put the negligible outlay I could cost her in the scales, shrugged, and instead of "No" said, "Why not?"

The theater was called the Chanticleer, and the play I chose was Cocteau's *Infernal Machine* because anything from France had a special intellectual glamour. It made a tiny stir, there were some good notices, some West End managers came, they were even complimentary, but it led to nothing. I had given up my job in films; now months went by, and nobody offered me any work. I used to pour my heart out to a friendly retired actress called Mary Grew, and when, thanks to the war, she was invited to return to the boards, touring army camps as a somewhat senior version of the little cockney flower girl in *Pygmalion*, she generously insisted that I should be engaged to direct the play, or rather "produce" it, as one said in those days.

ENSA, as the organization was called, had been created to bring entertainment to the troops. It had no glamour; it had even succeeded in draining the magic out of the Drury Lane Theatre by converting it into a drab series of temporary offices, part army, part low-grade touring agency, where the only concern was mass production and quality was unimportant. We were given few rehearsals, and the set had to be just a few doors and windows that could be easily transported from camp to camp. Today I would find these few bits and pieces far more than I need, but at that time to be denied scenery was a painful deprivation. Costumes, however, existed in some tawdry way, so we had a dress rehearsal in the barren, partly partitioned Drury Lane auditorium. A few bored members of the ENSA staff in uniform drifted in and out. The red plush stalls were empty apart from an old friend of Mary's, William Armstrong, a very successful West End director, whom she had coaxed to come watch her at work. He was a very refined elderly gentleman, whose bald head drooped sadly onto one shoulder. He took me by the arm, walked me up and down between the stalls, and although I cannot imagine what he could have seen in the ramshackle show, he was kind and complimentary, promising to recommend me to his friends.

Pygmalion left to tour with the troops in Germany, and in London bombs fell. The war was all around me, but I cannot say I was really involved. At the time, my essential discovery was that whatever the moment of danger, once it is over, ordinary life has no choice but to go on. This was something that films and fiction had not taught me, and I learned that life as it is lived is always life in between the high moments out of which stories are made. I think that my parents, with their Eastern European heritage of terrors and pogroms always imminent, silently absorbed the dreads of war for me, fearful when a letter from my brother in the army failed to arrive, fearful when I came home late during the Blitz. My father knew what a Nazi victory would mean, so he would sit tensely, raising a finger each time there was a distant explosion. Every night as he switched on the radio for the nine o'clock news, before the announcer could speak he would announce, "Hitler assassinated!," tirelessly repeating the formula in the hope that it might come true.

Then one night firebombs fell and my father's pharmaceutical business was burned to the ground. He took the disaster in his stride and in no time at all had everything reorganized in a place outside London. My mother evacuated with him to the country while I remained in our empty house in Chiswick, wondering where to turn for work. One morning, the postman knocked, the letter box clicked, and an envelope bearing a Birmingham post-mark dropped onto the mat. "We are preparing a production of Shaw's *Man and Superman*, to begin rehearsals in two weeks' time. On William Armstrong's recommendation, we can invite you to produce it. The fee will be £25." Signed: Barry Jackson.

Two days later I was in Birmingham, passing behind the rail-way station to the unassuming building on Station Street called the Birmingham Rep. In the office, a tall, ageless figure with clear blue eyes greeted me simply. I am not sure I even realized what a legendary person I was meeting: Sir Barry Jackson had been the pioneer, along with Granville-Barker, of serious drama in England between the wars. It was he who, with his own mon-ey, had first put on many of Shaw's plays in London, although he viewed the great city with suspicion and dislike. He was essential-ly a cautious Midlander with private means, and when he found that he had been cheated once too often in the capital, he with-drew to the security of his grimy but dependable Birmingham base. Here he could give free rein to his enthusiasms; from here he launched some of the finest actors on the English stage, and in his small office he quickly lost his reserve as he told me with boyish excitement of the new young actor for whom he wanted to stage the Shaw play. A moment later the door opened. "Ah, here he is!" said Sir Barry. "This is Paul Scofield."

As we shook hands, I looked into a face that unaccountably in a young man was streaked and mottled like an old rock, and I was instantly aware that something very deep lay hidden behind this ageless appearance. Paul was courteous, distant, but as we began to work an instant understanding arose between us, need-ing very few words, and I realized that beneath the gentle modes-ty of his behavior lay the absolute assurance of a born artist. This was the start of a partnership that lasted many years.

Sometime later H. M. Tennant's, the London management firm, asked me to direct my first West End production, *Ring Round the Moon*. Paul was already recognized as the most ex-traordinary young actor of his time, so although his movements were awkward and his voice grated and exploded uncontrollably, I went against all the rules of typecasting and asked him to play an elegant, Edwardian gentleman. In order for him to acquire the grace in his movements that this stylish comedy demanded, I asked Paul to take lessons from a ballet teacher. He looked at me strangely and was quiet for a long while, then he shook his head. "I can't do it that way. You must explain to me what impression of elegance you want me to give. Then I'll act it." This was what he then proceeded to do, day by day in rehearsal. And although his characteristic movements did not change, by a mysterious alchemy of the imagination, they ended by expressing the essence of the refinement that the part required. Later, when we rehearsed *King Lear*, he refused to be disturbed by my constant chiding that he was not portraying an old man. He remained himself, but by the force of inner conviction he projected to the audience the exact image that he had in mind. For me this was a first indication that the theater is the meeting place between imitation and a transforming power called imagination, which has no action if it stays in the mind. It must pervade the body. A seemingly abstract word, "incarnation," suddenly took on a meaning.

There was one time when I saw Paul nearly defeated. We were responsible together for a season of plays at the Phoenix Theatre, and Paul was playing *Hamlet* at night while we rehearsed our next production, Graham Greene's *The Power and the Glory*, during the day. The part of the humble Mexican whiskey-sodden priest attracted him greatly, and although in his imagination he saw the character with absolute clarity, somehow this never descended into his body. During the last performances of *Hamlet*, as we drew near to the end of rehearsals, the author was desperate, I was alarmed, even Paul was truly worried — the alchemy of his secret art was failing, and he could not even achieve a convincing external imitation of the part. Something was blocking his normal process, and neither of us could discover the cause. *Hamlet* closed on a Saturday, and we were due to open the new play on Monday, two days later. I spent Sunday in the auditorium with the sets and the lights, preparing for the dress rehearsal, and Paul went straight to his dressing room where a barber had been called to cut off the splendid romantic head of hair he had cultivated to play the prince. When the run-through started, I was sitting with Graham Greene and Denis Cannan, who had made the adaptation, in the stalls. The curtain rose on a seedy wharfside shack. Through a window there was a glimpse of a rusty steamer, a stagnant river, a Mexican sky; in the foreground a dentist was pulling out an Indian's teeth. The door at the back of the set opened, and a small man entered. He was wearing a black suit, steel-rimmed glasses, and holding a suitcase. For a moment we wondered who this stranger was and why he was wandering on to our stage. Then we realized that it was Paul, transformed. His tall body had shrunk; he had become insignificant. The new character now possessed him entirely. The obstacle had been his, or rather Hamlet's, noble head of hair. All through rehearsal his actor's instinct had told him that something was wrong, that the image he was carrying was false; intuitively he sensed that his silhouette was the antithesis of the role. It took only one lightning glimpse of his shorn head in the mirror for all the thoughts and feelings he had accumulated over weeks instantly to be distributed to the right places inside him, for him to discover organically the person he had been seeking in vain.

A decade later, *King Lear* enabled me to resume my partnership with Paul Scofield. The communication between us was now so deep that it required few words: gaps of time had made no difference. Neither of us worked much when rehearsals were over, we never discussed the theory or the meaning of what we were attempting, it was implied, unsaid, and the close friendship that existed between us never even required social relationships such as lunches or suppers to keep it alive.

One morning, I came to Paul with what seemed to me an illuminating discovery. "Lear is someone who wants to let go. But whatever he sacrifices, there is always something left to which he is attached. He gives up his kingdom, but still his authority remains. He must yield his authority, but there is still his trust in his daughters. This too must go, as must the protection of a roof over his head, but this is still not enough, as he has preserved his sanity. When his reason is sacrificed, there is still his profound attachment to his beloved Cordelia. And in the pitiless process of stripping away, inevitably she too must be lost. This is the pattern and the tragic action of the play." Paul did not react with enthusiasm. He gave a cautious "Mmm . . ." Then he said thoughtfully, "That may be true. But I mustn't think of it, as it can't help me as an actor. I can't play negative actions. I can't show *not* having. I have to find a different way to mobilize my energies, so as to be fully active, moment after moment, even in loss, even in defeat." At that moment I saw unforgettably the trap of yielding to the intellectual excitement of "having ideas." One word out of place in the director's explanations, and without noticing it he can block or hamper the actor's own creative process. The same is true for the director's relation to himself. Ideas must appear, they must be expressed, but he too must learn to separate the useful from the useless, the substance from the theory.

This opened very subtle areas of exploration, because the theater is made out of living material. Once, in a new play, Paul had to struggle day after day with one hurriedly written scene, with its threadbare and inadequate lines. Toward the end of rehearsals the author became conscious of this weakness and brought us a new version that was infinitely better. Paul and I were delighted, but after we had tried it out Paul shook his head. "I have now found all the strands that lead me from one line to another in the old version. These fibers now exist and through them I can make the old pattern real. The new scene is better, but it won't be as good to play."

When I moved to Birmingham, my father said to me, "Go to the best hotel," having always had a taste for big hotels wherever he went. So I moved into the Station Hotel, where Sir Barry kept a permanent room. Seeing me alone in a corner of the big empty dining room on my first night, he invited me to join him and his lifelong companion Scott Sunderland at dinner, and from then on I took every meal at their table. They were an old married couple, two very conventional British gentlemen in tweeds, liked and respected by the waiters who would accept the yearly tip of £1, to be shared among them all, with an appreciation they never gave to more lavish customers.

One day at dinner Sir Barry was preoccupied and hardly spoke. At the end of the meal Scott left us alone. "I've been asked to take over the Stratford festival," Sir Barry said hesitantly. Then he added, "I'm going over to Stratford tomorrow. Would you like to join me?"

I had never been to Stratford, and I spent the day following this quiet elderly figure as we pottered round the charmless red-brick building. The theater had been designed by a committee, none of whom had any connection with the stage, and it was said that they had chosen a design by an inexperienced lady. I'm not even sure she was an architect; according to legend it was her pretty watercolor sketches that had seduced them. We were shown the dock doors that had been knocked out of the wall in a last-minute panic when the builder found he had forgotten to provide an entry for scenery to come and go. We saw the cumbersome corner in which the switchboard was awkwardly housed, because the need for lighting had been overlooked until a few weeks before the opening of the building. As we strolled through the trees to the expanse of green lawn at the river's edge, Sir Barry murmured, "This place could be as important as Salzburg." Poor old man, I thought to myself condescendingly, how could a dull English provincial theater ever compete with the bold and sophisticated adventures that took place in that world called "The Continent," which for me stood for all the glamour that England lacked. "To begin with," he continued with calm conviction, "there shouldn't be one producer desperately rushing five productions onto the stage in the first five days, which is why the present system is so bad. There should be a different producer and a different designer for each play, and they should open every four weeks so that each work can be properly rehearsed. As a result, instead of just lasting three weeks, the season should stretch through to the end of the summer . . ." And so he went on, until in a few quiet phrases he had drawn the outline of what was to become the Stratford revolution that one day would put Warwickshire far ahead of Middle Europe.

The boldness of Jackson's thinking was not appreciated, and as he began to set his vision in motion, he was attacked from all sides. The town was up in arms, the city council claimed he was ruining the festival — no one would come from London more than once a year, they asserted, least of all the press — but Sir Barry went forward unshaken, putting his ideas into practice in his own way as he had done all his life.

In his first season, he invited me to stage *Love's Labour's Lost*, which was indeed a labor of love, and it enabled me to pour into the play all the dreamy romanticism that had been accumulating for so long. My production came third in the season and I was a little envious of another director, with far more experience, who had the glamorous task of opening the new season and launching the new regime with his production of *The Tempest*. However, as we were in the same building, for the first time I had the possibility of observing someone else at work. One evening I heard that there was going to be what was called a costume parade, and I slipped in to watch. Standing in the shadows, I was overwhelmed, both dazzled and at the same time secretly jealous as the actors proudly demonstrated their new clothes and one brilliantly colored confection of velvet and lace followed another. How dull the simple shapes we had chosen for *Love's Labour's Lost* were going to appear after this glittering display! Yet on the first night of *The Tempest*, seeing the overdressed figures in front of the elaborately painted scenery, I realized that nothing in the theater has any meaning out of its context in performance. Now that they were in action, the dresses had mysteriously lost all their beauty and had become an ugly impediment to the play, until the text was drowned like the great realistic galleon of the opening scene. This was an important lesson. The theater exists in movement: a color, a shape, a sound, or a beautiful phrase can make one impression in isolation and a quite different one when the action is unfolding. I now saw how I was spending long nights building up beautiful and somber lighting effects that were meaningless when placed the next day in the sequence of the play. My obsession with film was helping me to realize that a play is also a spool that unrolls; its truths come to life shot by shot.

For *Love's Labour's Lost*, I had decided to use Watteau's paintings as a basis. Although historically no connection could be found between an Elizabethan comedy and an eighteenth-century painter, intuitively I felt that Watteau's purely imaginary Golden Age was a world in which the action of this play would sit naturally, and I was convinced a fresh image was needed to get away from the inevitable Elizabethan doublet and hose of the time. The play was very well received, the reviews were excellent, and a few weeks after it opened, I met a Russian choreographer, Suria Magito, who was living with the then legendary director Michel St. Denis. She invited me to dinner and after the meal suggested that Michel give his comments on my work. For her, this was clearly a great gift she was offering to a raw beginner, even if I was not necessarily ready to have my first efforts analyzed by a master. He sat back in his chair, pulling on a pipe, and explained that it was a great mistake to imitate famous paintings, as the theater is theater in its own right and true theater art should not refer to anything outside itself. "I can see you in rehearsal," he added, "making your compositions and placing the actors with a book of Watteau in your hand." It was just this phrase, perhaps expressed a little too forcibly and not literally exact — I never had a book in hand — that allowed me to react with concealed fury, and as a result, many years went by before I could see the absolute truth of his criticism: theater is theater, not a synthesis of other arts.

In the second year I did a *Romeo and Juliet* that was hot, violent, and unromantic. It was much criticized, but Sir Barry loyally took any adverse criticism in his stride. What was far more serious, however, was that the designer and I spent too much money; we had scrapped a set at the dress rehearsal, and for this reason I was not invited back the following season. I had transgressed against a vital aspect of Sir Barry's values.

After a few years, Sir Barry in turn was pushed out by a group of governors, above all, I was told, because although he knew every stagehand and cleaning lady and would stop daily to inquire about their ailments, when he met a governor, he could never remember his name.

The words "the West End of London" exercised a powerful fascination on theater people: this seemed to them the only place in which to make a career. In the calm that followed the storm of war, the theater world to which I was now drawn was dominated by men with fastidiously draped muslin curtains at their windows. The pursuit of charm was a cult, and in its style there was an absolute conformity. The houses were small but elegant, they were carefully cluttered with well-chosen antiques, something indefinable called good taste ruled every detail, and the veiled windows were there to turn the interiors into invented worlds where the life of the street was never allowed to enter. The theater was a natural extension of this: when the curtain rose, we were drawn out of the everyday world into a world of grace and beauty where charming people with not-too-intense feelings played out unreal situations that never reflected the crude realities of life. This suited me well. I had once seen some Austrian puppets that played behind a kind of thick glass porthole; the experience for the spectator was like peering into a crystal ball, seeing in its mists strange images melting mysteriously into one another. At the time I too was only concerned with passing through a looking glass into a miraculous dream.

When I began a production I did not have any intellectual idea; I just followed an instinctive wish to make pictures that moved. The proscenium frame was like a stereoscopic cinema screen on which lights, music, and effects were all as important as acting, because my only wish was to conjure up a parallel and more seductive world.

Years later, when I had become established as a director, a middle-aged architect who had the exciting commission of building a new theater in a provincial town came to me for advice. The question that troubled him most concerned the proscenium. Tyrone Guthrie had just built his theater in Stratford, Ontario, bursting out of the proscenium arch onto a three-sided open Elizabethan platform. It had become fashionable for theater theorists to pour contempt on the "picture frame," but I remained deeply attached to it; the picture frame was all that I had ever experienced since the cardboard players in the toy theater production of *The Miller and His Men*. It was what had drawn me to theater as a substitute for filmmaking, and if my search was for energy and excitement, they were always to be found within that other world beyond the footlights. When I first heard of Guthrie's theater, despite my great admiration for his work I could not see myself even beginning to function in his space. A picture was all I had to lean on; without one I knew I would be lost. The work on the design, alone or with a designer, was the only key I knew to a production; finding the image was finding the blueprint out of which all subsequent meanings and actions would grow. If the blueprint was sound, the rest of the production would arise almost without effort in rehearsal. If the blueprint was unsound, then, however hard one searched and struggled, nothing would fall into place. I was fascinated by shapes, by the interrelation of forms in the flow of movement, by the patterns of crowd scenes and the breaking up of rigid lines of people until one formation would dissolve into another. I despised the drab shortcuts of the day, such as playing certain scenes before a set of front curtains while the next set was pushed into position behind. I had one criterion: if someone wandered into the auditorium at any point during a play, the image they saw should be complete and coherent; it should evoke the imaginary world in its entirety, in relief, in three dimensions. "The so-called picture frame is an instrument of focus," I told the architect. "It is foolish to throw it away. With an open stage, different parts of the audience see different images. With a picture frame, everyone sees the same thing."

"But what about contact?" he asked. "We hear a lot about contact nowadays. With a proscenium, everyone is cut off from the action."

"Nonsense," I said, "that's just a theory. Look at what happens when a great actor is in a picture frame. Every eye is focused on him. He holds the audience in the palm of his hand."

"But I'm told," pursued the architect, "that today one wants to feel that the actor is just like a member of the audience."

"In the theater in the round," I said scornfully, "you see an actor in costume, and as a background there is a crowd of people in suits and spectacles. Can you really prefer that to a beautiful set?"

"I have read," continued the architect, weakening, "that an audience in the dark is completely passive."

"The theater," I concluded forcefully, "is two places with two entries, one for the audience and one for the actors. There are two worlds. The people in the dark peer into another world. That is illusion. That is why they come."

The architect was convinced, and he thanked me profusely for giving him my time. Unfortunately, building a theater takes too long in a rapidly changing world. Ten years later, he had completed his building, and I had come to reject all the notions I had sold him with such force. At the time all my experiences had led me to believe in what I said, but over the years further experiences gradually led me to understand that having the performers share one space intimately with the audience offers an experience infinitely richer than dividing the space into what one can call two rooms.

A beautiful woman once said to me, "I can give you something no one else has ever given you."

My curiosity was irresistibly captured. "What is it?"

"Boredom," she answered.

It was not true, but I respected the way in which it was offered. Boredom has always seemed to me one of the most constructive states of mind. If I have had a guide that has helped me again and again in the theater, above all with productions of the classics and in the opera, it is my deep desire not to inflict on others that squirming and wriggling misery, that mind-killing ennui that was so often my experience during my first years of theatergoing.

When I began to work in the theater, I could not stand the polite and in most cases bloodless nature of the majority of English plays. Even though I was ready to tackle almost anything just for the experience of working, if I could not find some possibility of excitement in the piece, then participating in theater was meaningless.

The West End was dominated by one man, Binkie Beaumont, who produced almost all the successful plays in London. He had been adventurous enough to come to my first production of the *Infernal Machine* and had liked what he had seen. This made it possible for me, after much badgering, to get into his office, and I persuaded him to let me direct a very vigorous American play that attracted me greatly called *Dark of the Moon*, by two young authors, Howard Richardson and William Berney. This was a first opportunity to work with a cast of inexperienced actors of my own age. It was all about witches in the Smoky Mountains, full of crowd scenes and square dances, and I could let bold images arise from the tremendous outburst of energy that an enthusiastic group can bring. The play surprised and startled the stallgoers who were used to evenings far more genteel, but Binkie's intuition told him that he was on to something new.

This was the beginning of a long working relationship. Many people loved Binkie; many more hated him. He was a monopolist, a subtly concealed dictator, but his aim was not only power and riches; he also loved quality, and this is what brought us together. He wanted the theater to be a place of style and beauty, and as this was what I wanted too, there was nothing but agreement between us. He became a good, even endearing friend as well as an object of almost irresistible fascination. I studied him like a teacher, as he was the first example I had met of a man totally equipped to achieve his ends. He knew his world and he knew his people, and he could play on this keyboard with exquisite finesse. He was gentle, charming, and seemed to be totally self-effacing. He never made the managerial error of stealing the limelight from his performers, his name never appeared on the bills, he gave no interviews, he was rarely photographed, and in his quest for absolute power he could never be caught opposing anything head-on. He was a perfect listener and could improvise an interest in any subject, however remote from his own tastes, whether racing or football, politics or poetry, finding in the recesses of his memory just the bits of information needed to give a knowledgeable flavor to his conversation and in this way seduce someone who could be of use to him. He lived through the telephone, exploiting to the full the anonymity of the instrument, which would never reveal the true and sometimes chilling expression on his face but which instead carried to the listener's ear his purring, conciliatory tone repeating persuasively, "Yes, but you *do* see . . ." He amazed me time and again with a shameless trick that never failed. When an actress, writer, or designer categorically refused to accept an idea that Binkie with his unerring instinct knew to be vital to the success of the show — such as rewriting a scene or changing a dress or a hairstyle — he would say, pointing to the obstinate adversary, "My friend here has just made the most brilliant suggestion." The person in question would look surprised and flattered in anticipation. Then, quite unabashed, Binkie would put his own thoughts into the other person's mouth, and the poor victim, confused but beaming, would generally end by acknowledging ownership of the idea and accepting the congratulations of the rest of the cast.

Binkie would work on seven or eight productions at the same time, but he always gave the impression that the one you were concerned with was the only one that mattered. "We," he would say to each group — "they" being the others — and so we all felt loved. When we did *Ring Round the Moon*, he persuaded me to take out Anouilh's sharp reference to real life when the melancholy banker reveals he is Jewish. "Why Jewish? Not very nice!" said Binkie, rumored to be part Jewish himself, as he cut the words from the script, thus eliminating anything as ugly as real life. Perhaps "niceness" was the value that was most appreciated by the West End theater of the day.

One day, quite unaccountably since I had no qualifications whatsoever, the *Observer* invited me to be its ballet critic. Perhaps this was not after all so surprising, as one of the most influential drama critics at the time had only one field of professional knowledge, and that was cricket. At any rate, even if my judgments made the ballet world angry, it was a fascinating experience to be suddenly on the other side of the barrier, and I could now observe the temptations of the professional critic rising in myself: "I should mention him, but it'll make the paragraph end clumsily," or "I've given her good notices three times running, I can't go on or people will think . . ."

The job gave me free tickets to Covent Garden. One matinee as the audience crowded into the foyer for tea and plumcake during the interval, I was chatting with some friends when suddenly my attention was drawn toward a girl of unusual beauty standing by the bar. Moving nearer, I discovered to my delight that she was with someone I had recently met, a well-known film director, Anthony Asquith. Greeting him would clearly entitle me to be introduced to this timid, reserved young person with long dark hair and grave dark eyes. "This is Natasha," he said. Natasha? It was like hearing the echo of a distant bell. When I was twelve I had read *War and Peace* — or rather devoured it from end to end, swept heart and soul into the world inside the covers. I lived with and loved the heroine called Natasha, and before closing the book I had decided I would marry a girl of that name. And so it came about.

Not quite so easily as that, however. I lost sight of her and time went by. Then I badgered a mutual friend to invite her to a party and we exchanged a few timid words. Having pushed the hand of fate, I then phoned her house and discovered that she had left for Paris for a few days, address unknown. At once I took a plane and rushed to the headquarters of the French police at the Quai des Orfèvres to try to discover in which hotel she had registered. There the policemen were totally unimpressed by my breathless statements that this young girl was "suddenly needed urgently for a major movie." I returned again and again all through the day, trying different people at different windows. After these wild bursts of energy, I was just about to accept with bewilderment that for once I was not getting my way when a tender-hearted middle-aged lady who had watched my various visits from afar came over to the counter. The back of a hotel registration form dangled from her fingers. "I'm very sorry, monsieur," she commiserated. "You must understand. This is information we are not allowed to disclose." Then as though by chance she allowed the form to flop over for a moment, adding, "It's not allowed. I'm so sorry. I would so like to help." With a little conspiratorial smile she turned the form back again, but she had given me just enough time to note the name of a hotel and its address.

Not surprisingly, when I turned up in a state of romantic and possessive triumph, this excess of zeal was not only unwelcome but led to a year of misunderstanding. A year later, however, we met again and all came together harmoniously, as Destiny had willed. Another year later, we were married.

Life now seemed radiant and complete. Our first journey together was to Ischia and our honeymoon to Marrakech and Greece. We taught each other to swim all alone in the crystal-clear sea of a yet unknown and deserted island called Mykonos; we went on to Istanbul, and in the bazaars a determination to continue to travel the world took a firm root in us both.

Natasha was already listed among the world's great beauties, but she entered London's social life with fear and distaste. One night, soon after our wedding, she was flimsily clothed for the opera yet walked ahead of our car, guiding me with a flashlight through a dense and poisonous London fog. In this way the strains of tuberculosis were able to invade the terrain that had been busily prepared by the other sort of strain of being a hostess. Our little house became her hospital with two devoted Australian nurses in attendance and the kind and equally devoted owner of a West End restaurant regularly sending by taxi little offerings of butter, cream, and even steaks that were still unobtainable after the war. Slowly she recovered, then she had a relapse and recovered once more. Tender, graceful, silently elegant, she seemed a princess from another age — a rare princess with neither tantrums nor complaints — and disputes between us would never arise, even if later we both came to understand how much tension and conflict lay painfully concealed under the surface. Yet far below what timidity and self-restraint could hide existed an even deeper level, more fundamental than fragility, where an almost oriental wisdom recognized that in a relationship nothing is more precious than the patience that brings peace.

Like the homes of everyone else we knew in London, our house was tiny, with muslin curtains and antiques, and our friends were mainly theater people who spoke a very special jargon that covered private and unmentionable fears. Reality was often attenuated by the use of the prefix "What's laughingly known as . . . ," or "We read it in Auntie *Times*," "We went to Dolly Dentist," "We took Lily Lixen for our constipation"; plays and parties were "pure Boredomville" or even "Boredomville-on-

Sea," men were "Mrs.," and a talented but cadaverous male scenic designer I worked with was known as "the Coffin Maker's Daughter." We were adopted into this world as a phenomenon because we were so young, but I was regarded with a certain suspicion: "Has he *taste?*" the others would ask behind my back, and as my instinct was to travel and to introduce uncomfortably vigorous or realistic elements into the world of fantasy, they found a safe way of accepting me by labeling me an "enfant terrible."

I still wanted to work in films. Writing scripts and meeting American producers for long, pointless drinking sessions in big hotels, I began to feel more and more acutely the lack of any bold energy in what I was doing. My immediate ambition developed in a new direction: to stage an opera. The scale and vitality of a huge stage peopled with enormous crowds were irresistibly attractive, I had a love for music deeply inscribed in me since my early piano lessons, and so Covent Garden became my goal.

After being closed during the war, the opera season had just been revived by David Webster, a portly Liverpool businessman with a taste for music and a genial, slightly regal manner, who when approached proved very welcoming. I asked for a job, he said yes, then no, then yes again, and so, surprisingly, I found myself at the age of twenty-two the "director of production" — a title I think I invented for myself but which has since caught on — which meant that I was a resident producer at the Royal Opera House. Naturally, I had no qualifications, any more than I had as ballet critic, but I certainly did not feel at a loss, as the postwar repertoire at Covent Garden was unbelievably bad. The Royal Opera House had not undergone the drastic reappraisal of old methods that Sir Barry Jackson had brought to Stratford, so the productions were still thrown together in a week each, which was even worse than it sounds for it meant just five rehearsals, each of three hours, out of which fifteen minutes had to be lopped off for the chorus to have its tea. I entered the opera with one simple aim: to give this sleepy old-fashioned institution a series of shocks that would jolt it into the present-day world.

Now I encountered what tradition really meant and was surprised to discover that it had its own special charm, a charm that came from the scent of dust and ancient glue on the vast stage, from the stacks of painted frames creating a disorder of unrelated fragments, from trees leaning against columns, balustrades rising above clouds, rocks split raggedly down the middle. An eighty-year-old Dickensian cockney gentleman in a black suit and stiff white collar ruled over this collection: Mr. Ballard, whose word was law; shrewdly he had made himself impossible to replace as he had seen to it that nothing was ever recorded or catalogued. Only he knew, from one day to the next, where to find the borders for *Rigoletto* or the trick fountain for Marguerite's garden in *Faust*. "We had your namesake here," he said to me on the first day. "Mr. Brooks. Used to paint all the scenery. He'd arrive in his top hat, take off his white gloves, and set to work. Mr. Puccini had taken his own photographs, in Japan and in Paris. He'd give the slides to Mr. Brooks, who knew exactly how to paint them so they'd look real." Mr. Ballard and I got on very well until, for my first production, I proposed to build a solid set in wood. "Oh, no, Mr. Brook," he shook his head, "that's not opera-type work. Canvas, that's what we use. And if the painter knows his job, it'll look as built in wood as you could ever wish for, from the front."

I knew he was wrong. The great days of painted scenery belonged to the era of dim lighting from gas-fed footlights or candles, which flattened the performer so that he and the picture became one. The day the first spotlight was hung on the side of the proscenium, everything changed: the actor now stood out, was substantial, and a contradiction suddenly appeared between his roundness and the two-dimensional trompe l'oeil behind his back. The great innovators in the art of scenic design, Adolphe Appia and Gordon Craig, knew this before the First World War, but it took another half-century for their influence to penetrate the Royal Opera House walls. My first objective at Covent Garden now became to achieve the graceful retirement of Mr. Ballard. I did not succeed.

Lighting was my passion, and opera seemed to call for extraordinary effects of beauty and splendor. But to my dismay, always the same lurid filters would be brought out: royal blue for moonlight, bottle green for grottoes, canary yellow for sunshine, and what was called surprise pink for singers' faces. The chief electrician, a dear ineffectual man, agreed with every one of my propositions but somehow could never get them to work. Light cues in new places never seemed to happen, and this was so consistent that I determined to detect the reason. One day, I climbed on to the switchboard to spy on his assistant. Everything became clear. He would only execute a cue at dull moments in the music. When a great aria or a passage renowned for its difficulty would begin, he would lean over his rail, entranced. The stage manager dutifully sent him his signals, but behind the switchboard operator's back, red and green cue lights would flash in vain, for he was far away, in a gypsy camp or riding with the Valkyries into the clouds. His love of music was our undoing.

A certain Dr. Schramm was brought from Germany at great expense to produce the first postwar *Ring*. This was not because he was expected to bring any special creativity or new insights to the work; he was called in because he and he alone knew all the moves that the great star singers were likely to make. Dr. Schramm coached the chorus and the secondary roles, shouting, "Flagstad come down here and hold out left hand. So you must be ready give spear with right hand, so!"

Sometimes he would pause and add very dramatically, "Once in Göteborg in 1939 suddenly she went opposite way. And there was no one there! We need other man and other spear in case she does Göteborg. And if she does Hamburg, then . . ."

So the rehearsals went on day after day until the stars would fly in for the first night, meeting the rest of the cast for the first time onstage.

There was one disastrous lighting session when Dr. Schramm wanted the stage darker and a ladder to be removed. "That thing . . . die Leiter . . ." — pointing furiously at the ladder — "that Leiter off . . . nein, nein, nein! dunkler . . ." Leiter! Darker! Dunkler! No one could understand, and the stage grew alternately brighter or dimmed to blackout and then rose to full glare, the offending ladder remained untouched, the producer was screaming, the chaos was complete, and I watched in joy.

Dr. Schramm was very critical of my first production. "You make them move too much, and what they do is showing us the same as the musical phrase. That's ballet choreography. Opera choreography quite different." At the time I laughed behind his back, but later I came to see what an important lesson he was giving, helping me to understand that vitality and restlessness are not the same.

"She's so lovely," said a jovial old gentleman who had been at the Royal Opera House since time immemorial. The thought of an attractive woman excited me — I certainly hadn't seen many since entering the world of music — so I followed him into the rehearsal, but alas, my expectations were sadly let down. The plump lady in pale pink, waving a handkerchief girlishly, remains my first lesson in relativity, and I realized that if I stayed locked long enough in this sealed-off world of wing collars and formalities, I too might call beautiful what to my still-fresh eyes was tasteless and ugly. The relationship between opera professionals and sex is often difficult to fathom.

One day we were rehearsing *Figaro* and had reached the moment in one of the ensembles when in traditional productions the count puts his hand surreptitiously on Susanna's bosom, she slaps him, he snatches his hand away, and the audience chuckles with delight. This feeble piece of business could be witnessed in all European opera houses, but when I first saw it, I found it absurdly out of place in a beautiful passage of music, and now I prevented the singers from introducing it into our new production. At the end of the rehearsal the Austrian conductor was very agitated. "Mr. Brook, I am used to that joke. If you take it away, I am distracted, I can't conduct." I took it away, and he never forgave me.

I learned another aspect of the hidden mysteries of the Royal Opera House when I was given an office that was a sort of corridor leading to the Accounts Department. Day after day, a knock on my door would reveal an embarrassed or truculent creditor, who, a sheaf of papers in hand, in true comic opera style would mumble, "When the company was on tour last year, they ordered flowers" — or champagne or taxis — "and we've never been paid . . ." I would just point to the opposite door.

I also learned other more prosaic mysteries, as once a week I would join the musical director and the general administrator in agonizing sessions called planning. We sat with what was mysteriously named the N. A. book and sheets of squared paper, working out the opera repertoire for the coming months. Whenever anyone proposed a certain work for a particular day, there was invariably an obstacle.

"No, that will make seven *Toscas* in one season, but there's only enough audience for six. We could always do *Trovatore* — no, it's a Wednesday and we've got a matinee of *Carmen*, Mr. Ballard couldn't do the changeover in time — ah, but he could manage *Traviata*, let's see what cast we've got for *Traviata*." Out comes the N. A. book and I learn that the initials mean Not Available. "She's in Hamburg. And the tenor's got a *Messiah* in Huddersfield. *Aida?* Why not . . . ? But if the old cow lets us down at the last minute like she did on Thursday, and her cover's doing a B Minor Mass — no, let's forget *Aida* . . ." And so it went on.

I struggled for better conditions and longer rehearsals, and I gradually succeeded, but all the same, when I did a new production of *La Bohème*, I encountered many of the most fundamental opera house problems. I never had the four principal men together in rehearsal at the same time. If three of them were there, the fourth was inevitably away — not resting, as was always claimed to be so important for the voice, but flying to Paris for a quick morning recording or to a provincial German city to snap up an extra fee for a recital. Instead, a stage manager would stand in for the missing character, holding the large score and enthusiastically singing in out-of-tune Lancashire Italian. When the day of the premiere arrived and I still had not had one complete rehearsal of the fourth act, I went to see the administrator, angrily threatening to withdraw my name and make a statement to the press. He was exceptionally well-practiced at soothing temperaments — this was the major part of his job — and he swore to me that I would have a rehearsal that evening before the performance. He kept his word, being equally persuasive with the reluctant singers, who, half an hour before the curtain rose and as the white-tied audience was already taking its seats, were assembled on the other side of the thick red curtain in their silk dressing gowns and initialed bathrobes, with makeups unfinished, faces glistening with foundations of unpowdered greasepaint — and in stage whispers, without music, we solemnly went through the movements of the last act.

The reason for doing a hurried cut-price *Bohème* was a problem of repertoire. In every opera house, *Bohème* is a work that can easily be popped into any gap, because however many performances one gives in any one season, it never fails to draw an audience. In the hurriedly and haphazardly improvised postwar repertoire, we had not yet got ourselves a *Bohème* and desperately needed one, good or bad, to help us out of our planning problems. However, the season's budget had been spent, so I was persuaded against my will to use the ancient scenery that had not surfaced since before the war. Mr. Ballard was consulted and lovingly went to one of his special hiding places. What he brought out were the painted cloths from the very first *Bohème* at Covent

Garden, which showed the views of Paris that Puccini himself had photographed with his tripod and plate camera and which had been faithfully reproduced by my namesake, the scene painter with white gloves, Mr. Brooks. They were very faded, something between old picture postcards and early Utrillos, and they were magically beautiful. I had fumed against the idea, but I had tears in my eyes when I saw them. If I hated traditional operas, this was the exception. For me, *Bohème* will never look so good again, and I willingly accept that even the war against tradition has its exceptions.

My first big production was *Boris Godunov*. It was an opera I loved — it seemed like Shakespeare, with no exaggeration, no rhetoric, each phrase expressing a dramatic truth — and we were to present it for the first time in Mussorgsky's own austere orchestration instead of with Rimsky-Korsakov's lush revisions. My starting point was always the scenery, and as painted views of Russian folklore seemed woefully inadequate, I wanted a designer who could help me bring into the opera the earth and passion of the Russian revolutionary cinema that had burst so excitingly into my life when Stalin became our ally in the war. At the time, it was customary to use easel painters as stage designers, but my aim was to replace the flapping and unconvincing series of outsize paintings with a solid world of real structures. If I did not want a painter, I could not turn toward the professional theater designers either, as for the most part these were competent men who knew all the routines of their craft, could deliver ground plans and working drawings, and were popular with the technical staff because "they know what they want" — but for all these virtues their work sadly lacked the mystery that a real artist brings.

At the time, Roland Petit's company was visiting London, and I saw a performance of Cocteau's ballet *Le Jeune Homme et la Mort* where a three-dimensional attic flew up into the air to reveal, as solid as reality, the rooftops of Paris with the Eiffel Tower in the distance and a neon sign for "Citroën" winking up and down its structure, letter by letter. The decor was signed Wakhevitch, a name that was new to everyone I asked. But I was convinced that this was the designer for whom I had been waiting and set off for Paris to pick up his trail. "Cocteau always keeps a lot of young men around him," I was told. "He does all the work himself, but sometimes he lets one of the boys sign it, to give him a start in life." I could not believe that such strong architecture could have come into being in this way, and further inquiries revealed that though Wakhevitch was unknown in the theater, he was already famous for a triumphant series of very expensive film sets, including rebuilding a whole section of Montmartre on the lot at Billancourt Studios at the height of the war. I managed to reach him on the telephone, and we made an appointment to meet on the pavement outside the Théâtre Marigny where the performance I was attending ended at midnight.

The man who sprang out of his Citroën very late was certainly not one of Cocteau's boys. Georges Wakhevitch had close-cropped gray hair, a face textured like a walnut, warm quick eyes, and he was wearing the shiny though well-worn belted leather overcoat of the world of French movies. As we shook hands, a friendship was instantly created. We had coffee together in the Champs Élysées, and the working relationship was sealed.

When our *Boris* opened, an old-fashioned critic dismissed it as being "like a film," but this was exactly what we had wanted. A "film" meant replacing the wobbly artifices of operatic realism with a harsh Russia, where ferocity, oppression, and pain could be totally believable. Opera for us meant energy, the energy of revolution, of *Battleship Potemkin* and *Alexander Nevsky,* so we looked for an imagery that would go beyond the ordinary, that would fill the proportions of an operatic stage and create impressions that would catch the breath. For Georges and myself there was only one criterion — could we astonish?

Indeed, the images were unexpected: I had a first empty space for the scene of the revolution where, instead of the usual painted forest, there was nothing, just the gigantic Covent Garden stage, covered with a white cloth, and an idiot waiting alone in the falling snow. When Boris died, a deep perspective of double doors slid silently together, one by one, starting in the distance, until the last pair, as they met, formed a gigantic icon, a head of Christ whose enormous eyes towered over the tiny dying czar. Earlier in the opera, when Boris during his long monologue was frightened by the ticking of a clock, an ordinary timepiece somewhere in the room seemed suburban and trivial. So searching for an epic way of treating this idea, Georges created a circular dome, looking out over the spires of Moscow, to which the czar climbed to study maps and contemplate the vastness of his kingdom. Above his head, a system of huge interfitting cogwheels disappeared into the flies, as though part of the mechanism of a medieval clock.

As night fell, iron grilles slowly rose up shuttering out all the openings of the dome, and we bullied the chorus into becoming the starving population climbing nightmarishly onto the bars. At the same time, the sharp-toothed machinery began to revolve, and suddenly a huge pendulum plunged down like a blade, sweeping across the full length of the stage. This seemed to us to be in keeping with the scale of the music, and naturally we were rather proud of the result, taking the inevitable cries of protest in our stride.

The production was sufficiently well received for it to be revived a year later, and this time a young Bulgarian singer, Boris Christoff, who was beginning to be known on the Continent, was invited to make his debut with us in the leading role.

He did not take kindly to these new scenic effects, which in his eyes risked stealing some of the glory from the star performer. As soon as I had described the production to him, we were at war. At every rehearsal, he opposed each direction with a "no," hoping to bring the production into line with the traditional stagings he had already performed in Europe. For both of us, the quarrel became a basic matter of principle, and neither was prepared to yield an inch. When Christoff learned that all the seats had been sold because of his already considerable reputation, he played his trump card: he would not perform unless I changed the production. Immediately, we were in the general administrator's office, with agents, managers, the conductor, and once again all of David Webster's conciliatory skills were needed.

"It seems that the main problem is the clock."

"Yes," said Christoff, "I am used to having a clock where I can see it, on my right. Otherwise I can't sing the scene."

"And you," Webster continued, turning to me, "you insist that the big clock is an integral part of the set and the production?"

"Yes."

Webster knew that Christoff longed to perform but had got himself locked in a situation from which he could not withdraw, and he also realized that I had no intention of giving in.

"Then, Mr. Christoff, if we give you a clock of your own . . . " he proposed.

"That's all I need! No problem."

Webster had him trapped.

"One clock for you, one for Mr. Brook?"

He could not refuse.

So the matter was settled, but I am afraid that Christoff's compromise did not leave me generously disposed. I asked our prop maker to make the tiniest clock he could imagine, as for a doll's house. He agreed and produced for me an exquisite miniature. A few mornings later came the big moment, the general rehearsal, far more important than the first night, because it was a social event for all musical London. The theater was full of singers, and even the wings were crowded with jealous rival basses, wanting to take the measure of this new foreign prodigy. The first act went off without incident. But when the interval was finished and the conductor was already back in the pit, I was not surprised to hear a voice shouting, "Where is Mr. Brook?" I went on stage to face a Boris shaking with fury.

"Mr. Brook, you have not kept your agreement. Where is my clock?"

I pointed to the tiny object on the table.

"Ridiculous! No one will be able to see it!"

"You never mentioned a particular size," I answered.

"Very well. I won't sing." He strode off the stage to his dressing room and locked the door, paying no attention to the stage manager's knocks and entreaties.

By now, the audience, the orchestra, and the conductor were growing restive. Looking round the wings, my eye fell on a young Polish bass with a magnificent voice. He had longed to be considered for the role but unfortunately had absolutely no acting ability. When I asked him if he would like to take over, he leaped forward joyfully, and as Christoff sat convinced that the performance could not proceed without him, through the dressing-room speakers came a rich and powerful Slavonic bass, generously amplified by the sound system. What followed that day was exceptional, even in opera history. Suddenly, the poor Polish singer in his everyday suit, his mouth wide open, his larynx vibrating, his arms outstretched, was elbowed off the stage by a furious Bulgarian in costume and makeup, who proceeded to both sing and act the scene with such power, passion, and conviction that the two clocks and the full battery of scenic effects only added to his triumph, and the scene ended with one of the greatest ovations of his career.

Some years after I had left Covent Garden, I went into a little Italian restaurant in Kensington, and at a table by the wall I saw a man who seemed very familiar. I had a feeling that I knew him well, and when he looked up and caught my eye I saw that he too had a similar reaction. He came rapidly toward me opening his arms. I did likewise, we hugged and patted each other, and only then did we realize that he was Christoff and I was me. We had both mistaken one powerful flood of feeling for its opposite — it was hate not love — but there was no turning back. We hugged each other once more and we never met again; when recently I heard the sad news that he had died, I felt I had lost a good friend.

Someone I knew well who had been a tenor in his youth gave me one essential piece of advice that carried me through my short opera career. "Flatter," he said. "Flatter all the time, flatter shamelessly, never ask yourself if you are overdoing it, because that's not possible, go on flattering." I learned many other important lessons — not only how to practice the subtle techniques of diplomacy that I had observed in Binkie Beaumont but also when to shout, when to threaten — in fact, all the repertoire of roles an opera director has to play.

During one of my rehearsals I overheard two famous German sopranos whispering together on the other side of a piece of scenery. "It's our first London season, so let's do what he asks. Later, we can dictate." In this case, I struck first, acting like an angry fascist in rehearsal, and of course they were very impressed.

Fortunately, these lessons were only of use in the hysterical opera world. Ever since, I have found that in the rest of theater, no violent or aggressive tactics have the remotest chance of producing any good result. On the rare occasions when I have lost my temper, or bullied, or reduced an actor to tears, I have deeply regretted it. A French actress once told me of a director who would noisily eat sandwiches and then crumple the paper bag during her scenes just to create a climate of irritation so that out of frayed nerves something unexpected might explode. This method may have worked for him, but in my experience tension and friction in rehearsal help no one — only calm, quiet, and great confidence can bring about the slightest glimmer of creativity.

At Covent Garden, out of necessity and despair, for the first time I found myself taking an interest in training. I made experiments with the principal singers, but soon saw that there was nothing I could do to improve their lamentable efforts to act. A tenor I worked with was an ex-policeman, and all he could do was to move his arms stiffly up and down as though directing traffic. I even tried hanging on to them with both hands, only to discover that they were totally and inseparably locked in his brain to the pattern of the score. If the musical phrase rose, then the stiff outstretched arm would go up proportionately, and nothing could check its movement. In his case, I accepted defeat and turned my attention to the chorus. Every Saturday morning I held sessions in the long, narrow bar behind the Dress Circle — one hour for the men, one hour for the women. The men were mostly Welsh miners, who stood in surly groups as though they were at a pithead union meeting, grudgingly responding to my instruction to run, fall on the ground, then leap to their feet, in ways that could express pleasure or fear. The ladies, however, were very enthusiastic; they came in hats with tiny veils, decorated with paper flowers or dangling clusters of cherries. They would listen eagerly as I explained, "You are all slaves in an ancient Egyptian harem," and the cherries would bobble with delight.

The turmoil I had brought into the Royal Opera House was beginning to prove too much for the ever-anxious administration. My production of *Salome* was the last straw. I did not set out to shock, but followed a line of reasoning that was exactly the same as it is today: if the stage image is ugly or inappropriate, it distracts from the music; if it is boldly in tune with the music, then one can listen fully engaged. Unaccountably, opera lovers do not seem to be distracted by ugliness, only by the unfamiliar. Even more strangely, many of the same audiences who are very sophisticated in their visual judgment at the ballet allow their sensibility to be blinkered when they go to the opera. I had seen the conventional stagings of *Salome* in a so-called realistic set with colonnades and a large well, reconstructing antiquity in the same way as Henry Irving's panoramas had done for Shakespeare in the previous century, and was absolutely certain that Wilde's bizarre imagery drenched in Strauss's heavily erotic score could not be banalized in this way, and felt that the stage picture needed to be as daring and imaginative and even as complicated as the music. No living artist seemed better equipped to provide this than Salvador Dalí. I had seen several of Dalí's designs for the ballet, and he clearly had the freedom, the decadence, the obsessive sense of the erotic, and the unpredictable fantasy that would correspond perfectly to this task. In fact, what he invented for *Salome* was quite amazing, but it only reached the stage in a very diluted form. When I delivered Dalí's designs, the conductor, the musical staff, plus the production and wardrobe departments were all outraged by his iconoclastic visions, and Dalí refused to come to battle on the spot himself. Desperate telegrams to him yielded no other result than a message advising me to get a rhinoceros to take his place. I could never leave the rehearsals, even for a moment, as relations with the conductor had so deteriorated that he would only speak to me through an assistant. Gradually each department chipped Dalí down to size, until outrageous costumes became normal and his fantastic architectures tame. On the first night I was booed off the stage for a scandal that was not even there, and the next day I was out on my ear.

Even before meeting Wakhevitch and Dalí, I had sought out every occasion to travel. The Europe I had known as a child was an unlit quayside, a long black silhouette of warehouses, and when the channel steamer drifted in to Calais, it still revealed a brooding continent of postwar darkness. Often I had found excuses to visit Paris: the sharp scent of Gauloises was strangely exciting, and everything from the Métro to the cafés had a special sexual glow. And if Paris was the films of Carné and the photos of Brassaï, when I went on to Madrid I discovered how the streets belonged to the Middle Ages, while the botanical gardens were nostalgically Proustian, dusty as an old picture postcard, with nursemaids pushing prams along the rusty railings while soldiers in faded uniforms walked by hand in hand. The Russia of nineteenth-century novels seemed to have been transported to the great Spanish estates, where the gracefully desperate and elegantly tragic rich relieved their boredom in feverish nights with gypsies. In Barcelona I found my favorite world of the thriller and moved into a seedy hotel called the Hotel of the Orient for no other reason than to write to all my friends with this name on the letterhead. In Lisbon my introductions were to theater people, but the fascination of the city was the discovery of whole streets of whorehouses — something for which Oxford, Birmingham, and Stratford-upon-

Avon had no equivalent. I was stranded for a time in Tangier, and it was here that I had my first taste of the East, of heat and dust, of swarming children in narrow streets, of shady men approaching me in cafés to ask if I could help them import contraceptives or barbed wire, while my immediate concern was to buy olive oil for my mother from old women sitting on the ground, concealing large illegal jars beneath their voluminous black skirts.

Initially, Salvador Dalí had seemed a good pretext for visiting Spain, but in fact it was back in Paris that we met for the first time. In an elegant drawing room in Neuilly, with a countess of his acquaintance in attendance, we listened together as a pianist played and sang his way through the score of *Salome*. What gave me weight in his eyes was that I represented Covent Garden — he was very susceptible to prestige. He spoke enthusiastically of his wish to make effects in the theater that no one had ever seen before. This established him as a man very much to my taste, and when he described his ideas of making scenery out of firemen's hoses that when the water was turned on, would swell, leap, and twist into fantastic shapes, or of a proscenium constructed out of porcelain plates that would suddenly splinter and crash to the ground, or of dancers in a ballet he had designed who scattered hundreds of furled black umbrellas on the stage to make a lake so that when the hero, Ludwig of Bavaria, drowned himself, the great black lake of umbrellas would rise and snap open, making a funeral pall over his body, I was rapidly convinced that he could be the greatest inventor of stage effects and machinery since the baroque masques. He invited me to stay with him in his home in Cadaqués, and there he proved to be both a thoughtful host and an admirably serious collaborator. To be with the great surrealist and find no trace of eccentricity in his behavior was oddly disappointing nonetheless, until the morning I found him with two flowers in his nostrils. He raised a finger: "We have guests."

During lunch, he spoke of the film he wanted to direct. It is a ridiculous convention in the cinema, he said, for the camera always to be present at dramatic moments in a story. This is not like life; he would do away with the convention of aiming the camera at the center of the action. Instead, the spectator would watch a banal, meaningless setup — the camera perhaps focused on a bit of wall — and occasionally an elbow or a scrap of nose would jut momentarily into the frame, suggesting passionately exciting events just out of our reach. Then he went on to describe a project he had thought up that very morning as a result of his new connection with Covent Garden. *Salome,* he hoped, would put him in a position to insist that the Royal Opera in the future place at his disposal unlimited funds. Then he would announce to the press that for the first time ever he was going to bring a real ocean liner onto the operatic stage. With the maximum of publicity, he would build a great ramp from the Thames up to the theater. He would demolish the back wall, giant, costly winches would be installed, and cables would be attached to the ship. The date of one unique performance would be announced, and inevitably all elite London would rush to buy exorbitantly priced seats. When the night came, the curtain would rise and — what would the audience see? Here he stopped dramatically, and we knew he had a trick up his sleeve. It would see no more than what it always sees each time the ballet performs, he continued: the cracks and creases that always disfigure the canvas of the permanent Covent Garden cyclorama. As the great ship made its slow stately journey up the ramp, the audience would hear the growing percussion of creaks, groans, and bumps heralding its approach, the excitement would grow, the tension would become unendurable, and suddenly there would be a *new vertical crease* in the pattern of cracks, as the nose of the liner pushed against the canvas sky. That would be all — just a new dent. But the dent would be the expression of the immensity of the enterprise that lay behind it and would be all the more extraordinary and unforgettable because the object itself would remain unseen. "To show people what they expect," Dalí said, flicking his mustache, "would be very disappointing." His exaggerations and absurdities made sense to me; they displayed a kind of logic that seemed more penetrating than the tepid attitudes on which the conventional theater thrived.

Dalí lodged me in a little fisherman's hut on the bay that he kept for his friends. On a shelf, I found a book called *Essais sur la proportion,* by Prince Matila Ghika. Had it not been for Dalí's hut, I might never have come across this work. As I turned the pages, the first thing to catch my eye was the picture of a magnificent piece of classical architecture with a geometrical grille superimposed on it. Then I found an analysis of the relationships between arches, vaults, and colonnades, showing them to be equal to the proportions in faces; the distances from eyebrow to nose, from chin to lip were linked to famous paintings, which were in turn linked to architecture, all of them referring to geometry, their harmony inseparable from numbers, their beauty subject to laws. For the first time I heard a spellbinding term, "the Golden Section." Dalí, *Salome*, the opera, suddenly receded, for I knew I had found a work that revived all my deepest preoccupations.

"What are you going to study?" we used to be asked at school. "Science or literature? If you take biology, you needn't do religion. If you take physics, then you drop art." I could not understand how experience could be divided into two opposing categories, into what can be felt and what can be defined. All the explanations of the fascinating mysteries of the universe were always in terms of numbers, and it was the coldness of these equations that repelled me. I wondered what could give a number the warmth that would link it to the living world.

As I had no formal training when I began to work in the theater, I used feelings and intuitions as my guide. This did not lead me to despise reason; on the contrary, I respected its value as a tool that could discriminate, organize, and clarify, but I observed with astonishment that decisions taken by pure instinct seemed to reflect a hidden order that the conscious mind was unable to define. I noticed that when I was working with a designer, pushing pieces of cardboard across a model stage, empirically seeking what would look right, we would suddenly stop and cry out together, "Six is too many, let's try five!" Why? I asked myself. Why did three arches seem more harmonious than four? This is "cultural," I was told, but I couldn't believe it. Why in rehearsal did I ask the actors to step closer to one another, or move apart, until the distance had a rightness that could be neither more nor less? Why did one sound seem truer than another? I became more and more convinced that behind taste, artistic judgment, and cultural habits lay certain proportions and relationships that touched us because a quality of emotion is integral to their nature.

When I first read a book about Einstein, the notion of relativity immediately caught my imagination because it showed how lurking inside every measurement was a factor that classical physics had ignored and that the unshakable two plus two I had learned since childhood only made four in a relative way. The moment I learned that two plus two is not necessarily four, science sprang to life; it became pure poetry, ordinary commonsense logic was shattered, the vastness of the unknown reasserted itself, and wonder was there once more. Could there not be another unknown factor, I began to speculate, that sits unseen within every measurement, which we could call the factor of feeling, the indefinable quality that binds the workings of the atom to the experience of life? Having been conditioned since childhood to assume that each number is the same as the next, I was now discovering in my daily experience that every figure is alive; it carries within it its own emotional power. I knew nothing of numerology; this was based on practical observation. So I invented for myself a new post-Einsteinian theory in which all equations had to include a factor that I called the "dimension of quality." All I cared about was to break through the divisions among science, art, and religion and unite them within the same observable, understandable experience. I was so amazed by my discovery that I wanted to shout from the rooftops, "Eureka! Quality exists! Differences of quality are real!" Ghika's book came as an unexpected confirmation of my first naive intuitions. On returning home I tried to find a copy of the work for myself, but without success.

Sometime later, when I was again in Paris, I called Georges Wakhevitch, who said that he was going to dine with some friends and would I join them? We met in a small uninteresting two-room flat, and the couple, not so young, were busy with Georges in the kitchen. As they had left me alone with a drink in their living room, I looked idly at a book that was lying open on the table. If it had not been for Dalí and the work by Ghika that I had studied, I might not have paused in front of a simple diagram that seemed at first sight to be connected to the Golden Section. However, as I read the accompanying text, I realized that the author was doing something different and even more unexpected. He was referring to the musical scale and using the octave to express an amazing idea: the nature and quality of human experience are exactly determined by their place in a rising and falling scale of energies of differing intensities. This meant that even when life is in its crudest state, a process exists through which the coarse can become finer, and this process is not haphazard. For the first time I encountered in a clear contemporary language something that corresponded to the question that concerned me most. I had always been troubled by the fact that science has no way of recognizing that human experiences rise and fall in quality all the time. Everything at one moment is acutely sensed as "better" or "worse," and this is not just a "value judgment." It is a real judgment based on a deep sense of hidden values, without which no human life would have any meaning. For every artist, levels of goodness and badness — levels of quality — exist all the time. This is the guide behind artistic creation. For science, levels of quality have no measurable reality and consequently they are dismissed with the portmanteau word "subjective." Now here was a presentation of the great space around us in terms that were neither cold nor impersonal. It expressed, in concrete practical terms, a new way of understanding how a sense of values can depend on something more objective than likes, dislikes, and personal taste. It bridged the gap between the vagueness of our inner experiences, however intensely they are felt, and the rigorous outlines of the observable world. At last I was stumbling on a knowledge in which observer and observed were united, where science was human, and where the levels of quality of human experience were inseparable from the structures of measurable reality.

Now, in front of my eyes, someone was actually describing this intuition in very precise terms, and in my excitement it never occurred to me that this new discovery was merely feeding my already overactive interest in theoretical ideas. The fact that the greatest theories about the nature of life are meaningless unless they are integrated into hard-gained personal experience was something I was not yet prepared to accept. Learning to assemble ideas and thereby live in a palace of glittering thoughts seemed an end in itself.

All this occurred at a time that seemed filled with joyful coincidences. During these years, events would occur as though by chance, but each seemed to have a storybook symmetry. My life was often like a well-built unfolding scenario, and I welcomed each surprising twist, becoming dangerously confident that whatever my immediate obstacle, somehow a hidden author would bring about a neat solution.

In between meeting Natasha and our marriage, I had lived with a young woman named Jean in a relationship that was sadly crumbling away. To mend it, we set off for Paris, but we quarreled all the way, and in a further attempt to escape from our disputes, we took the night train to Florence. The journey was even more unhappily agitated, and as we stepped off the train our relationship had reached the breaking point. Neither of us knew the city, but we walked side by side in hurt silence along the platform, out of the station, into the street. We still walked straight ahead, until we came to a point where the road divided. I branched to the right, determined not to turn my head to see if my companion was following. Only after several minutes did I allow myself to look round. She was gone and I was filled with a sudden sense of elation, in which relief was coupled with a sense of freedom. Resolving not to risk seeing her again, I took the most obscure side streets until on the far side of the town I found a small hotel. Later in the afternoon, I pressed the button for the lift. The old wooden cabin creaked painfully down to my level, and as I opened the outside door, Jean opened the inner one. Fate seemed to be dangling reconciliation in front of us, but we were icily unresponsive. However, destiny had other aims, for the coincidence served to keep us in touch, and this made it possible many months later, on a sudden impulse, to phone Jean and go over to her flat. A newspaper cutting was lying on her mantelpiece. As we spoke, I looked at it idly, until I realized that it was a review of the book I had seen in Paris at the home of Wakhevitch's friends. In the book, *In Search of the Miraculous*, its author, a Russian philosopher named Ouspensky, claimed that the ancient teaching had been transmitted to him orally by a figure whom he indicated only by the initial G. In reading the book, I had wondered what name lay behind this enigmatic letter, and Jean now explained to me that G. stood for Gurdjieff and went on to say, "A book is one thing; direct teaching is quite different."

"What do you mean?" I asked.

"There is a person in London who is responsible for this teaching," she said.

"Why did you never tell me about it?"

"It's not something to talk about — it's far too personal. It is very difficult, but if you want, I can put you in touch."

There is an old tradition that says that every night before going to sleep one should thank the person who leads one to one's teacher. I cannot say I have been very faithful to this suggestion, but as I write, the gratitude is there. A few evenings later, I was walking through the gate of a large old London house in a quiet tree-lined street called Hamilton Terrace. The front door had frosted glass plates set in vertical panels, and in one of them was silhouetted the shadow of a waiting figure. The image inflamed my imagination, exciting me with a sense of mystery and at the same time arousing my suspicion. Part of me was longing for a chance to scoff at this adventure that another part had accepted so readily.

A moment later, all strangeness vanished as the shadow became a normal person, who quite simply was waiting to admit the visitors. Now description becomes unimportant. There was a room, there were people, but this is not what matters. The setting was quite ordinary, but the quality of the encounter was unique. I heard simple words that at once rang true, words that spoke of an understanding that can only be communicated directly, not by writing or by theory, and whose basic principle is that nothing must be accepted passively, everything must be questioned and verified, for a truth only acquires meaning and conviction if it has been tested, rediscovered, and proved step by step within one's own experience.

I had many layers of resistance, but there was no mumbo jumbo, which was reassuring; instead, I was being asked to work with ordinary people, with no flights of fantasy, no romance — something that forced me to face and accept, with difficulty, my own essential ordinariness.

The teacher was Jane Heap. She was American, short, dressed like a man, with closely cropped gray hair. At the time of Gertrude Stein and James Joyce she had been a brilliant literary figure in Paris. There she first met Gurdjieff, and she saw at once that all the efforts and activities that had so richly filled her life thus far were simply part of a search that had not yet found its direction. Deep down she had always felt a need for a quality of understanding that could give meaning to her various talents and link the outer world to another purpose for existence. "We have a world outside us, a universe within," she would often say, and in George Ivanovitch Gurdjieff she found the guide she needed to penetrate into this enigmatic space. She was gentle, ferocious, and compassionate. When she spoke, taking as her starting point any simple question, she would open great vistas of understanding, linking the tiniest detail of everyday life to the laws and the forces that condition all humanity. Her idiom was a rich slangy vernacular from the Midwest, bringing an earthy common sense to everything she proposed; when need be she could give her listener a sudden shock, like the grand slam of the bat on a Ping-Pong ball when it is close to the net. Through her, I began to discover that "tradition" had another meaning from the sterile old-fashionedness I so detested in the theater. I learned to understand the oriental way of hiding knowledge like a precious stone, of concealing its sources, of making it hard to discover, so that its value can be truly appreciated by the searcher who has been willing to pay the price. She showed how every religion rapidly destroys the purity of its origins by offering too readily to others what one has not made one's own by hard practical work.

There are many admirable books that give an indication of what this teaching can mean, and it is not for me to try to add more words to what must be experienced for oneself. It seemed to me at the very first meeting to contain essential truths, and this seems equally so more than forty years later. A school of work based on esoteric ideas is not like an ordinary school. One does not progress grade by grade. It is not a clinic, for one is never cured. At first a higher reality seems to be somewhere out there, in space. Gradually, painfully, wondrously one comes to see where it really lies.

"What is my biggest obstacle to a real understanding?" I asked Jane after a few weeks. The reply was instantaneous: "Peter."

Was it true that I would never again be as close to the truth as at that moment at the age of fourteen when, lying on the ground, I could feel the earth beat? Now my experience was swinging like a great pendulum, pulling me between countries and people, between travel and theater, between various ways of life. I have always been suspicious of any creed, of any conviction, of any program that ignores contradictions. The meaning of chaos, the need for order; the wish for action, the power of inaction; the silence that alone gives sense to sound; the necessity to intervene and the virtue of letting go; the balance between inner and outer life; the dilemma of what to give and what to withhold, of what to take and what to decline — then, as now, I was driven by these shifting themes. The changing of styles, places, and rhythms created a willful, joyful way of life, but the sense of being a swinging ball also carried with it a deep need for the ball to be attached to a thread, a thread that should be there at all costs to save the ball from spinning irretrievably into outer space.

There is a picture I bought from a small boy of nine or ten when I was on my first holiday with Natasha in Ischia. How he managed to conceive such a strange image I will never know, but it haunts me to this day. In strong strokes of Prussian blue, it shows a great horse in full gallop, leaping toward the sky, hooves rampant, its head tossed back in splendor, while a second neck curves downward from the same powerful body over other stumbling legs so that the horse seems both to rise and at the same time to lurch toward the ground. The two movements are equally dynamic, one matching the other, so that the leap and the fall are suspended in midair, never to be resolved.

The image has stayed bright and present on the wall of my mind as one of the most treasured and most personal symbols, rich in ambiguity. Did the small boy, by some intuition buried deep in his subconscious, recognize that all that aspires upward must also fall? Was the stumble tragic, or did some other intuition tell him that within the inevitable curve toward the ground another head, another pair of legs always has the possibility to leap again toward the sky? Did the image speak to me so deeply at the time because in it all possibilities coexist — the leap, the stumble, the need to look upward, the urge to fly, the inevitability of the fall, followed by the leap renewed? The double horse was like a mirror, or even a map on which both my past and future were already drawn.

Once I had to change into evening clothes in a taxi, rushing at breakneck speed from Glasgow airport to the premiere of the Edinburgh Festival, and as I twisted myself into a scissor position on the backseat, my legs in the air, trying to perform the incredibly difficult acrobatics of changing trousers upside down with arms too short, a ceiling too low, and an angry Scots driver shouting, "Not now, sir, not when we go through a village!," I felt I had turned myself into a hieroglyph of the life I was leading at the time. Then I believed, perhaps excessively, in "experience"; today I would be more critical and question the choice of experiences and the aim that they might serve—then I plunged in headfirst. I followed every attraction. There were few temptations or excesses I refused, wishing to live simultaneously as many parallel lives as I could encompass. In the theater, the thrill was in the activity, never in the result. It was the involvement with others, the process day by day that enthralled me. When a show had gone well, friends would say, "You must be feeling pleased" or "proud" or "satisfied," and not to disappoint them I would usually answer, "Yes." But in fact I never experienced the end of work in this way; what was done was done, and the emotion was one of release or of rediscovering that all possibilities were wide open once again. I always made sure that I had another production already set up before the current one was ended, to cover the danger of failure, and I even made myself ill once when rehearsals were going badly to be sure that I would at least be praised for continuing heroically to the end. After most first nights I would go on a journey, reading the notices in the plane, and I would have to be dragged back almost by force to revisit the cast. It's over, I would say to myself, it's done.

Life was intense, coming in short bursts, and the immediacy of the goals provided the stimulus. After Covent Garden came Stratford again, then London—play after play—and I lived from production to production, which meant rehearsal periods that never exceeded three or four weeks, so I felt no need for long-term aims. Each new project had its virgin beginning, its time of preparation, and an all-engrossing crescendo as the active work began with the completion already in sight, the premiere an unmovable date that seemed to race toward one like the buffers looming before the driver at the end of the railroad track. From the start there was an urgency, and each day the pressure would increase until, at maximum heat, there was an exceptional tempo of creativity, creating combustion that led to explosion, followed by climax and release.

One path led to another, taking me naively into fields where I had neither special knowledge nor experience: tinkering with odd musical instruments; experimenting with large clumsy tape recorders; finding odd places for a microphone, sticking it inside the piano or under the pedal to make *musique concrète*; spending happy hours with a model theater tearing and folding scraps of cardboard, moving them into different configurations of scenery; taking photographs, cropping and editing enlargements; passing from film to opera, to light comedy, to the classics, to television, each burst of energy producing more energy, one area feeding another. But it was only in travel that I felt myself complete.

In 1951 Germany was still a dead sea of destruction whose waves were rubble out of which rose a feverish life that infected me with its excitements. This was my first trip to Berlin, and here I met Brecht. What fascinated me had nothing to do with his theories — in the pragmatic climate of English theater I never read books about the stage — it was the man, it was the melodrama of having to meet Brecht in secret, of not being allowed by the British military authorities to be seen speaking to this notorious Communist in public when he came to the first night of the *Measure for Measure* I had just staged in Stratford. There was some incomprehensible fear that a handshake could be interpreted politically by the West German press and embarrass whatever Allied policy was at the time. So I sat with this cool ironic man and his walnut-wrinkled wife, Helene Weigel, in a private dining room in a Berlin hotel whose special entrance gave onto a back alley, eating a lavish meal laid on apologetically by the same military authorities at the army's expense, and it was this atmosphere of a spy movie that I relished rather than what he said.

Brecht described to me his theory of "alienation." He spoke of his ideal audience: two peasants, sitting side by side in the front row, discussing the action with irony, never caught up in the make-believe. He was articulate and entertaining, but I was quite unconvinced. For me the stage was still the world of illusion I had cherished from childhood. Brecht's attempts to question the value of this magic place beyond the looking glass found no response in my experience, and his social concepts were very far from my own. On the other hand, I was spellbound by the richness and dazzling theatricality of his work as a director. At his suggestion I made a special trip to Munich to see his production of *Mother Courage*. The first moments — when from the depths of a bare stage, pressing against the turning of a revolve, a powerful old woman dragged her vast cart laden with goods toward us — captured my imagination in exactly the same way as the approach of the cardboard bandit in the boat had done in the toy theater I had seen as a child. The following hours seemed at the time very turgid — today, I would be more respectful — and my interest only returned with the last moments, when the first image was reversed and the tough unbreakable Mother dragged her cart away into the infinite white distance.

Brecht also invited me to his theater in East Berlin, the home of the Berliner Ensemble, to see his new production, *Der Hofmeister*. The play is a satirical account of a young man's humiliating experiences as tutor in a rich house, leading to his castrating himself in the last scene when he realizes that the education he is expected to deliver is mutilated at the source. Brecht's staging, with elegant revolving scenery and slyly sardonic music, threw into relief a form of stylized acting that I had never encountered before. In the first scene, where the tutor is being interviewed by a monstrous rich lady, his inner states were directly mirrored by contorted and grotesque body movements, executed by a young actor of incredible dexterity. One hand clutched a handkerchief behind his back, and in between each answer he gave to the lady he would mop his brow, at the same time bending his knees, bowing lower and lower, then straightening to squeeze out the next obsequious phrase in a strangulated high-pitched gasp. The same actor delivered monologues in other scenes in a voice from which all natural inflections had been eliminated, making a sound pattern that mirrored his jerky marionette-like gestures. The result was as though a powerful caricaturist's vision had been stamped onto a human form; every muscle was disciplined to serve the grotesque vision, brilliantly executed and purely theatrical. The experience was totally unexpected, and the shock of it opened possibilities and questions about acting that were completely new and far from anything the theater at home was providing.

Many years later when we were in Berlin with *King Lear* I went again to visit the Berliner Ensemble. Brecht had died, but his widow Helene Weigel had taken over the company and for a year had been rehearsing one of his last projects, an adaptation of Shakespeare's *Coriolanus*. The auditorium was virtually sliced in half by a long table. The English system, where the director is backed by a long table with stage managers and their assistants noting down every move, is already alarming, but here, along the

length of the table were six people — Helene Weigel, two directors, two dramaturgs, and another man of undefined function —
each apparently with equal weight and authority, all controlling
the rehearsal together. As the main actor entered the stage, I recognized him as one of the European heavyweights, middle-aged,
of peasant stock, shrewd and commanding, a type of actor for
which England had few equivalents. I had seen him many times
playing magnificently in other Brecht productions, so I was very
intrigued to know how he worked. "No!" cried an overexcited
dramaturg as the actor spoke the first line. "Say it like this!" and
he proceeded to show how the words should be spoken, deliv-
ering them in a tense, high-pitched, singsong voice. For many
years, it had been anathema in the English theater to "give an
intonation" to an actor, and few directors would dare attempt it.
Here to my astonishment the performer, one of the pillars of the
ensemble, immediately complied. As he repeated the line exactly
as he had been told, there came another cry, this time from one
of the two directors, who instructed him to raise his arm and
point his fingers in a certain way to match the rising inflection.
Then Weigel drily intervened to launch a discussion on the
meaning of the scene. I had difficulty remembering that the play
had been in rehearsal for over a year, as one could easily have
taken it for a very first day on the stage with a cast of beginners.
The actors were pummeled, shaken, provoked, and ordered
around to such a degree that I began to wonder whether Gordon
Craig's dream of having a theater entirely played by marionettes
had not at last come true. At the end of the session, less than half
of a very short scene had been explored, and as the lights came
up I could not wait to put to Weigel what seemed to me to be the
vital question: "When you next come back to the scene, do you
expect the actor to reproduce all that you've made him do
today?"

"Of course not," she answered. "This is how we work in order
to stimulate the actor. Now he must digest the rehearsal and
come back with his own propositions."

I was not convinced that this answer was completely genuine
and left wondering how much freedom the actor was eventually
allowed. But what I had seen made one thing very clear. Brecht
himself stressed the importance of selecting, with a critical sense
of political meaning, the revealing details, the precise gestures
that placed the actor firmly in the social context of the action he

was portraying. This has led to a great deal of misunderstanding all over the world, for it has produced a cold, intellectual, even theoretical form of playing Brecht. Brecht's own actors, however, were never cold or abstract; they were nourished by the rich Central European tradition of dense and psychologically fed naturalism. When Brecht — like the panel I saw in action — constructed with his actors an external pattern of behavior, never discussing the characters' inner life or their psychology, for such terms were taboo, the actors themselves had the training and the intuition secretly to fill these schematic blueprints with their own inner creative material, humanizing them with the warmth of their own private cuisine.

Walking through the streets of East Berlin, I liked most the crumbling facades, the decrepitude, and the shadows. Communism was a romance, as though a strangely insidious sexuality was hidden beneath its drab conformity, in its slogans and heroes. It was not that I felt remote from politics. On the contrary, when very young I would make passionate socialist speeches in our home about poverty and injustice, reproaching my father for abandoning the militant positions of his youth. He would smile tolerantly and explain his view of society with a grown-up moderation that made me boil with impatience. Later, when I left Oxford, I tried to be taken on as an actor in the one Communist theater of the time, called the Unity. I went to an audition and read, with what I thought was great passion, the speech of a young man denouncing capitalist society, and for the first time I heard the phrase that I would utter myself so often in the years to come: "Thank you. We'll be in touch." At the time, I believed and waited, but I never heard from them, so I neither joined the Communist party nor ever again tried to act. Instead, a sense of the relativity of all positions prevented me from attaching myself to any political conviction. I simply observed events with journalistic interest and journalistic skepticism.

After the excitements of Berlin, with its nightclubs where naked women on horseback could be called by telephone to one's table and where trim young men in business suits bowed to one another and fox-trotted discreetly in each other's arms, the long-awaited first trip to New York was a disappointment, for everything there seemed very conventional and slow. Today, I love New York and have some difficulty in reconstructing the elements that seemed so alien at the time, but I remember the hostility of all the square corners, the harshness of a city that had no curves, the apartments that seemed identical — I could have sworn they had the same Renoirs or Cézannes on the walls — so that I no longer knew whether I was visiting someone for the first time or whether I had been there before. When I dared to criticize the mediocrity of one of the great hits on Broadway, I would be told reproachfully, as though this closed all argument, "It's the hottest seat in town." The tiny square of light cut off in the glittering facade of a sky-scraper at night could easily mean a life extinguishing itself, as one human story switched off and another flashed on, and the painful weight of the overfriendly hospitality created such a gap-ing hole of loneliness in me that one night I sat in my bed and could not check a flood of tears, though for what or for whom even at the time I could not tell.

New York was a cliché: it was parties where famous actresses threw off their shoes and screamed, it was the Stork Club, 21, El Morocco, and supper with movie stars, even with foreign royalty; each day had its element of caricature, from the body I passed on the sidewalk on my first day, which had just jumped from the fiftieth story, to the great house on Christmas Day in front of which stood the owner's present to his daughter, a shining Cadil-lac tied up in Christmas ribbon. At the time it was unprecedent-ed for a director to be very young. I had skipped all the stages of apprenticeship, learning as I went along; thus I had no rivals and was taken up by the profession as a sort of pet freak. Now, perhaps unfairly, I was tasting the rewards of success without having had the tough fight to achieve them. My status was indeed a gift from the gods, and I was offered the chance to see that such rewards are of no true interest or value. If one has had to fight ferociously to reach the top, it is hard to accept this simple truth. As my suc-cess had come about quickly, my own impressions were merci-fully direct.

I met a much-admired writer famous for his witticisms, who would set out in the afternoon alone with his chauffeur in his great black Rolls-Royce to cruise round the house on Long Island where he was due to dine; the car would silently glide up the drive and out again while the tense, tortured celebrity would try to imagine the people he would meet and rehearse his jokes in the terror that one of them might misfire. He talked to me kindly, but all I could retain was his empty sadness.

If success and money failed to convince me that they were worthwhile goals in life, my sense of romance, so deeply rooted in childhood, was utterly captivated by something equally vague called beauty. Influenced by the drabness of the wartime years, I reacted against all that was crude and ordinary. I had no respect for the harsh texture of real life, I still looked at the world through muslin curtains like my London friends, and the theater seemed to exist to create fleeting images of delight. So a Proustian sense of nostalgia attracted me to those who could afford elegance, to fashion magazines, dress designers, and photographers, where ephemeral beauty, charm, and style all intertwined. Paris natural-ly seemed the best place on earth; even its smells and its shadows had poetry — and it took me many years to understand what the director I most admired, Tyrone Guthrie, meant when he told me he disliked Paris and preferred the roughness of Belfast. Why roughness rather than beauty? I wondered. It is very hard to be so open to life that one accepts it in whatever form it takes, and when early in my relationship with my teacher, Jane asked me what the greatest aim in life could be, I answered immediately, "Happiness!" She looked at me with wryness and compassion but did not say a word.

When, just after our marriage, tuberculosis was diagnosed in Natasha, my immediate question had been "Should I take her to Switzerland?" The Harley Street doctor had looked at me over the top of his glasses. "Streptomycin," he said adventurously, for antibiotics were still very new, and he added an unforgettable phrase: "If I had TB I would rather be treated with an antibiotic in a coal cellar than breathe the finest mountain air." These words resonated in me long after Natasha's successful recovery in our London home, for they conjured up the power of rough-ness and the flimsiness of beauty.

In the same way, our work with Jane Heap — for Natasha had joined me in her groups — was making us recognize that spiritual meaning can only be found in the thick of life. Her teaching left no room for dreams and self-indulgences; it was sober and aus-tere. There was no proselytizing — it was the very opposite of a sect. It was a school in the true sense of the word, and as an ardent individualist I was reluctantly coming to see how important it is to work with others and not try to make up a spiritual recipe of my own by taking just the bits of the various traditions that seemed to please me at the time. On the other hand, there didn't seem any great difficulty in accepting that a tradition, fed by centuries of revelation and hard-earned formulating, has to be studied and accepted in humility and ignorance; I recognized that the pupil's place is to listen and to learn. A way is proposed to him, and he has the privilege of being allowed to follow — not to criticize and invent his own path. This appeared to be the very meaning of initiation.

To my surprise, one day I heard a very sensitive person who had followed Gurdjieff's teaching since childhood use the phrase "my own personal search," and for a moment I was totally confused. I had become convinced that there is no progress in real understanding, that many thousands of years ago human beings had already reached the summit of intelligence and awareness, and that a teaching based on ancient knowledge stays eternally valid. If each person tried to invent his or her personal approach and interpretation, this could only lead to confusion.

So what could my friend have meant by "his personal search"? Gradually it became clear to me that following a teaching is not just a matter of listening and following obediently. A passive respect is not enough. Both passivity and activity are needed, and both refer to very intense conditions that are far from the crude oppositions these words suggest.

A truly personal research begins when one realizes that to make the process real, one has no choice but to enter into its rediscovery, step by step, accepting nothing as true until it has become true in one's own experience. One must start from zero, clear an empty space in oneself, and painfully struggle to rewrite within one's own organism the whole journey of the very first searcher who paved the way. Only then can one come to the point when if one's teacher raises his right arm and affirms with all his authority, "This is my left arm," the only possible and even respectful answer is "No!"

My first enthusiastic impulse on encountering a spiritual teaching had been to give up everything, to reject the world, to devote myself to a life of metaphysical search, only to discover to my surprise and in a way to my disappointment that this was not expected. Sacrifice without understanding leads to fanaticism, and the first difficult sacrifice one must make is of one's eagerness, of one's confused idea of what it means to be "involved." What is called in esoteric jargon "the fourth way" is neither the way of mortification of the body nor the way of withdrawal from the world, nor the way of high intellectual investigation. It is a term that has caused every possible shade of misunderstanding and distortion — and demands only one thing: understanding. This means a conscious, independently gained understanding that denies credulity — an understanding that cannot be reached simply through ideas, through the mind. It cannot be discovered alone, neither in a study, nor in a desert, nor in a hermitage, but only by long patient work with others under the near-impossible conditions of everyday life. In the coal cellar.

Conventional religion attempts to console; Gurdjieff, on the other hand, said, "I am here to tread on people's corns," and Jane certainly followed him in this way. She was very kind, but she had no indulgence. I would come into a gathering, once even in black tie dressed for a late-night party, locked in my social personality, and would receive jolt after jolt. "It is not possible in a group to have one person making clever and malicious observations about the others," she once said. Immediately I spoke up, protesting, "Whoever amongst us here is malicious?" Jane seized the moment: "You!" she thundered. I can still feel the tremors of my startled ego slapped into recognizing its blindness. I learned dimly to appreciate why in Japan if a pupil is hit by his master he bows in gratitude. "I can see you coming toward this work from a long way off," she would say to me, and I would be pleased, taking it as a compliment. One day it dawned on me that I was indeed a very long way off. "Drowning in life," she would say. "Listen to the way you speak. You can hear in the sound of your voice that you are drowning in life." This image frightened me, and I could not understand why she said this. Everyday life was needed — she was not even suggesting that I give up my basic activity — so I asked myself incessantly, what proportion of time and energy should go to inner work, how much to the outside? I was the double horse, or rather a chariot with many horses pulling in every direction, and it never occurred to me that the driver was missing. When I did a production of *Hamlet*, the line that touched me most deeply came from the king praying, "My words fly up, my thoughts remain below." I saw again the proud head of the double horse and knew that to leap upward a new force was needed. But where to find it? I had no clue.

For a long time, what entered through the eye had been my principal motivating force. The root of my attraction to cinema, ballet, and design was that I saw daily life as a moving pattern. Walking through a bar or among trees, life was a long tracking shot in which shapes, lines, and structures never ceased to evolve and interweave. Certainly, I never stopped thinking up theories and ideas, but in staging a scene, the fascination with the abstract beauty of the actors' positioning was so strong that it would often carry me away from any real interest in the content of the play.

On one occasion, close to the opening night of a play I was directing, Binkie Beaumont came to watch a rehearsal, and although he was by my side, we were not seeing the same thing. What I proudly saw was pure imagery, a triangle of actors melting effortlessly into a quartet of moving torsos that imperceptibly became a duo of backs. As the last actor turned his head, making a line with his body that perfectly completed the curve of his partner's arm, the cadence was satisfying, as in a ballet, and as I still loved ballet, I felt my work had been truly well done. So I turned to Binkie for the praise that I did not doubt would be forthcoming. "We're in serious trouble," he murmured. I was so surprised that I listened intently. Then he began to ask me unfamiliar questions — about the text, about the characters, about what the scene was supposed to express, about where the play was leading — and I recognized with a painful shock I had given no attention to any of this, that my fluid geometry, the picture-making that had carried me through Shakespeare and the opera, was of no interest at all to him without the dramatic substance that alone could give a play its life and meaning.

Another time, the shock was even more revealing. John Whiting had written an enchanting fantasy, *Penny for a Song*, and in the manuscript the words danced across the page with delicious lightness. There was a Mozartian elegance in their pattern, and when at the final rehearsal I found the play depressingly earthbound, I blamed the actors vigorously. "You're heavy and clumsy," I told them, then believing in the directorial technique of aggression. "Sit in a row on these chairs, speak the lines quietly, and we'll be able to taste the rhythm of the writing." This time it was not love of ballet but love of music that guided me. I gesticulated to them like a conductor, they followed, and soon, as in a radio play, the words were tumbling out one after the other, nimble and feather-light. "You see!" I said, and the actors left chastened, half-willing to believe that a director who sees it "from out front" must always be right. A few days later, the first performance in Brighton was disastrously flat, and I could not understand why. Long afterward, I came to realize that the actors had tried loyally to reproduce in the big space what we had rehearsed in a small room, and that the energy was not sufficient for an impression of vitality to cross the footlights and reach the audience.

It takes a long while for a director to cease thinking in terms of the result he desires and instead concentrate on discovering the source of energy in the actor from which true impulses can arise. If one describes or demonstrates the result one is seeking, an actor can for a moment reproduce it. To be able to do so a second time with sufficient energy, however, the actor must have such conviction that the impulse becomes truly his or her own. Invariably, for actors, this sense of conviction comes from their inner sense of reality, not from obedience to a director's ideas. When I blamed the actors for letting down the performance, Binkie understood intuitively where I had gone astray, and in his tortuously roundabout way he led me to a point of no escape. "I asked Alan," he said, referring to one of the actors, "why he hadn't a growing relationship with the other characters, why his scene hadn't moved to its proper climax. And Alan answered, 'Peter never worked on such things; he only talked about moves, style, and the music of the words.'" Binkie looked me straight in the eye but still expressed himself in his indirect way. "I was astonished and said: 'Surely, Alan, our friend the director was there to teach you how to play?'" To teach Alan how to play! These words came as one of those jolts that change one's thinking. Never had I thought of my job in this way; I had always worked with experienced actors on well-built texts—what did I know about acting, what could I give to them, let alone teach? I had neither the wish nor the experience to become a teacher. Surely the actors were there to act, the writer to write, and the director to bring to an audience his pictures, his energy, his surprises, his sounds? However, once an essential question is opened, it cannot be closed, and I now saw before me a labyrinth of contradictions that clamored for attention. I realized I could never teach an actor his job—I had never acted and knew I never could. The choice of the word *teach* was wrong, yet it implied something quite precise that I needed to understand. Between the large initial conception and what reaches an audience, all manner of specific articulations must be found, and every detail must belong to a pattern of human actions that the director stimulates into life. For the first time the word *specifics* took on an immediate practical meaning as hooks onto which truths can hang: character specifics, psychological specifics, plot specifics — all elements I had often discussed with the actor in general terms but would leave him alone to discover in detail. Now these became areas where I needed to be fully involved. But what sort of involvement? All I knew was that doing too little leads to too little, but being overaffirmative, whether in argument or work, at once slams shut the very doors that need to stay open.

Then one evening the question was illuminated in a very unexpected way. Natasha and I were present at one of Toscanini's last concerts. I had always been fascinated by the act of conducting; as a child I had longed to be a conductor, standing beside our gramophone, pausing to wind the handle, beating time with a pencil while leaning over a printed score balanced on the arm of a settee. We had never seen this legendary conductor before and came prepared for the spectacular whirlwind of passionate gesticulation and demonic movement for which Toscanini was famous. To our amazement, the frail figure stayed perfectly poised, simply beating time with tiny, almost imperceptible movements of one hand. And he listened. He listened through the whole of his vibrant stillness and drew from the instruments an incredibly detailed, completely transparent texture of sound in which each thread was clear and present, each player being transported way beyond his best. The almost motionless old man was all attention, and such was the clarity of his mind, such was the intensity of his feeling, that there was nothing further he had to do. He needed only to listen, to let the music take shape for his inner ear, and the outer sound called toward him by his listening matched what he needed to hear.

I tried to apply this technique to directing a play, intervening minimally, listening and watching, without realizing that I was far from being prepared, and the result was a disaster. I did not know in depth how to listen and what I was listening for, and had to acknowledge that Toscanini only reached this possibility at the end of a long life of passionate gesture and action. Simplicity is not simple to achieve; it is the end result of a dynamic process that encompasses both excess and the gradual withering away of excess. Toscanini showed me that one cannot imitate someone else's lifeline; certain experiences have to be relived on one's own, and it is dangerous to try, out of misplaced admiration, to leap to the final stretch.

Listening is a mystery. For a body to be able to listen motionless, it must first be developed in movement. It is no coincidence that conductors live so long, as they spend their life constantly exercising and bringing into harmony body, emotion, and thought. The effort of rehearsing and performing draws on all these parts of them — on their bodies like athletes and dancers, on their feelings like singers and lovers, and on their minds like mathematicians and thinkers — simultaneously and in equal proportions. A body developed in this way can eventually stand still and listen.

Early on as I began to study with Jane, I made a promise to myself to keep my deepest aspirations and the inner work to which I was committed completely separate from my theater activities so as not to cheapen and exploit what I was still so far from understanding in myself.

A series of invitations came to do a play, an opera, and *King Lear* on television in New York, and I knew that this meant leaving my regular meetings with our group for several months. An obscure feeling of guilt arose in me with the murmur: "Is this betraying a commitment?" Should I refuse everything that beckoned from the outside, just because it glittered? Was this at last a temptation to be resisted? I had no yardstick — no reference — and there had never once been the least suggestion that renunciation was expected. The natural answer would have been to talk this over with Jane, and perhaps for this very reason I was embarrassed by my own confusion, afraid she might say something I did not want to hear or tell me not to go — and I badly wanted to go. So I persuaded myself each day that I was going to phone her, and as each day ended I told myself I had not had time but would indeed phone tomorrow. This went on day after day until Natasha and I were on the boat train to Southampton and the call had not been made. When we reached the docks, the great ocean liner was throbbing with the unique and thrilling pulse of ships about to leave. We found our cabin, settled in with our luggage, and saw on the table, unexpected luxury, a telephone. Now there was no excuse. I lifted the receiver. An operator answered and I asked for the number. Then came the sound that only those who have lived in England can understand, that leisurely and infinitely reasurring burr-burr that conjures up all the security of our island, followed by the sound of Jane's voice. "I'm going away," I said. "I'm leaving for several months." Jane answered warmly, there was no reproach in her tones, but after a few words the line went dead. I flashed the operator. "What's happened? Get the number again. I've been cut off." As I spoke, through the porthole I saw the quayside draw away, and when the explanation came, it was unnecessary: "We're leaving port." The cable had been disconnected, but another lifeline had not been broken. When Theseus went into the labyrinth he unrolled the thread that Ariadne had given him, and thanks to it he found his way back to daylight. So it was that although the pendulum swung irresistibly and I swung with it, I kept in touch with my teacher and, through her, with the teaching and, through that, with the inner point in oneself where the only true teacher hides.

Many years later when I left again on another long journey, I was able to speak openly and confidently to Jane about these many conflicting thrusts and urges. Her last words were "If you are on a desert island, just remember two words: 'Be present,' and the rest will follow." It was all she said, after which she came to the door to say good-bye. When I reached the gate, I looked back; she was still there. She raised an arm high above her head in a movement of farewell. The powerful rectangle of the body, the strong line reaching upward, the gesture, the feeling, the person, and the moment were one single expression of presence, of being. With this image engraved on my mind, even on a desert island I would have known where to start.

Night was falling on the beach in Tamariù as I walked out of our tiny flat and down to the water's edge. All was quiet, except for the sound of the waves and the occasional cry of a bird. But the world I had left behind was as noisy as ever in my head. I had believed that the simple decision to go to Spain, forsaking the ambitions and excitements of show business in order to sit on a rock and write a novel would be sufficient; instead, I experienced directly how we always carry the whole of our lives with us everywhere we go.

This acute sense of being at a turning point is something I have known many times before and since, yet it is always unexpected. Once it occurred in winter, when as I jumped over a stream, the moment of suspension seemed to stretch indefinitely; in midair the whole of past and future became present, illuminating the remaining half hour of walking, transforming a random scrapbook of happenings into a pattern whose order seemed to have meaning. Now, as the waves broke on the beach, the contradictions of the years past rose and broke with the same intensity, hissing forward into consciousness, drawing back into limbo. Peering into all my activities, I saw double. Each thrust forward was countered by its opposite. If there was a tug in one direction, then the pull went on equally in another: for each belief there was a disbelief, for each wish a refusal. Working in theater made stronger my longing for films; if I was working joyfully with others while directing, then a need for the solitude of writing grew as well. If I was securely living at home, then the restless urge rose for adventure abroad; if withdrawn into an inner quiet, then a passionate plunging into life was irresistible.

Each day I would wake with a burning sense of gratitude to life, unable to understand why I had been given so much and filled with thirst for a still unknown way in which I could repay my debt. But to whom, where, with what? There was no answer, yet the question could not be stifled, except through new activity. Then another burst of energy would sweep all introspection away and, as it spent itself, as though between one crashing wave and another the give-it-all-up impulse would recur. With dreams of something purer than my normal occupations, I would be enticed by the desert-island fiction, the Gauguin myth, the obsession with "somewhere else." Eventually I would come to realize that this is the most treacherous of all illusions because it does not take into account the power of our deep conditioning that inevitably dictates what we are and where we are, most of all when we are dreaming of where we are not. It is easy in the mind to go to India or to Africa to treat the lepers, but a true change of direction in life only occurs when a long period of friction has created an intensity through which the options drop away by themselves. Now, making long lines of footprints in the sand, I wondered whether this moment had come.

Natasha treasured home and the meaning of home while I valued nothing more than the freedom to live a loose bond of separation and reunion, but like so many actresses, she found the complement to her timidity in the freedom of the stage. She had acted since she was twelve and was at the start of a film career when her independent life was broken by her TB. Then it was interrupted again and again by my own constant movements, so each time she returned to acting, she faced new fears. Now the possibility of swinging away toward another life was as attractive to her as it was to me.

This break had been carefully planned. Our aim was to taste together the joy of absolute solitude, even though a little farther up the coast lived some Spanish friends to whom I had become very attached a few years before on my visit to Dalí. On arrival, I had called them, politely explaining we had decided to live a hermit's life. The attractive Spanish wife must have smiled as she said, "You will come to dinner, though. I'll phone you on Wednesday evening." Our friends had a beautiful property, their dinners were always big social events, they knew everyone on the coast, and inevitably one would leave with further invitations to drinks and dinners from their guests. I knew that if I accepted even one invitation, the whole social scene of the Costa Brava would follow, so my new resolution was already in danger, and as I walked up and down the beach in the half-light on that fateful Wednesday evening, I felt that this was one of the occasions about which my divinity teacher at school had warned me: "If you let this moment pass, it may never return." Each passing second dramatized the question: would I answer the telephone? It was as though my future depended uniquely on this decision. Where was strength, where was weakness? Was I prepared to give up the life I knew so as to dedicate all my energies to another way of life that seemed more real? I was back once again in army uniform on the tree across the river, trying vainly to let go of a leaf.

I reviewed every possibility but never considered the one factor that eventually resolved the argument: the phone never rang. The waves splashed, the odd bird cried, and the whole dark comedy of questioning had no conclusion—so I made the unexpected discovery that the crucial moment that may never recur is recurring all the time.

More days went by in the little house on the beach in Spain, and when the phone rang, now unexpectedly, and I finally heard the warm voice of my friend asking us to come to dinner, the immediate answer was "yes." Later a publisher refused my novel, and when Natasha and I went back to London, I was left querying the meaning of questioning and doubting the process of doubt, both rendered suspect by the teasing ring of a Spanish telephone across a beach.

We do not make decisions, decisions make themselves, but only if we've allowed ourselves to prepare the ground by passionately exploring all the options. This was something that the theater had taught me. I could recognize it in planning a production, in working on a model, in rehearsing. The mind has many layers, and to reach the layer that is most operative, a struggle must take place between the submerged impulses in a hidden zone and the confident voices from a more superficial level that claim to know best. It is above all the terror of demonstrating indecision in front of judging faces and the need for reassurance that push one toward pretending to know what one wants. If one doesn't yet know what one wants, I came to realize, why pretend? The phrase "thinking aloud" is full of meaning; rehearsing began to teach me that there is a way of thinking aloud with others that goes much farther than thinking by oneself. I was already discovering in my work with actors how important it is to encourage them to share their uncertainties and to invite them to join in a process of endless changes of mind. The way is then prepared for the distracting and irrelevant thought-waves to calm down, allowing coherent patterns to rise from a more buried level.

Sometimes it was even possible in my work to see that the result I was trying to achieve was there before the start, that time was reversed and the search was not to create but to unravel what was already coiled—a common experience, I believe, for sculptors, for whom the form is already in the block of stone, waiting for the chisel to cut away the irrelevant disguise. One of my early productions at Stratford had been Shakespeare's *Titus Andronicus*, for which I had also designed the scenery. Months after its last performance, I looked by chance at my original copy of the play and found on the back page a forgotten sketch, scribbled in the heat of the moment as I had finished the very first reading. There, already complete, was the set that I had seemed to discover months later after a long series of painful trials and errors, with models made and torn apart and painted cardboard scattered on the floor. Yet there is no reason to be ashamed of such chaos; indeed, a certain chaos has at last become respectable, recognized as part of the universal pattern, firmly ensconced in the multitude of unknown layers of the mind.

Natasha and I had a small house with a miniature front garden in the quiet and charm of Kensington. We saw many friends, entertained a lot, went to opera, ballet, and exhibitions, and were not surprised when in a thank-you note a dinner guest wrote to say how much he had appreciated such a "civilized" evening. In fact, this civilized London life was a necessary reaction after the war, but already its attractive surface was beginning to break up, revealing the basic social conflicts underneath. This was also the London of Soho, of sleazy and unhappy nightclubs, Francis Bacon, and despair. Elizabethan London, Dickensian London had always encompassed these extremes: when evening came, there was a moment in Hyde Park when the gently beautiful half-light would show the nannies, with their well-bred children, quietly pushing their prams past the women in tight sweaters and short skirts who arrived as the others were leaving, the stiletto heels followed by silently gliding cars.

At this time, the friction between our lives in Paris and in London was only just beginning, and although Natasha and I were already asking ourselves, as a game, which of the two cities we preferred, it would be many years before the underlying issues would come to the boil, making a decision possible. Every time we came home to London, we felt we never wanted to travel again. Then we would go to Paris for a couple of days and find ourselves acting as though we were never going to leave, getting deeply involved in plans, projects, and passionate relationships that implied we would be there all the time. Two horses were galloping furiously, pulling us in different directions on opposite sides of the Channel.

A city can be seen in many ways: one person is struck by the dirt and the violence, another by the historical beauty. Despite the undertones of anger, London was still a place of reassuring slowness and calm. Paris was restless, feverish; a true Parisian was expected to be nervous and uneasy, and the city itself had a sensuality for which London had no equivalent.

In London, for instance, the very best house of costume making, situated near Covent Garden, was unchanged since the eighteenth century. Its anterooms had red velvet furniture and vast gilt mirrors, and a formally dressed very superior gentleman would always attend to one with a gently condescending smile. When a play needed beggars in rags, their costumes had first to be presented to the designer in an immaculate state, carefully pinned and fitted with meticulous care, before being dirtied and pulled to shreds, proving that however unattractive the designer's demands, the house still maintained for itself its unique standards of perfection.

The construction of scenery carried with it a similar ritual. To get good results, one had to strike up a respectful relationship with an honorable Victorian firm of builders, and the plans one presented had to be as precise as those a gentleman would demand were he installing a new library in his house, where every piece of carpentry would be made to last a lifetime. At Covent Garden, I had watched the irascible red-bearded production manager throw out beautiful but imprecise designs because he sensed at once that they originated with "artists" as opposed to "practical men." In France, however, the shambling genius of theater design, Christian Bérard, would scribble an idea on the paper tablecloth in a café, then hand it to the canny old *machinistes* of the theater to work out the technical details for him. When, the night before the opening, he suddenly decided to change it all, this did not lead to anger, to strikes, or to hard-bargained overtime deals but only to a few bottles of red wine that made the same *machinistes* work happily till dawn, with a genuine satisfaction in bringing their skills to a creation that they loved and shared. This was a way of work that I could understand.

Anyone who has a taste for old French movies, for the Brassaï photographs of Paris cafés by night, or for the songs of Piaf will see why the cramped and dated mustiness of a little boulevard theater, with bent and rusty spotlights and a cracked canvas curtain painted to look like velvet brocade, had a special charm that London or New York could not equal. They seemed on another planet, at another moment in history; in Paris there were no managements, no producers, agents had hardly been invented, let alone unions, and each theater had its own identity, its own idiosyncrasies, and its own audience. Many were run like private dwellings by difficult ladies, whose choices were based on alternating bursts of love and hate, elation and despair.

To my good fortune, one of these ladies took me up. She was a legend called Simone Berriau, famous for her large hats held in place by a black velvet ribbon tied beneath the chin, which she never removed — not even, it is said, when she had to oblige a volatile leading actor, who as the first-night audience waited, refused to descend to the stage until she had sacrificed herself to calm his nerves. The moment we met, chastely but with the same lack of hesitation, she adopted me and instantly became a devoted friend. I would lunch and dine in her apartment in the sixteenth arrondissement at a mirror-topped table, encircled by even more mirrors, with some rich corpulent friends, her masseur, and an elderly boulevardier in an elegant pearl-gray suit, shining boots, and a finely turned mustache, whose eye had the well-primed gleam of someone from whom wit was always expected, and although he seldom spoke, when he did, his words were savored like wine.

At our first audition for *Cat on a Hot Tin Roof*, Simone made the unsurprised, uncomplaining actresses lift their skirts, turn, and show calves and thighs for her approval. Only then would she allow them to read their lines. This was indeed very far from the England I knew, and true to the tradition of the British abroad, I was delighted by the novelty and easily outraged by the barbarity of foreign ways.

A few days before rehearsals were due to begin, it was announced that Jeanne Moreau, who was in the cast, had signed up for a film for the same dates, and although Simone, unperturbed, assured me that Jeanne would surely find odd moments to rehearse, I reacted in a transatlantic, show-business way, threatening press conferences and lawsuits. This surprised everyone so much that we won and the film was postponed.

Nonetheless, the relationship with Jeanne seemed to start badly: she was late for the first rehearsal. She was already something of a star and as I was discovering how nineteenth-century habits still prevailed in the French theater with leading ladies, I resolved to institute a climate of firm discipline from the beginning. The rest of the cast was assembled on the bare stage of the Théâtre Antoine, and as I sat on the side, my watch in hand, a silence fell, no one moved, the tension grew. Ten minutes went by — no sign of Jeanne. I simply waited, watched uneasily by the others. After fifteen minutes, she made a splendid entrance, unconcerned, chattering excitedly, kissing those nearest the door. Then she noticed me, and as she began to run across the stage holding out her arms, I spoke icily. "If you play the leading part, you need far more rehearsals than the others, not less. If you are late, you will be the loser." She stopped short as though she had been slapped, apologized profusely to the other actors and to me in such a spontaneous and modest way that the atmosphere was lightened, and we set to work. At the end of the day, the old administrator of the theater, with the air of one who has seen everything in his time, took me by the arm. "Ah, you the English! You and punctuality. You are terrible." "Why?" I protested. "Do you think I went too far?" He shrugged. "For thirty seconds . . ." "For thirty seconds?" I repeated in astonishment. We compared watches. I was exactly fourteen and a half minutes fast. We never told the truth to Jeanne, and I think that the whole company left with a healthy respect for implacable British ways. After all, there is nothing the law-resenting French appreciate more than severity and rigor.

This was the first time that I worked with Jeanne Moreau, and the relationship between us was telepathic. We hardly spoke in rehearsals, but we understood each other through a gesture or a glance. Our worst problem lay in the script, and here I encountered for the first time the intrinsic incompatibilities of English and French. Our translation of Cat had been made by a distinguished author who knew no word of English; in the hope that I could persuade him to correct some flagrant errors, I called on him in his small house in an outer suburb. He received me courteously and showed me how he worked. His method was simple, for he just walked up and down while his lady friend who knew some English tossed word-for-word renderings of each line into the air. The author had no knowledge either of the play or of Tennesee Williams but had an inborn conviction that nothing Anglo-Saxon could have real literary merit. He would catch the line on the wing, roll it on the tongue, then exclaim, "This is what I'd say," while his lady friend would scribble it down. As this text was quite unusable, Simone, counting on the fact that the author would never even notice the difference, set up a little committee, consisting of a Polish literary agent who had lived in the States, her old boulevardier friend, the masseur, and myself. With her at the head, we sat deep into the night round her mirrored table struggling with phrases like "I'll hump her from hell to breakfast," which the logical French language had no possible way of accepting.

As I had been told that Simone was in the habit of sitting in at rehearsals, usually with a number of friends, I firmly forbade her to come into the auditorium. Simone was delighted, proudly telling her friends she had been turned out of her own theater. After a few days, however, she asked me to join her after rehearsal for a drink in her office, which she insisted on calling her dressing room. After we had chatted for a while and I had given her some impressions of how things were going, she commented on one of the actors, "I don't like the way he does that speech." I looked at her in amazement. She was very confused and tried unconvincingly to cover up this slip of the tongue, leaving me very perplexed. As I had been sure she would try to make her way unseen into the back of the house, I had prudently rehearsed with the curtain down. Now I went rapidly back onstage to discover where she could have been hidden. At first, there seemed no solution; then I noticed that there was the tiniest of gaps where the curtain did not quite touch the floor. If someone was in the prompter's box, which was placed in the middle of the footlights, he or she could by straining forward just manage to peer underneath the frayed canvas edge. The thought of this large, middle-aged lady in her inevitable hat creeping along a narrow passage into the tiny cubicle out of an irresistible need to follow what was going on touched me deeply. I still did not make the mistake of letting her come to watch, but I greatly admired a tradition of theater where passion still ruled.

Although the rehearsals for *Cat* were vivid and enjoyable, we still did not succeed in building a bridge that would allow the skeptical French entry into a script whose situation tore at the guts of a Broadway audience. During the premiere, when the heroine describes how her husband, desperate because of a sexual weakness on their wedding night, blew out his brains, I heard a voice behind me murmur, "When that happens to me, a strong cup of coffee usually puts things right." And I knew we had lost.

Nevertheless, Simone loyally asked me to return the following season to stage Arthur Miller's *A View from the Bridge*, which I had just put on in London. I was very reluctant to repeat work that was already in the past, and despite all the emotional pressure she brought, I refused. Then a forceful young woman who was just beginning her career as an agent came to see me in my Paris hotel. "Don't be under any illusions," she began bluntly. "Your work hasn't made a good impression here. If you want to work again in Paris, do *A View from the Bridge*. It can't fail to be a big hit." Her name was Micheline Rozan, and her frankness so impressed me that I listened. We have been working together ever since.

Even more than theater, I wished above all to make a film in France, not only because of my permanent love for the cinema but also because I felt I could do better work there than in England. Before my attempt to give up everything and move to Spain, a deep conflict with Laurence Olivier had turned my first film, *The Beggar's Opera*, into an ugly battlefield. The choice of subject had already been a compromise; I had really wanted to work on a contemporary theme, where there could be cars and motorcycles, as I had a passionate wish to escape from the world of scene paint and false hair. However, Shakespeare and Covent Garden had already labeled me, so among the sheaf of proposals that I was hawking around, it was a classical subject that caught the attention of a producer, and I was too excited to refuse. Herbert Wilcox was of a very different world indeed; he had spent his life making second-rate commercial successes, mostly with his wife Anna Neagle as the star. These films were never taken seriously by anyone except his backers, who had absolute faith in his box-office flair. When we first met, I found him an endearingly ordinary man. He was always in a dark blue business suit, a carnation in the buttonhole, and even in the studio when he directed his own productions, he would stand beside the camera in his formal clothes speaking to the actors in a plummy and slightly cockney tone as though he were the mayor of an outer London borough. He produced bottles of champagne on the slightest occasion, he never raised his voice, and as far as I could discover his ultimate business secret was continually to preface the shameless evasions of a true producer with a modestly understated and thus totally convincing "I think I can safely say . . ." When I came to him with my project, he thought a connection with culture would make a comfortable conclusion to his career, so he welcomed me with open arms, and I was included in his new program of future box-office hits.

The first discussions went very smoothly. I wanted Christopher Fry and Denis Cannan to write the script and Sir Arthur Bliss to arrange the music, and as these were prestigious names Herbert agreed at once. And he needed a star, a big star for Macheath. I saw in my mind a rough energetic film in black and white, with a coarse and virile highwayman in the lead. There was a young actor named Richard Burton who seemed perfect for the role, but the time was not ripe, his name not sufficiently known to make the investors and distributors feel secure. On the other hand, Laurence Olivier was at the height of his success, both as an actor and filmmaker. In the way one throws a bottle into the sea, I sent him a telegram asking if by any chance Macheath was a part he had ever wanted to play. Fortunately and calamitously this struck too good a note, for apparently *The Beggar's Opera* had been a project he had been nursing for many years, hoping to act, direct, and produce it himself. His "yes" rejoiced us all and was an early lesson in how one must never celebrate too soon. Certainly he was more than eager to play the part, but was furious that he had let his own project slip out of his fingers, and so he insisted on being coproducer as well, a distinguished partnership that filled Wilcox with pride and that I had neither the grounds nor the authority to oppose, although it was obviously a dangerous partnership for a director to have the star both as his actor and as his boss. In fact, I was so thrilled to have the finest actor of the day for my first film that I quickly forgot my apprehensions.

Peter, age twelve

Peter's father and mother

Peter's brother Alexis
during the war

1944

Filming *A Sentimental Journey* at nineteen

With John Gielgud
during rehearsals of
*Measure for
Measure*, 1950

Peter and Natasha

Peter and Natasha with Fidel Castro in Cuba

© Angus McBean

Paul Scofield as Lear

Lord of the Flies

Tell Me Lies

A *Midsummer Night's Dream*, London, August 1972: Alan Howard as Oberon (LEFT) and Robert Lloyd as Puck

Peter and Natasha with daughter Irina

Peter with son Simon

Ted Hughes's play *Orghast* at Persepolis

In Africa, 1972–73

The Conference of the Birds, Avignon, 1979; LEFT TO RIGHT:
Bruce Myers, Alain Maratrat, Mireille Maalouf

First rehearsals at the
Bouffes du Nord, 1974

With
Natasha,
rehearsing
*The
Cherry
Orchard*,
1981

Rehearsing the *Mahabharata*

A scene from the *Mahabharata*

A scene from
the *Mahabharata*

Lord Ganesha
in the *Mahabharata*

Bakary Sangaré in *The Tempest*

The Man Who; LEFT TO RIGHT: Yoshi Oida, Bruce Myers

Natasha Parry in Beckett's *Happy Days*

But I did not know Olivier. He was a strangely hidden man. Onstage and on the screen he could give an impression of openness, brilliance, lightness, and speed. In fact, he was the opposite. His great strength was that of an ox. He always reminded me of a countryman, of a shrewd, suspicious peasant taking his time. When he tried to catch up with a new idea, his forehead would seem to shine, as though from determination not to be outwitted. The dazzling virtuosity of his acting came from a painstakingly composed mosaic of tiny details, which when finally assembled could flash by in sequence with breathtaking speed, giving the illusion of glittering thought. What I never realized was that once a conception had taken root in him, no power could change the direction in which the ox would pull the cart. If one was with him on the same track, an understanding was easy. But if not, no meeting of minds was possible.

Slowly, day after day, during the preparation and shooting, our mutual misunderstanding drew us further and further apart. For him *The Beggar's Opera* was a masterpiece of eighteenth-century elegance and artificiality, in the tradition of a very famous production in London in the twenties that was still remembered for its grace and charm. As he had only just been knighted, Olivier saw the work as an urbane and stylish jeu d'esprit that would suit his new gentlemanly status well. For me, ignorant of these traditions, the work breathed the stinking air of Hogarth. It was a robber's tale for beggars, and it needed to be violent and harsh. In the half-expressed exchanges of the British, it took almost all the filming for the nature of our differences to become clear. On the floor, Olivier with exquisite politeness would ask my permission to peer through the viewfinder. After a long silence he would turn to me and ask, tapping the camera, "Is this really the setup you want?" When I answered yes, he would return to his place, the whole of his actor's body expressing the disapproval that he did not need to put into words.

On the first day of shooting, wandering around the set with a portable viewfinder, I discovered with dismay that the entire crew was following me, with an assistant ready to drop a piece of chalk to mark the precise position where the camera was to be installed. Following what had already become a fundamental need, I wanted to explore countless options before settling on an angle, but clearly I was not to be allowed to do this, and day after day I was paralyzed by a sort of football team hovering behind

my back. In the canteen and round the studio, the joke was repeated: "On *The Beggar's Opera*, they have had to send the viewfinder back to the garage for an overhaul." Eventually, Olivier
tried to use his producer's prerogative to fire me and take over
the direction himself. Somehow, I resisted, but between us we
spoiled much of the picture.

When a couple of years later, Glen Byam Shaw, who was now
in charge of the theater at Stratford, invited me to direct *Titus
Andronicus* with Olivier in the lead, it was a hard decision to take.
This was a play that had long fascinated me, and I had a very firm
intuition about the dark ritual that I was convinced lay behind
the words. If I accepted, I was not prepared to let Olivier in any
way confuse my search for the strange image that I wished to
discover, one that I was certain would give a primeval coherence
and meaning to the seemingly gratuitous succession of horrors.
But English good manners can have surprising effects. Ever since
The Beggar's Opera, a feeling of constraint and embarrassment
had made both Olivier and me play the role of devoted friends.
Natasha and I were very fond of Vivien Leigh, and we would
spend weekends with her and Larry in their very aristocratic
country retreat, Notley Abbey. We would sup together in town,
exchange notes, and send one another little presents in order to
disguise deep hurts. When I came to the first rehearsal of *Titus*, I
was for once well prepared and determined to bring all latent
feuds right out into the open. Armed with a battering ram, I was
prepared to charge at Olivier, little guessing that he was already
an open door, for he had made up his mind to show himself a
model of acceptance and flexibility, partly, I think, under Vivien's influence and partly because of a sense of generalized guilt
that was a permanent part of his nature. From the first surprising
moment, our relationship was transformed, the partnership was
ideal, and daily we worked together in perfect harmony. It made
me wonder how the same two people could relate to one another
so differently, and if living down a first bad experience had
helped, I think the real key lay in the invisible area where con-
ceptions and images are formed. This time, by coincidence, we
were both on parallel rails, and so we could advance together in
mutual confidence. Not only could I understand and admire his
amazing talent but the way he played the central role also gave
the whole production an intensity and a reality that no other
actor at the time could have brought. Unfortunately, I cannot say

that I ever felt close to Olivier in human terms. He was most polite and attentive, but behind the gesture there was always a sense of strain; even his laughter was acted, as though he never ceased remaking and polishing his mask.

On the other hand, working with John Gielgud led me back to my own interrogation. What are these different levels, clumsily called "better" and "worse," that give meaning to our work? What is the passage that leads from one to the other? In *Measure for Measure* at Stratford, then in London with *The Winter's Tale* and again with *Venice Preserved*, I was able to enter a unique and endlessly inventive mind, always open to change. John had become notorious for never knowing what he wanted, but this was quite untrue. I felt very close to him and would easily follow his restless hesitations as he had only one reference: an intuitive sense of quality. Everything that he questioned and discarded related to an impossibly exacting standard that he could never reach. This indecision is far from the confusion that comes from weakness, for when John directed a company, the rejection of the mediocre, the constant demand to go further, to do better, the sensitive awareness of every fine detail always led to an impressive unity. Something very precise was taking place through which the "quality" was being transformed. A mystery, certainly, but also a process. Where could one find the key?

A defrocked priest, one would say, and perhaps that is what he was: pink and gentle, ever so gentle, with a name like a flower, Jean Genet, with a humorous look from blue eyes as wide as innocence. He would sit tenderly massaging Natasha's feet, and as he spoke, the edge of the voice betrayed a mordant intelligence. I had read his play *The Balcony* when we came to Paris with *Titus Andronicus* and was astonished by the purity of theatrical thought that it revealed. Conditioned by the tolerance of English liberal thinking, far from the intense partisan climate of French politics that colored that country's intellectual life, I could not understand why no theater had taken up this bold and subversive work by an already famous author. I took this to be my good fortune. Genet had just seen *Titus*, and what appealed to him was the way in which pure violence had been translated into a language of signs and suggestions, so from the start we shared the same conviction that the theater needed to emancipate itself both from naturalistic and from classical conventions. As *A View from the Bridge* had filled the house for two seasons, this left me with some credit with the Théâtre Antoine, but I soon discovered how deeply politics penetrated the French cultural scene. Attempts to stage *The Balcony* there failed dismally after my friend Simone Berriau received a personal warning from the police, so I made melodramatic statements to the press that I would not work in France again until justice had been done to Genet.

Soon Genet and I began meeting in cafés to discuss strategy. I had heard and read of his belief in the absolute necessity for total betrayal, especially in friendship, but as we were now comrades-in-arms against other betrayers, our own relationship seemed firm as a rock, especially as one after the other even the tiniest avant-garde theaters refused to become involved with this work. Then suddenly a large boulevard theater called the Gymnase — or the Gymnase–Marie Bell, as it is called today in the Paris tradition of theaters with double names — came to our rescue. Marie Bell had stepped straight out of the nineteenth century: she had played all the great leads at the Comédie Française, there were leopard-skin rugs over the divan in her dressing room, she had an apartment on the Champs Élysées that was draped in crimson velvet, she wore large hats, strong makeup, had the panache and style that belonged to her role, and in her extravagant diva way was a free woman. "At my age," she used to say to me, "my aim in life is *me perfectionner*," and I would admire the implication in this often-used French phrase that all we need are the finishing touches to bring ourselves to perfection. As she had a great respect for Genet, she was delighted to wage a battle on his behalf, being fearless for herself and contemptuous of the police. She wanted to play the overliterary part of the *maîtresse du bordel*, and later she proved to be one of the few actresses I have known with the practical sense to urge me to cut more and more of her lines: "The less I say," she would insist, "the better I will appear." I cut her to the bone, dressed her in a flamboyant robe made out of an old flag — a genuine Union Jack — and she was very effective indeed. Once the play was announced, the major battle was won, so in the logic of his beliefs all possibility of friendship with Genet was over. He took a plane to Athens, and I never saw or heard from him again.

Once, late in rehearsal, Marie Bell did succeed in getting him on a faint long-distance line, and I listened in on the extra receiver designed for eavesdroppers that used to be part of the French telephone tradition. She asked him if he would come to a rehearsal or at least to the opening. He refused acidly: it was of no interest. "Would you like to speak to Peter?" "On no account. You know he's someone I never could bear." Perhaps this had been true from the start, for although we were in perfect agreement artistically, I was very far from the furious climate of rebellion and political violence that his whole way of life had pushed to an absolute extreme.

In England, I had never been given more than four weeks' rehearsal, always with a new cast gathered for the purpose, and I had accepted this as a fact of life. Genet, however, had sworn that his play could only be performed by a homogeneous group, working together over several years in order to master styles not normally in a professional actor's range. This seemed a very pretentious claim, yet I was convinced that he was right and for the first time began to feel the necessity for an ensemble. This sort of group did not exist, however, and as no one was prepared to pay for the long preparation the formation of an ensemble would entail, I chose instead unconventional casting so that at least the routine of conventional acting would be shaken, if only by the friction that came from mixing together boulevard actors, avant-garde actors, the great ballet dancer Jean Babilée, and many amateurs, including an exceptionally beautiful girl whose only experience had been acquired as mistress to a wealthy biscuit manufacturer, and the totally inhibited but quite fascinating wife of a fashion photographer whom an assistant had accosted for me one night in a bar.

It was an odd assembly, and as necessity called for a special method that would make it into an ensemble in a short time, I conducted my very first experiment with an unknown new tool called improvisation. This opened up many fascinating directions that I was to continue to explore in the years to come. Improvising can take a limitless number of forms with very different applications, and I had heard that now in the fifties the American theater, in particular the Actors Studio, was already using improvisations based on everyday situations — "You are in the dentist's waiting room," "There are two of you on a park bench" — to encourage the actor's sense of the character's life continuing into the wings. This followed Stanislavsky's conviction that the more actors learn to improvise scenes that are not in the text, the more they will be able to believe in the human reality of the characters and situations they play. I had a hunch, however, that this was not applicable to a nonnaturalistic play and so we did not look for realism in our games but merely improvised freely and outrageously around the theme of brothel life, not caring a jot about psychological accuracy. Certainly, the enjoyable moments we spent did not help any of the performers to act better, nor did they make more real a highly literary text. Yet the work in improvisation proved irreplaceable and precious for a different reason: it was liberating through the sheer delight of playing for the sake of playing, and as we laughed and entertained one another, a large degree of coherence appeared in this very eccentric band of performers, creating a sort of ensemble.

In the original version of *The Balcony*, everything took place within the fetid upholstered intimacy of the brothel. This was one of the last productions for which I designed the scenery myself, and I found a particular interest in constructing a labyrinth of picture frames covered with velvets in deep primary colors. They turned slowly as the actors passed through them, giving the impression of a constantly changing play of mirrors. Wishing to show still another reflection in his mirrors, Genet had added a new scene, moving the action to a café where the revolutionaries were preparing their coup in the hothouse of their own rhetoric. Many new characters appeared for this scene, demanding extra actors, and the problem of breaking out of the unity of empty velvet mirrors alarmed me until I devised a new series of picture frames coated in yellowed newsprint. When the set was in place, I was delighted as designer, but as director I could find no way of making the scene itself come to life. "All must be beautiful," Genet had said, "like a funeral," but the words he gave to the revolutionaries were far more prosaic than his intentions. A few days before the premiere, we had a run-through for some invited intellectuals. Genet's friends were unanimous that his revolution scene was a great mistake and that it endangered the rest of the play.

Although in France producers and directors never dare to tamper with an author's script, as Genet could not be traced anywhere I needed little persuasion to take a ruthless Broadway attitude. "The scene is cut!" I announced to the cast the night before the opening. As on a pre-Broadway tour, drastic actions are seldom good ones; there is a mixture of manic excitement and simple hysteria that comes with fatigue, and a director must be wary of his dangerously destructive impulses when faced with last-minute decisions. If I had paused quietly for a moment, I might well have realized the human cost that this decision entailed, but it was only the following evening when I saw bouquets of flowers arriving for the actress who was no longer going to appear that I awoke to a different heartbreaking reality. If the play was only a lukewarm success, certainly cutting this scene had done little to change the overall impression it made; now what troubled me most was the distress of the discarded actors loitering in the wings and the destruction of the ensemble we had so carefully and joyfully built. Once and for all I realized that it is not true that everything must be sacrificed in the name of success. On the contrary, perfectionism is often an arrogance and a folly: nothing in a theater performance is more important than the people of whom it is composed. I suddenly recognized that I had accepted a flimsy half-truth: the "show must go on." But why must the show go on? Most directors at some time or another are compelled to fire actors — or more elegantly, to ask them to withdraw. I am always uncomfortable when I hear the American producer's jargon: "I hired him, I fired him." This is never a relationship that is desirable in a theater. There are no easy solutions — casting mistakes can be made and someone has to take the responsibility — but in each case a balance has to be found between the distress of the actor on the one hand and on the other the damage done by allowing one incompetent person to undermine the general work. Sometimes one finds that the actor or actress is secretly longing to be freed from an excessive strain and is relieved when asked to leave, but there is no rule. One marriage can be saved and another must be broken. Sometimes a breach can be healed, and sometimes a divorce is the only salvation for one or both partners. Whatever the solution, the formula "the play comes first" is too hollow to be applied glibly.

At that time, however, a first night marked a kind of ending, the anguishes of the past were quickly forgotten, and another project with other people was already taking shape. While *The Balcony* was in rehearsal, I was preparing to shoot Marguerite Duras's novel *Moderato Cantabile*, fulfilling my ardent wish to make a film in France. *Moderato* was indeed a labor of love. The ever-inventive Micheline Rozan had brought it into existence, uniting me with Marguerite Duras and Jeanne Moreau in a project that stemmed entirely from the heart, and in the shooting I found a freedom that was far from the rigid conditions of the British studios of the day. Here no one said, "It's not possible," or followed me around with sticks of chalk. The small unit was always prepared to improvise, to respond with enthusiasm to a change of plan, foreseeing the needs of a shot and laying tracks for the camera in exactly the right place long before I had found it by myself. When we needed a little platform, no plumb line and spirit level were required; a piece of wood was retrieved from the roadside, a few stones, a couple of nails — no time wasted and it was there, ready to last for no more than the duration of the shot rather than a theoretical lifetime, as it would have been if a British studio carpenter had felt that his professional reputation was at stake.

Actors sometimes speak of being like putty in a director's hands, and this is not a very attractive image. Jeanne Moreau was not putty; she was unlike any actress I had ever known for she was totally fluid — she could, right away, be anything she was asked to be. It hardly mattered whether the suggestion was good or bad as it immediately became her own, as though a natural part of herself, and if it was unexpected, then the psychological meaning had to catch up without explanation. In this way, surprising actions that most actors would have considered "out of character" became, as they do in life, the revelation of an unexpected facet of the same person.

During the shooting she never came to rushes, and when I eventually showed her a rough cut she was not interested to see how she had acted a scene. What fascinated her was how her character had behaved. Watching the scene in which she meets her fellow actor Jean-Paul Belmondo for the first time in a café, she laughed with excitement because she noticed that her eyes had dropped for a second onto his ring finger. "Of course!" she cried. "That's just what she would do!" and added, "But it happened without my knowing it." With one phrase, she cut through all the traps that intellectualizing and analysis can bring into a field where true human behavior can only be caught in a deeper and more mysterious way.

Marguerite Duras also was hypersensitive to each passing moment. She was constantly surrounded by a small intense circle of friends, and she lived their lives with them and for them, detail by detail. At lunch in her apartment in the rue Saint Benoît there were always several former lovers, for not only did she never wish to discard anyone but they in turn could never endure to be deprived of the intense climate that Marguerite had created during their intimacy. Like Chekhov, she entered so fully into every minute detail of banal existence that it became charged with significance, and her art was merely a dramatized image of the way she lived her day. A door opening, a curtain being drawn, a phone ringing, a cup of coffee nearly overturned, a hesitation in the middle of a sentence, a yes or no were all extraordinary events. If for most of us our yesses and noes are casual, for Marguerite they were absolutes; this is what made her writing so simple and so intense.

When we worked together on the script, she would often pause dramatically and raise her finger, sensing some shattering implication hidden in a trivial detail. Once after a long silence, she said, "Can we dare?"

"Dare what?"

"Perhaps it's going too far?"

I encouraged her to speak her thoughts.

"In the script, when Jeanne meets Belmondo for the first time, he asks her if she would like a glass of wine and she merely answers, 'Oui' . . ."

I nodded, wondering what else Jeanne could say.

"What if . . ." Marguerite paused. "What if . . . but then we'd really show what a whore she is . . . What if after 'Oui,' she adds, 'Monsieur' . . ." and Marguerite's softly rising tone showed how insinuating and revealing that simple word could be.

After *The Balcony* and *Moderato Cantabile*, commuting between London and Paris made me even more restless; although I was enjoying each moment to the full, I was still fully dissatisfied, so I made another attempt at breaking away from show business. This time, Natasha and I traveled through Mexico and Cuba, absorbing new impressions, convinced that our old life had now been left behind for good. Then, on a wicker table of a small hotel run by a German anthropologist, I chanced on a well-worn copy of *L'Express*, a French magazine I used to read every week in Paris. As I flicked through it, page after page acted like magnets; words, names, associations from the past reached out, and as they grabbed me, my theoretical calm vanished and I could feel the return of other tastes and other desires, the need to be on the move again. They say a man can spend half his life in a monastery, weeding out all his attachments, until the day he returns to the world and then they reappear stronger than ever. Where actors are concerned, the need is to escape into other lives, to be "someone else." In my own case, it was not that; it was a permanent need for "something else," which, despite *L'Express*, soon proved to be neither in Paris nor in London. Once again, it was travel, not theater, that seemed to offer the most convincing passage to another world.

We had spent months poring over maps, I had done a series of lectures that eventually became a book, *The Empty Space*, to pay for the trip, and now there were four of us, two men and two women, traveling in Afghanistan in search of the sacred, hoping to find traces of ancient, forgotten traditions. My friend and I had grown beards because we had been told that this would make us appear more serious; his wife and Natasha had carefully experimented with Turkish trousers and instant food and even a self-sufficient toothpaste from Israel that needed neither brush nor water, while I had spent six months at home learning Persian. We had studied road maps only to find, once we arrived, that there were few roads, sometimes none at all, so a *bashi* was essential. *Bashi* means "chief driver," and the garage in Kabul where we were renting a Land Rover presented him as a man who could be useful. A tall, thin, sad figure, he stooped toward us, crushing a felt hat in his hands; he was humped like a camel, but an unusual sort of camel, apologizing for its own existence.

"A few crumbs," said the American owner of the garage, patting him on the back, "all he needs are a few crumbs." The driver nodded and bowed modestly. Over the weeks that followed we learned that our *bashi* was a consummate actor. The Western idea of a loyal bearer was a part he was prepared to play — and if simplemindedness was meant to go with it, he would play that too. He stood, his hands hanging by his sides, while we looked through a wallet of letters of recommendation from expedition leaders: "the *bashi* is honest and reliable" and so on.

"They live on credit, these chaps," said the Indian foreman.

"Don't let him touch the motor," said the mechanic.

Driving through the night across the desert, the wheels leaping, skidding, he danced a wild version of the twist with a thumb-slicer of a steering wheel. Obstinate, flintlike, refusing to speak, refusing rest; taking no food in case it made him sleepy, just accepting cigarettes or, newly discovered joy, a handful of caffeine pellets; now gloomy, muttering introspectively, now elated, leaping from the car, fiddling, tightening, cooling, repairing—veering from triumphant to punch-drunk, he would endure twenty-two hours at the wheel. There were two orders of happenings in his world—*khob* and *kharab*, good and bad—and from his lips continually came one of these words: a man, a track, a noise from the motor—*kharab*—but when the situation changed, there was never any hangover of despair; if one thing was *khob*, then all the world was *khob* once more.

In Afghanistan the roads are justly infamous; when there are tracks, they are a bewildering choice of furrows, deep in gray powder, parting and coming together again over infinitely long scrubby plains. Sometimes the tracks vanish into dried-up riverbeds, and you pick your way among the pebbles and rocks. The country is bony and ancient, *khak* is the Persian word for dust, and khaki is the color of these humps and spines from prehistory, for it is as though the mountains were the fossilized shapes of dinosaurs and pterodactyls.

Sometimes the mountainsides seem blown with lavender, and a pastel down on the slopes glows with gentle pinks and grays; then the valleys appear Irish and emerald green. But dust is the recurrent theme; clouding round the passing vehicle, swirling under the occasional rider, and crossing the distant plain in whirling cones, it can hover so low on the horizon that it seems like the mist of a winter's dawn.

The special Afghan quality is a gravity that is never lost. When we prepared for the journey, I read a phrase from the journal of the first Englishman to visit Kabul: "I have found," he wrote, "the organic remains of a former world." This indeed is what made our journey worthwhile, in a country where there were no ruins to admire but which was organically linked to traces of a living whole. Since then the current has been broken again and again, the former world has been violently wrenched apart by horrifying conflicts, and the remains, organic no longer, are now scattered into a limbo of pain and darkness.

Kabul in those days had magic—not the dreamlike magic of white walls and perfumes that we project onto the *Thousand and*

One Nights but a rough brown magic, brown like the mud walls and the mud lanes, a magic firmly of this world, rude and hard, transformed by a quality brought by the people themselves. The wonder of Afghanistan that was to draw me back there years later to film *Meetings with Remarkable Men* lay in the people, in the unseen quality of their relationships, in an openly acknowledged sense of religious presence — something we had so often talked about and searched for over the years at home, as though it was a quality the world had lost. Here we saw how it really existed and could pervade all of daily life.

Walking in the covered bazaar of Kabul, an obscurity sliced by great shafts of brilliant sunlight from circular holes in the roof, I passed an old cobbler sitting cross-legged in his stall, pouring out tea. His head was so noble and dignified that I could not resist pausing just to watch. He caught my eye as his hand was moving the cup to his lips. In a complete unbroken gesture his movement changed its direction, and the cup was now held out to me — an offering that was the natural answer to my indiscreet stare.

Another time, I saw a dwarf with a proud head and a magnificent long black beard sitting cross-legged, motionless and upright, in front of the great mosque of Kabul. Day after day, as I passed, I would pause to observe him from the corner of my eye with a special sense of respect, and long after the journey ended his image remained with me as the embodiment of strength, for here was a man accepting totally who he was, where he was, what he was. A dwarf placed in infinity, like us all.

In a way incomprehensible to the Western mind, a newcomer in an Eastern country is sized up and weighed on arrival. If one wants to be taken seriously, it is important just to wait. If one is patient and above all respectful, coincidences happen and doors open by themselves.

After a while, we learned that in Kabul there was a remarkable young Sufi known as the Black Dervish, the Tour Malang. Discreet inquiries led us from one person to another until one day we found ourselves crossing a little wooden bridge over a small river on the outskirts of the city. In typical Afghan fashion a small boy appeared from nowhere to lead us to a house, where in the hallway a quiet elderly man greeted us, hand on heart. "He's not back. You can wait." We sat on the ground in a tiny outer room, sensing an invisible activity on the other side of the walls. Tea was brought, we sat in silence, afternoon became evening, the sun went down, the small boy came in to light a lamp, and night fell. Then suddenly, the dervish was there; older people were rushing forward from the unseen inner part of the house to touch the feet of what at first sight was simply an unshaven young man with the wild-eyed stare of someone back from fighting in the street. Seeing us, he sat down, and giving us all his attention he began to ask questions.

To prepare for our encounter with the dervish, the four of us had, the night before, discussed what questions we could put. We agreed that we should avoid Western-style formulations, and naively I proposed to open the discussion in what seemed to be an appropriately oriental metaphoric language. I wished to ask my eternal question: how to respond to the obscure intimations one has that there is a "something else" beyond the everyday world. So, preparing my poetic imagery, I leaned toward the dervish, "In my House," I said, trying to give a special symbolic resonance to the word, "there are many rooms, crammed with a jumble of unnecessary objects."

He nodded and I felt that he was following my metaphor.

"Occasionally," I went on, "I seem to hear sounds. I don't know where they come from, nor what they are —"

He was clearly interested and interrupted me. "What sort of sounds? Could they come from the pipes? Have you called in a builder?"

I was astonished, convinced he was making fun of me, but as he continued I realized that he was a practical man accustomed to giving his pupils practical advice, and my companions quickly rescued me by rephrasing the question in clear unpoetic terms. The words we received in return are long since forgotten; in their place remains something far more direct, which became an answer to my clumsily phrased question.

When he heard that we were leaving Kabul the following morning to drive to Kandahar, he made a suggestion. "It will involve a small detour." Then the dervish gave us the name of a village. "Just before you enter the village, on your right you will see an old white building. This is a prison. On the other side of the road, you will find a man sitting, watching the prison. Go and speak to him. He is my pupil." He went on to explain that the man had been his pupil for many years but was the victim of a nature so violent that it led him to outbursts that he always regretted but could never control. One day he had committed a terrible crime—perhaps he had killed someone, I no longer remember—and shocked by his action, he had rushed to the dervish to pour out the full incoherence of his distress. Tour Malang knew that if the man were sent to prison, this would only feed the fury in his nature and that a last chance of escape from his inner darkness would be lost, but in working with him for so long, the dervish had seen a hidden side to the man's nature and was certain that if this side could be strengthened, everything else would be transformed. "I had to find a way in which he could be fortified, not destroyed," he continued, "and fortunately I had another pupil, an elderly judge."

"There is no question, the law says the boy must be punished and this is right," he told the judge, "but I want you to give him to me to punish. I promise you, my punishment will be harder than yours."

As the judge had complete confidence in the dervish, he agreed, finding a way to twist the letter of the law and release the prisoner who was in his custody. The dervish then pronounced his sentence. The young criminal was to go find a prison; he was to place himself in front of the prison and stay there voluntarily for the full length of whatever the maximum sentence would be, facing the prison wall of his own free will, never losing sight of his crime.

We eagerly made the detour, and we found the place without difficulty. On the right side of the road were the walls of the prison, on the left a few big stones were half buried in the thick white dust, and two sticks held up a piece of torn cloth to make a thin band of protection against the noonday sun. Here a man in rags was sitting in front of a fire, stirring the contents of a large metal bowl. Leaving the Land Rover, I approached him, murmuring the name of Tour Malang. As he raised his eyes, the look that came through the filthy matted confusion of hair and beard was shocking in its strength. It was like scraping the embers of a dying fire and suddenly uncovering a red-hot piece of coal. The quiet but powerful figure who sat there in front of the prison was clearly going through a passionate ordeal of inner transformation; if ever it were possible for him to master his demon, clearly it would be through the process that was now under way. Courteously holding out his ladle, he invited me to share his meal, but when I looked into the cauldron what I saw filled me with nausea and my courage failed. To my shame, I put my hand on my heart and regretfully shook my head.

What is that strange and secret struggle that one can employ against one's own weakness, turning weakness into strength? Acceptance always sounds timid and passive; submission seems to evoke the bowed head of the conquered slave. But this prisoner's head was not bowed, and his acceptance was an act of strength because it was voluntary; at any moment he could get up and escape, back into weakness. To stay in front of himself, in front of a prison that constantly reflected back to him an awareness of the terrible prison in himself, must have cost him an equally terrible price. This was a punishment that he could never have invented alone; the order had to come from someone stronger whom he respected, someone who had his trust. He needed to understand the meaning of his situation, and only then could a true, dynamic acceptance enable him to find the forces necessary to stay with himself, face to face. The look in the eyes of the prisoner and the way he sat facing the jail made an image that has never left me.

Once, many years later, in Kyoto, I put to a Zen master the same question I had asked the Tour Malang, though I managed to formulate it in a better way. "My wish to struggle with myself is weak. How can one intensify the will?"

"You can do nothing," he answered. "No one can 'do' anything. If you try to force yourself, this leads to nothing. But the will can intensify itself on its own, if it is placed again and again in front of real obstacles."

A remarkable African Sufi, Amadou Hampaté Ba, was asked one evening at a gathering of friends in Paris what destiny meant to him. Was it true that the Eastern view of implacable destiny was fatalistic and led to accepting everything with equal passivity? "Of course not," he answered firmly. "When you are in front of a crisis, a painful situation, a potential tragedy, you must struggle to prevent it with everything in your power. Man has a warrior's nature, and he must fight against destiny and never give up. This is his freedom. It is only when the inevitable occurs that everything changes. Then the past cannot be altered, neither by prayer nor curses nor regrets, and at that moment man must accept destiny absolutely, without looking back. There is no other way in which he can be free." Of course, today he would have added gently, "Man means woman as well."

Our journey took us deeper and deeper into an Afghanistan that mountains and poverty had so far preserved from strangers, for even the hippies had not yet made their trail through the land. We were looking for monasteries, or whatever structures and communities existed here to meet the monastic need. These places, we discovered, are called *khanakars*, literally "houses of work," the "work" meaning the devotional activities of the members of a Sufi order that take place within a rigorously guarded space. For this reason, nothing from the outside indicated that these places were in any way different from other buildings, but as we gradually and patiently penetrated into the Afghan way of life, it became easier to sense the presence of a *khanakar*. Often there would be a bazaar touching its walls, and although the *khanakar* and the bazaar were quite distinct, as we walked in the narrow alleys a special quality of energy became perceptible in the rhythm and movement flowing from stall to stall. In this way, a bazaar peopled with artisans practicing their normal trade became a link between the activities of the outside world and the sacred devotions hidden by the walls. It seemed to express for me in a vivid way how a craft can serve both its practical purpose and yet be impregnated with a quality that it manages to transmit.

Here in Afghanistan I began to wonder whether a theater, like the bazaar, could both stay in the everyday world and yet touch a monastery wall. Could it be normal and down-to-earth — and also have a quality that comes from a finer source? The source is what matters, and we soon had a sharp experience of what can happen when a source becomes impure.

We went from one *khanakar* to another, always welcomed with dignity and simplicity, and were more and more moved by the fine quality in every detail of what we encountered. Then one day we were admitted to a waiting room where the furniture was ornate and not very well kept; the heavy Victorian sofas with antimacassars and the armchairs with doilies seemed oddly out of place, and instead of the silent attentive young man who invariably welcomed guests, a pale somewhat plump young woman greeted us. Normally, when tea is offered in a *khanakar*, the exquisite care in its presentation directly reflects the level of dedication with which the spiritual work is maintained, but this time flies buzzed round the far-from-clean tray, which seemed to correspond to the overall impression of slovenliness and decay. An elderly man came through the door with hesitant steps. From his clothes we knew he was the dervish, so we rose to our feet respectfully. "Sit," he gestured, and as he took his place in front of us, he seemed strangely ill at ease. We had prepared many questions, ones that had grown and deepened through the experiences of the journey, and the old man answered us without conviction. I noticed that the young woman had stayed, and against all tradition, she was following our conversation. Suddenly, the old man burst into tears. "Ah! . . . ," he cried, beating his breast, while tears rolled down his cheeks and into his white beard. He looked at the woman, but she did not react. After a long moment of embarrassment, we got to our feet, while he continued to sob heavily. Gradually, the loud sobbing turned into silent weeping, and as neither he nor the woman made the least sign to retain us, we bowed and left. As we drove away, we tried to understand what had happened. Was it the arrival of foreigners with their questions that had shocked him into a realization of his situation in a *khanakar* falling into decay? Or were such bursts of self-pity and self-accusation part of his daily routine? While we had no way of telling, the flies clearly knew that something essential was missing.

The Sufi poem *The Conference of the Birds* tells of a man weeping true tears of remorse, but the tears, as they touch the ground, turn into stones. He collects the stones, mistaking their frozen beauty for the feeling that had been there while they flowed. The whole history of religions and traditions has always seemed to me to be captured in this tale — and also of art, of writing, of theater, of life. Unless a special quality of life is present all the time, forms lose their meaning; they rot and only attract the flies.

A wise old fairy tale that exists in many cultures tells of the man seeking everywhere for the priceless treasure — a blue flower or a magic mushroom — only to find that it has been on his doorstep all the time. Despite all my youthful dreams of an illumination arising in the exotic decor of high mountains or distant temples, it was a very ordinary car handle that one day gave me the most direct experience of the "here and now." I had grasped it to open the door of the first car I possessed, and suddenly within the movement of my hand a conviction affirmed itself: "This moment contains the whole of everything. There is nothing to look for, nothing to find." Then as the car door swung open, the moment was gone, but I had tasted what a moment can mean.

This precious sensation reappeared fugitively at different times: in a café at the corner of the Avenue Carnot in Paris when for a few exceptional minutes I was part of the whole skein of life with sounds, movements, events passing in a vibrant unity through a body that had become momentarily transparent. Another time I was digging in an orchard when there was a sudden sense of relationship with earth, muscle, and sky, which someone who had had a similar experience described as a "flowing stillness." Unexpectedly, this sense recurred standing on the deck of a ship crossing from Jutland to Norway. At other times it would be evoked by places with their own magnetic power — ruins like Persepolis, where the life of the stone clears the mind and calms the spirit. In an African forest there is a lake that is regarded as specially sacred, and the impression here is very powerful; it is a lake like other lakes, yet so strong is its presence that the insects skimming across the surface seem inseparable parts of the lake's being. Standing in front of a great painting can produce this sensation, or before a vast Buddha whose hard stone seems to breathe. I found it once on a Christmas Day when the whole of Europe momentarily ceased its busy agitation, and a silence lay on the land as gently as the snow.

But these scattered moments of grace are crumbs dropped from the table, mirages that melt away. Dimly I sensed that their intoxication had its dangers and the relish I experienced was a trap. It may be a blessing to have a certain artistic sensibility, but just like drugs, art takes away as much as it brings. It is a struggle to remember that what the artist regards so naturally as his strength is also the rope that ties him to his prison. Every success, every word of praise has to be taken with a large pinch of salt, for artistic experience is just a reflection, an intimation of "something else"; it must never be confused with the indefinable thing itself.

In the search for the indefinable, the first condition is silence, silence as the equal opposite of activity, silence that neither opposes action nor rejects it. In the Sahara one day, I climbed over a dune to descend into a deep bowl of sand. Sitting at the bottom I encountered for the first time absolute silence, stillness that is indivisible. For there are two silences: a silence can be no more than the absence of noise, it can be inert, or at the other end of the scale, there is a nothingness that is infinitely alive, and every cell in the body can be penetrated and vivified by this second silence's activity. The body then knows the difference between two relaxations — the soft floppiness of a body weary of stress telling itself to relax, and the relaxation of an alert body when tensions have been swept away by the intensity of being. The two silences, enclosed within an even greater silence, are poles apart.

Near Bogotá, there is an underground cathedral that Indian workers hacked out of the rock in a disused gold mine. To enter it you leave the hillside to go along a tunnel that grows darker and darker until the daylight vanishes. For some twenty minutes you advance in a blackness that eventually opens up into what is called a cathedral, but there is no art, no beauty in the big clumsy pillars. The cathedral is a parody, a woeful series of dark holes into which someone has placed an altar and some candles; dim electric light reveals further dugouts pretending to be chapels in a world from which daylight has been banished. It is as though oxygen had been sucked away and replaced with pure nitrogen, or as if after a nuclear war, survivors had made a way of life under the earth, cut off forever from air, light, color, radiance, so that in this dungeon only the lowest of human feelings could subsist — as though gold in an inverted alchemy had been downgraded into lead. For a long while I stood motionless, inhabited by these somber feelings. Then unaccountably, without any intervention on my part, at the nadir of the experience, somewhere a sense of life was reborn — within the nitrogen the oxygen breathed again; in the dark, a captive light was released. I had needed to come here to perceive that a cathedral can grow even in a tomb.

Now I understand better how it was that when my father died, I stood silent by his body and for an extraordinary instant I could feel that this inanimate form had its own rightness. It had now become the firm support from which life could rise, as though from the bottom of a chain, upward and then descending again. The most acute sense of life is always found in the presence of death.

In Benares as dusk falls there is a time of reconciliation with the dead. The waning light turns yellow, the Ganges flows, the lines of smoke carry the remains of the corpses on the funeral pyres upward into the air, a dog barks, children play and shout in the distance. Silence absorbs everything and all is in its place, as it should be, with one exception — fear. Fear has vanished like a shadow that was never there.

Early one morning, time stopped. I picked up the phone, then turned to Natasha to tell her that Jane Heap had died. The powerful magnet at the center of every activity was gone. "What were her last words?" we asked, only to realize at once the absurdity of the question, because the whole of a teacher's lifework is her only statement. There was grief, there was emptiness and a useless scramble to fill the void. But the pain of deprivation needed to be cherished and respected, and only after mourning was allowed its time and place could new lines of life emerge with their own determination.

"You will see," said a friend when I first met Madame de Salzmann, "she is like a fan, which gradually opens until more and more is revealed." After Jane's death, Natasha and I went frequently to Paris, where Gurdjieff's work was being maintained with increasing intensity by Madame de Salzmann, who had been close to Gurdjieff since she had met him in the Caucasus during the First World War. Through her own unremitting struggle, she had gained the capacity to transmit to others a unique quality of experience, and I now made a vow to myself always to be available whenever the opportunity arose to be near her.

I would like to be able to draw a portrait with words of this remarkable person, but I know how inadequate this will be. In my work with actors, I have learned that impersonation only succeeds if it can capture the rigid areas in which a personality is imprisoned. Someone whose life flows freely has none of the rigidities on which imitations or even descriptions can comfortably hang.

Madame de Salzmann had achieved this freedom through a life devoted to the service of that unknown source of finer energy that can only become manifest when the human organism is completely open — open in body, feeling, and thought. When this condition is reached, the individuality does not vanish; it is illuminated in every aspect and can play its true role, which is to bend and adapt to every changing need.

Madame de Salzmann would always rise graciously to welcome a visitor. She would sit upright, still and contained, and would respond with laughter or seriousness, finding precisely the words and the idiom that corresponded to the age and understanding of the listener. Her speaking was not for herself, she was never carried away by her own memories or her ideas; out of an awareness of what was needed, out of listening to the other person's state, she would speak directly to the person so as to evoke a meaning or encourage an action to arise. She was always present, as close as the need demanded—yet in this closeness she was never to be grasped. No one could hold her, and she held on to no one.

There are many reasons for describing a human being as "remarkable"; for Gurdjieff the essential quality of a remarkable man or woman was the capacity to watch equally over "the lamb and the wolf" in his or her care. To cherish the tenderness of the one and the ferocity of the other, to give to each its place, is only possible if there is a special kind of presence that reconciles, unites, and holds them both in balance. Often Madame de Salzmann would describe how at her first meeting with Gurdjieff, she had immediately recognized this remarkableness in him. From then on she had stayed by his side, working with him through a multitude of forms of teaching and conditions of life, watching over both the wolf and lamb.

At Gurdjieff's death, Madame de Salzmann found herself virtually alone, inheriting the gigantic and volcanic output that Gurdjieff had left behind. All over the world there were groups of students left rudderless, in a state of confusion that seemed destined to splinter, distort, and degrade the material that they had been given. There were unpublished writings, a bewildering quantity of musical compositions, an even greater number of dances, movements, and exercises that she herself had taught and of which she had the truest living memory. Recognizing that uniting all these strands was now her unavoidable role, she devoted all her energy to this task, traveling indefatigably between Europe and America. I would meet her often and was always fascinated by the same observation. Wherever she went, she seemed always in the same place, her stability unaffected by outer change.

One day, I asked Madame de Salzmann a question that gnawed at me constantly, for it was connected to all my major decisions in life. On the surface, all seemed balanced and harmonious, and I certainly had no right to complain. But, deep down, nothing could quench a sense of meaninglessness, both in my own activities and in the world around me—yet to solve this by breaking away or dropping out seemed arrogant and futile. It was a personal version of the ancient dilemma of determining what belongs to Caesar and what truly belongs to that "something else." "I have an inner search that I cherish and respect but also a work in life for which I am grateful and cannot despise. Both seem valuable, but in different ways," I said. "What can help me to assess how much I should legitimately give to each, so as to maintain a balance?" She looked at me for a moment, then answered quite simply, "Come back at nine o'clock tonight." When I returned, to my bewilderment it was not to resume our conversation but to find myself included with others in a session that she guided, leading step by step to a complete silence.

I had expected something to be said that would clarify my question; only as time went by did I see how precise and practical her seemingly indirect answer had been. It was the answer of direct experience. It became clear that it is the quality of silent wakefulness, informing and uniting the organism from moment to moment, that gives meaning to each choice and to every action. On an ordinary level of awareness, all choices will suffer from one's lack of true vision, and as I had so often painfully experienced, we torture ourselves with decisions that in fact we are in no position to take. The purer the inner state, the clearer the vision. That evening she led us step by step to taste what that state might be and how in it contradictions can be resolved and priorities become real. In a cruder state, all arguments are valid because all choices are the same. The enigma is how to discover what can lead us to another, deeper, truer state. I still believed that somehow or other I could fabricate this state for myself, and I had to face the awkward truth that even this natural desire can become the greatest of obstacles; even the sincerest of wishes can block that special opening toward which all aspiration tends. Effort only has a place if it leads to a mystery called noneffort, and then if for a short instant one's perception is transformed, this is an act of grace. Although grace cannot be attained, it may sometimes be granted. One has to let go of the leaf to which one is clinging, but it takes no more than another leaf to blow by for one to drop again into the usual state of confusion.

Even while special moments were now making the inner world more real, outside life was once more taking on its necessary and irresistible attraction, involving a constant rotation through big cities — London, Paris, and New York — where Natasha and I had become sucked inexorably into an ever-widening circle of friends. Friends — one uses the word lightly; in fact they were the acquaintances in the artistic, fashion, literary, and show-business worlds whom one hugs, who give friendly parties and handsome presents, and who, it seems, can neither understand nor forgive if one does not phone the moment one arrives in their town. One day, I realized that the phone calls, the inevitable invitations leading to obligations of hospitality in return, were filling up the day and then the week; a choice had to be made between these activities and the moments of quiet that mattered most, so I decided to make a complete break. Arriving in New York to prepare the script for the film of *Lord of the Flies*, I went to the then obscure Chelsea Hotel on West Twenty-third Street, and for the first time told no one I knew that I was in town.

One old friend, to my great irritation, traced me and called just to say jokingly, "You see, my detective service is very efficient." Otherwise, no one found me. I had assumed I would be giving great offense but discovered I was mistaken. I was quickly forgotten, and there are many acquaintances of the past whom I have never seen again. I tried the same technique in London and Paris; people dropped me as easily as I dropped them, and no one seemed hurt.

The Chelsea Hotel was a unique hiding place. It had not yet been discovered by the press but was already well known in certain circles. Dylan Thomas had lived there; Tennessee Williams and Arthur Miller disappeared into its thousand rooms when the need for anonymity became pressing. I had an enormous sitting room with ugly orange tiles round the fireplace, reminding me of a room in an Oxford college. In fact, it was here that Thomas Wolfe had written *Look Homeward, Angel.* Along the corridor was a paneled library belonging to the composer Virgil Thomson, and on the next floor was a man who had come for two weeks and then stayed for fifty years and had installed a jungle, complete with trees, ponds, and live serpents. There was a floor for prostitutes, another for junkies, which combined later to give the hotel its exotic reputation, but in fact in the lobby and in the aging elevators that rose with such reluctance, one would mostly rub shoulders with sadly ordinary New Yorkers, with dogs and packages and well-worn overcoats. The original owner, Mr. Bart, unwilling to accept their money and touchingly affectionate, remembered and loved them all.

Natasha was filming in London, and it was during my months in the Chelsea, cut off from all the circles to which I used to belong, that I learned to appreciate New York. Eating in the Automat, walking and traveling on the subway, I found that the town lost not only its glamour, which I had so resented at first, but also its inhumanity. Sitting in the Horn and Hardart with a corned-beef hash, looking round at the lonely figures at each table, any one of whom could clutch his heart, choke, and drop dead at any moment without perhaps disturbing the isolation of the others, I found paradoxically a warmth and an honesty in loneliness that had so far escaped me; it gave a particular humanity to the city.

One night in New York, I said to one of the few close friends with whom I kept in touch, "I'm giving up the theater."

"Don't be so foolish!" He shook his head. "You have made a field for yourself. Perhaps you can now do something special within your field."

But I was not ready to listen to this good advice, and anyway, it was filming that still attracted me most.

Finding the money for *Lord of the Flies*, with the attendant feuds, elations, and disappointments, took two years. It was followed by shooting on a threadbare budget and editing in a cutting room in a Paris suburb alone with one close friend, Gerry Feil. Natasha, radiantly pregnant, meanwhile shivered in our first Paris apartment, a tiny triangle that looked out over a courtyard on the Boulevard Saint Germain. The winter of 1961 was harsh, coal was short, and bombs exploded in doorways as an extreme right-wing organization called the OAS tried miserably to save Algeria for France. During this time, I was glad to be away from the theater and passionately interested again in the director's dilemma of when to intervene and when to let things happen, this time in relation to film. The power of the accidental and the

principle of uncertainty were now highly regarded. Cinema véri-
té was in the air; cameras were held in the hand or clutched by
cameramen who were pushed around in invalid chairs, and
sound was now recorded on the spot so that the accidental noises
of the street made speech refreshingly incomprehensible. Filmmaking was finding a new freedom and excitement. In New York
I had run into a well-known British cameraman, Richard Lea-
cock, who told me that in the past he had carefully studied all
the rules of exposure — lighting, emulsion curves, and processing
times. Now, he said, he just pointed his camera in the direction
of the event and only bothered with two possibilities for his dia-
phragm — wide open or tightly closed.

This chance and humorous remark made a great impression on
me, since with *Lord of the Flies* all the conditions, not only financial, indicated that we should work with whatever in Puerto Rico
was at hand, so I picked a still photographer who had never oper-
ated a movie camera in his life and a largely amateur crew. We had
to rediscover the laws of cinema virtually from scratch, inventing
way-out techniques of our own so that the camera could follow the
children as they scrambled over rocks and across the sand, or reconstruct voices that had been drowned by the crashing of the
waves. Time was short; we were lent the children by unexpectedly
eager parents just for the duration of the summer holidays. As we
could never see rushes, we needed to cover ourselves with a great
amount of footage, so a second camera was indispensable. My
friend Gerry Feil, a skillful documentary filmmaker, had been
closely involved in all the preparation of the film, so I asked him to
take the second camera, with complete freedom to snatch, grab, or
follow whatever viewpoint he chose. In the meantime, I stayed
with the principal camera, carefully framing the shots according to
my own view of the story and my own pictorial values. When we
came to the editing, I was fascinated to discover how often I preferred and chose Gerry's camera's point of view to my own. Naturally, without the carefully constructed and rehearsed material of
the shot, Gerry would have had nothing to film, so he was benefit-
ing from what had been composed for the main camera. Yet I was
shown in a striking way how the inevitable directorial act of intervention can be counterbalanced by a viewpoint that is free from
tyranny. Afterward I learned that Renoir had once said to Matisse,
"When I have arranged a bouquet for the purpose of painting it, I
always turn it round and paint the side I didn't plan."

I applied this as a conscious method a few years later when I had to find a way of filming *Marat/Sade* in a studio in fifteen days. This time, I asked the cameraman, David Watkins, to do a prelighting that would leave him completely free during the shooting period, so that holding a second camera himself, he could choose his own shots. In the editing, a large amount of the most useful and expressive material came from this roving eye. The eternally nagging question of intervention, of when to give and when to take, was now emerging in a new guise.

In filmmaking, our desire for perfection can easily lead us to retake the same scene without realizing that we are chasing an abstract idea with which we have become identified and which can prevent us from seeing the true event that is taking place in front of the lens. It is only during the rushes — and later in the calm and detachment of the cutting room — that we can see how very seldom our final take is the best. There is a natural organic curve in the sequence of shots; the living material grows and reaches its plenitude, after which further takes become an attempt to hammer reality into conformity with one's own vision, which is so often narrower than the roughness and range of the real thing.

The dilemma arises when one recognizes that nonintervention does not mean sitting back, doing nothing, and letting everything happen by itself. Samuel Beckett once explained to me that when he writes a play, he sees it as a series of tensions, in the sense of taut steel wires that link one unit to the next. In fact, in all playwriting, whatever the style, each phrase must contain the trigger that sets off the following line. In this way, a good performance is like a game of Ping-Pong, and the five acts of a play by Shakespeare make up one long phrase, a phrase that accelerates, slows down, pauses, but never stops. When the first word is spoken, an invisible spool begins to unroll, and the structure of speech and silence must then flow inexorably to the end of the very last line. Whatever the way in which it is staged, even when the order of the scenes is rearranged or the text is drastically cut, this pulse needs to be there, for a performing art is life with the flabbiness removed. In the cinema as well, the chain of images must never be broken. Film editors have known for nearly a century that a fade-out has to be rapidly followed by a fade-in; if the duration of blackness in between the two is even a trifle too long, the flow of impressions will be broken and the spectator's interest will be lost. The great father of mime, Étienne Decroux, with a mordant sense of paradox, once said to me, "People believe that mime is the art of silence, but this is seldom true. Usually it is endlessly talkative, because the performer daren't let his hold over the audience drop for one moment. He has to make signals all the time; otherwise they will no longer watch."

On the day long ago when I was starting to shoot my first film, *The Beggar's Opera*, I ran into John Huston on the Shepperton Studios lot, where he was making *Moulin Rouge*. "However many films I do," he told me, "on the first day, my directing is always too slow. I watch the actors, give them moves and actions, and without realizing it I am still in the tempo of everyday life. It looks good on the floor, but when I see the rushes I get a shock, because what seemed natural is intolerably lethargic on the screen. Then I find a way of heightening my concentration on the tiny area within the viewfinder, and I begin to find a tempo where there is no longer any slack." For his medium, Huston was describing Beckett's tensions of steel. Working between the theater and the cinema, I was becoming more and more aware of the importance of being sensitive to an underlying tempo, hard to uncover yet always waiting to be heard.

Long ago my perceptive schoolteacher had pointed out that rhythm is the common factor in all the arts, but he had failed to add, or had left me to discover in adult life, that it is also the common factor that underlies all human experience. I now crept toward a recognition that this is what makes or destroys each instant of our lives. Living in the "here and now" is a beautifully vague phrase, concealing the fact that both "here" and "now" are always arising out of what was and transforming themselves into what will be. They are part of a continuity, and if the tempo is slack, any succession of moments loses its meaning.

How can one live one single day in its true rhythm, a day composed of a multitude of finely intertwining rhythms? To recognize the problem is not to know the answer, only to acknowledge that each wasted moment will never return.

There are private events that I cannot refrain from recording, because in my chronology these are large watersheds — the arrival of our two children, Irina in 1962, Simon in 1966. Their emerging into this life evoked a feeling of awe both for Natasha and for me that is far beyond any other experience I have tried to describe. When the ball of an anonymous head thrusts itself into a blood-stained world, followed by a tiny corner of shoulder, the amazement seems complete — but when all of a sudden a miniature human hand appears, tears flow and wonder can then go no further. For a moment, one knows with certainty that one is part of the great chain of existence.

And as I write this, I also realize that there is another book that is not to be written, a book of memories that belong only to those who share them. This is the secret book of all the long days and nights, the holidays, the journeys, the birthdays, the treats, the tears, the jokes, the games, the bedtime stories, the separations, the reunions, the special occasions with the children, the family, the closest friends, which are not for other eyes or other ears, which are to be told if at all at night in bed to oneself or occasionally just to the few who can follow the references. This other book has no substance; it is what is called the film of memory, for which no celluloid is needed.

My swinging pendulum was now changing its trajectory — its circular motion was becoming a closing spiral, still carrying me through the same rings of travel, personal relationships, and adventures, but in a new and more concentrated way. The gaps were not so far apart, because the questions overlapped, making the need to face them more acute.

For years, I had rigorously kept my inner explorations and my theater experiments apart, recognizing the danger of mixtures and not wishing to make a confused mess of either. However, nothing can stay for long in watertight compartments, and I began to see that in the theater I was now exploring with increasing precision the hunch that had been with me when I was sitting in Salvador Dalí's beach hut avidly absorbing Matila Ghika's description of how proportions contain qualities that in turn are the expression of natural laws. As a result, the theater was becoming a practical field in which the possibility existed of observing laws and structures parallel to those found in traditional teachings. The same action, the same gesture, the same sound, the same phrase can be commonplace, vulgar, or uniquely touching depending on what illuminates it. There is multiplicity, there is unity — what can link them? The more I approached this question, the more I was becoming conscious of a fundamental weakness in my own position. I was still the observer sitting in one room, peering into the other — on one side the director, on the other, the actors — and the artificial nature of this separation, which I had always taken for granted, began to be disturbing.

I had never really questioned the idea of working in "two rooms" as this was the only theater I had known: on one side was the stage, on the other the auditorium. Actor was opposed to spectator, it was them or us, and we were like motorists who when they drive scorn pedestrians but feel a solidarity with pedestrians when on foot; whether on one side of the proscenium or the other, each side was there to conquer or be conquered. Now the moment had come when I no longer wanted to peer into another world from a seat in the darkness; a far richer experience could be found if spectator and performer were both within the same field of life. Not knowing how to go about this, I could only recognize the need.

When Peter Hall, with a warmth and generosity for which I will always be grateful, asked me at this time to join him in the direction of the Royal Shakespeare Company at Stratford, I made it a condition that I could have an independent unit of research so as to be able to explore in practice what was still just a troubling idea. The first step was to find someone with whom to share the difficulties, and as some articles I had written had brought me into contact with Charles Marowitz, the very rebellious editor of an off-beat theater magazine called *Encore*, I asked if he would join me in forming a group to put radical ideas into a concrete form.

We called it "the Theater of Cruelty" as a salute to Antonin Artaud, for although theater theory had never interested me much and I found in Artaud's extreme visions very few of the specifics that practical work demands, both Marowitz and I admired the burning intensity of the positions Artaud took in relation to the safe theater of his day. Our own Shakespeare theater was playing comfortably to tourists in a reassuring way, but in many of us there was a nagging suspicion that this was very far from the daring of the Elizabethan Age, with its passionate inquiry into individual and social experience and its metaphysical sense of terror and amazement.

Certain questions had to be asked. First of all, why play theater at all? The usual answer — because there are great texts and an audience wants to hear them — seemed insufficient. The real inquiry had to begin very far back indeed. What is a written word? What is a spoken word? When is it weak? When is it strong? Why does a certain sound concern us more than another?

The exercises that we devised, whether for the voice or the body, were designed to lead us into areas about which we knew nothing, of which we had no firsthand experience. And with them came an absolute renunciation of the director's privilege to decide in advance what results he is seeking. This inevitably led us away from the proscenium that divides theaters into two rooms. I also no longer felt the need to invent a new world out of my imagination, and as a result we could observe the infinite possibilities within the actor when he is on his own and unsupported by directorial devices.

Friends would ask us what we were aiming at, but since we were groping in the dark, we had to discover our aims as we went along. We were very clumsy, even reckless in the way we plunged into areas of which we were completely ignorant, and I was forced to recognize painfully that if one leads a group of any description, from mountain climbing to theater exercises, enthusiasm must be viewed with suspicion, and one must be very aware of the responsibility one assumes. Both actors and directors can drag up from the dark regions of the subconscious suppressed images that are so disturbing that we must rigorously question the right to impose them on others.

Over many years and many trials and errors, we learned that sensitivity at every moment to one another and to the audience is more important than the wish for self-expression. In the early sixties this was new territory, there were no models, so it was with great relief that after a time I learned of a fellow seeker, Jerzy Grotowski in Poland, making very precise experiments, far more systematic than our own. He had an astonishing command of political strategy that allowed him to get support from a Communist regime for a search that was surreptitiously mystical at the core.

The chief accent of our early work in London, around 1965, was an exploration of all that the normal production's four or five weeks of rehearsal never left time to examine. *Experimental* is a misleading word; even in the most conventional circumstances,

all healthy work should be experimental, so the opposition between *experimental* and *traditional* is quite artificial. The true
meaning of "research" is not that it is more experimental but
simply that time is open-ended and one is under no pressure to
produce a good result by a certain date.

As our group had all the time it needed, we could explore what
otherwise must be taken for granted. In the English theater of
the day, communication meant words, so our first investigation
focused on what remains when words are taken away. For this we
needed actors who were young, talented, and unafraid. One day
while Charles and I were auditioning for our group, a very
strange girl appeared. I had seldom encountered anyone so determined to be concealed. She hid behind an ugly thick overcoat,
a scarf, a woolen hat, a scowl, half-closed eyes, and a sarcastic,
defensive voice. We asked her to improvise various ideas, and
there was no hesitation, nothing seemed to daunt her. We had
almost completed our group, there was only one place left, so
now we had to choose between another very talented young actress and this unpredictable apparition. Which would be better
for the work we wished to do? It was a knife-edge decision. Someone had told Charles that the girl's marriage had just broken up
and that she was at a stage of acute depression and confusion.
This later turned out to be quite untrue, but it just served to tip
the scales and gave the necessary edge to our preferring her to
the one who seemed more normal and in our terms less interesting. Even more important to me was the fact that despite her
determined efforts to present herself to the world in the worst
possible way, she was none the less powerfully attractive. So it
was that Glenda Jackson joined our work.

As with Jeanne Moreau, there was between us an instant complicity, a telepathic communication needing a minimum of explanations. Like Jeanne, Glenda seized any suggestion and at
once made it her own. But her special quality was an organic
originality that made whatever she did unexpected, different,
though never quirky — she bypassed clichés to reveal a truer and
more sharply observed facet of human behavior. But the image I
carry most vividly from all the work we have done together is not
of her in performance — it is of Glenda watching. For hours
on end, starting with the first Theater of Cruelty, I see Glenda,
huddled in a corner, motionless, silent, critical, missing nothing.

Our first activities took place in a small space in South Kensington, watched from afar with the deepest suspicion by the members of the main Aldwych and Stratford-upon-Avon Shakespeare companies. Our only public performances must indeed have seemed very strange, for they presented unearthly cries, long silences, splashes of red paint, Glenda Jackson stark naked, and lines of *Hamlet* shuffled out of all apparent order. This gave further nourishment to the many raised eyebrows and humorous green-room asides. However, actors are highly pragmatic beings, and when a year later the experimental group merged with the mainstream of the company to rehearse *Marat/Sade*, the new ways of working began to seem interesting even to the most skeptical.

On the first day of rehearsal of *Marat/Sade*, I asked the actors to improvise their ideas of insanity. We were all shocked by the ridiculous eye-rolling clichés of madness that appeared and realized that we needed to know more precisely what so-called madness really is. So we went to see. As a result, I received for the first time the true shocks that come from direct contact with the physically atrocious conditions of inmates in mental hospitals, in geriatric wards, and, subsequently, in prisons — images of real life for which pictures on film are no substitute. Crime, madness, political violence were there, tapping on the window, pushing open the door. There was no way out. It was not enough to remain in the second room, on the other side of the threshold. A different involvement was needed.

The closed world of the West End theater, the search for prettiness and charm were dying, and the fine muslin curtains over the windows in the beautifully decorated terrace houses had to be pulled back. This was the parting of the ways with old friends and colleagues who did not want to look out into the street. The war in Vietnam was at the other end of the world, but the meaningless massacre seemed infinitely closer to us than formal questions of culture and style. A number of friends, some from the original Theater of Cruelty group — the designer Sally Jacobs, the musician Richard Peaslee, and others involved in the Royal Shakespeare Company, Michael Kustow, Albert Hunt, Adrian Mitchell, and Denis Cannan — were very disturbed to see that in the length and breadth of the English theater there was hardly any reflection of this terrifying reality, for a play on the subject of the Vietnam War did not exist. This inexplicable fact shamed us into trying to make one collectively as quickly as possible, giving ourselves a deadline, believing that if one side of the research coin is to spend infinite time on a single gesture, the other side of the same coin is speed. In this case urgency outweighed art. The actors were largely those who had been in previous experiments, and from the start we settled on the two-way title *US* to underline that the agony of the United States could not be written off conveniently as a problem for "them" over there: "U.S." is also "US."

The members of the team were not at all in agreement about the meaning of political theater. My own conviction was that to be socially useful a theater needs to go beyond polemics; my early meeting with Brecht had left me with a strong distaste for anything didactic. As even the longest play is far too short to give a comprehensive analysis of a situation, it must make drastic simplifications and set up crude categories of right and wrong.

Certainly, my own attitude was not due to a feeling that I was outside politics. If anything, on visits to Russia and Cuba I had reacted with an excess of admiration, and while my stand was theoretically to the left, it was more of a skeptical anarchy in the face of the so-called Establishment values of the right than a belief in any party or program. On the *US* team, many of the co-authors were dedicated socialists, while the politics of the actors were mostly emotional, responding instantly to injustice and suffering. Ideologically, we had no basis for agreement, but the agonizing immediacy of the senseless destruction brought us together. This took us through territories that were very new at the time: we improvised, however inadequately, the brutal cruelties that we wished to portray by doing exercises that simulated mutilation, self-immolation, death. We got hold of documents that enabled us to reconstruct in a precise way many terrifying American army techniques that were used for training in torture. We puzzled over the blind search for aesthetics in many of the war photographers' prize-winning images and heard on tape the delighted schoolboy laughter of bomber crews watching the colored flashes and little puffs of white smoke that made a toy town of the villages and the human lives that they were destroying. At the same time we tried to enter into the spirit of Vietnam itself through studying its popular theater and exploring the Asiatic

techniques with which ancient legends were still being performed behind the battlefield.

The lunch break, when visitors would come by to talk to us,
was always a time of special interest. We had visits from war corre-
spondents, subversive militants, committed writers proposing
sketches to be included in our material. One day a young Indian
slipped me a copy of a five-page playlet he had written about the
Bhagavad-Gita. The name meant nothing to me at the time, but
the central image of the short, sparsely written text burned its way
into my memory. It described a great warrior who when poised to
give the signal that would launch a terrible battle of destruction,
unexpectedly stopped his chariot between the two armies and
asked, "Why must we fight?" We asked ourselves what would happen if the general in charge of the American forces were suddenly to pause and allow himself to ponder this question. Then
we realized that this could never happen outside poetic fiction,
as the wheel of war to which a general is chained can never stop
turning even for a moment, so we did not try to introduce this
idea into our show. However, for many years this amazing image
nagged at me, reappearing at unexpected intervals, calling to be
explored as the basis for a play, until the day when I sought out
a Sanskrit scholar to ask him where it came from. He then began to tell a story with a strange, seemingly unpronounceable
name — the *Mahabharata* — and I was hooked for years to come.

As we worked on *US*, again and again we would be asked, "Do
you imagine your play will stop the war?" The need to answer
this absurd question was a great help in reassessing the meaning
of political theater. This was in the sixties, when a critical and
intelligent new generation in the theater was becoming increasingly concerned with the state of the world and refusing to accept
that art provided an excuse to hide in an ivory tower. However,
making plays to preach a political solution always implies that
one is in the right, and in a great majority of cases a real situation
of social injustice would become simply a pretext for working out
one's private angers and frustrations.

The question can be approached in quite another way. If de-
mocracy means respect for the individual, true political theater
means trusting each individual in the audience to reach his or
her own conclusions, once the act of theater has performed its
legitimate function of bringing the hidden complexities of a situation into light. Thus political theater is the exact opposite of

politics; it cannot serve a party line. A politician is a professional who lives by making absolute affirmations that have little chance of being true. Good theater, on the contrary, must show that political absolutes are painfully relative and many commitments dangerously naive. A politician in a speech today makes promises that he believes at the time but that he no longer needs to keep when at a future date conditions have changed. In the theater, every conviction is in the present or else it is nowhere, so every affirmation must be given the flesh and blood of reality at the moment it is expressed.

In life the heat of conflict makes it almost impossible to enter into the logic of one's adversary, but a great dramatist can without judgment launch opposing characters against one another, so an audience can be at one and the same time inside and outside them both, successively for, against, and neutral. Thanks to these dynamic changes of sympathy and attitude, spectators can be given a moment of perception beyond their normal vision. If no act of theater can stop a war, if it can neither influence a nation nor a government nor a city, this does not mean that it is impossible for a theater to be both objective and political. An auditorium is like a small restaurant whose responsibility is to nourish its customers. In a theater perhaps a hundred and rarely more than a thousand people come to a performance; the field is circumscribed by the walls of the place and by the duration of the event — this is precisely where our responsibility to provide good food begins and ends.

All this may sound humble and modest, but in fact it is a far vaster challenge than trying to save humanity. For a few hours, it is possible to go very far; social experiments can take place that are far more radical than any that a national leader could propose. Utopian experiences that we will never see in our lifetime can become real within the time span of a performance, and underworlds from which no one returns can be visited in safety. Together with the audience we can make temporary models to remind ourselves of the possibilities that we constantly ignore. A performance has the possibility to turn words about a better life into direct experience, and in this way it can be a powerful antidote to despair. There is only one test: do the spectators leave the playhouse with slightly more courage, more strength than when they came in? If the answer is yes, then the food is healthy.

In the sixties, many people — not just the young — felt the need for a communal life. Even if within theater groups this often led to a confusion of relationships that could seldom last, the sincere and intense searching for contact among the performers was something that an audience could not fail to perceive. There is a cliché that backstage feuds make for great performances. I have never known this to be true. Once we see how easily our own angers and negativity can seep into the spectator and through him or her send a further drop of poison into the world, a new sense of responsibility begins to influence our choice of subject and our ways of work. Perhaps in an audience only a handful of people can be sufficiently touched to leave the theater in some way renewed. But when this does happen, then all the efforts of the cast and crew have not been in vain.

At the conclusion of *US*, which had no formal end, a player took out a lighter and burned a butterfly. Night after night we shocked the audience with the sacrifice, even though secretly it was only a folded scrap of white paper. After this moment no one on the stage moved, the action froze, leaving actors and audience in front of the play's interrogation: "What is this endless chain of slaughter? How can we live with it?" On the first night, Kenneth Tynan, a dear friend but one deeply impatient with what he considered our unclear political commitments, shouted at the immobile group onstage: "Are you waiting for us, or are we waiting for you?" Far beyond what he intended, the question rang true. This was the uncomfortable moment of doubt that a political performance should arouse, one that needs to be carried away into the street, where hopefully it can continue to nag.

In Paris in 1968, I stepped tentatively into a new experiment without realizing how far it would take me in the future. We were living in a small flat that became a bigger one in the rue Guéné-gaud — two floors and a little terrace on the rooftops looking out toward the Panthéon — and Natasha and I were crossing the Channel regularly. Our aim was to spend more time in Paris around the luminous presence of Madame de Salzmann, where a remarkable corps of people was exploring the rich and complex material that Gurdjieff had left behind.

At the same time, Jean-Louis Barrault, who had been running

a festival called the "Théâtre des Nations," asked me to do a Shakespeare production for him. I suggested that in keeping with the spirit of his festival it would be more interesting to invite actors and directors from many different cultures to take part in a workshop. This interested me far more than staging a play, as the work we had begun in London with the Theater of Cruelty had already revealed some surprising resources within a human body. But those bodies had all been British, and now like an Elizabethan explorer I wished to discover continents remote from my native land. For this, companions were needed to make up a team that was as diverse as possible. There were two young directors, Joe Chaikin and Victor Garcia, whose work was strikingly original and free, and I asked them if they would join the expedition. Each of them within his own group was trying to explore new ways of working, convinced that the moment had come to break away from accepted notions of what "theater" had to be.

Then, in Barrault's office, I met an immaculate and formal young Japanese actor. He had no language at his disposal other than bowing, but he gradually emerged as the invaluable, irreplaceable Yoshi Oida, an integral part of all our adventures to this day. The other actors came from many varied sources, and as a gesture to Barrault we made the central theme of our work the many different ways of approaching Shakespeare, taking *The Tempest* as a basis. A first vital question was how to portray satisfactorily on the stage spirits, fairies, and witches. We knew that our debunking and skeptical age gave us no clue, but unless this question was faced, any new production of *The Tempest* would from the start be loaded with old clichés. "Ariel!" I said early on to Yoshi. "Play Ariel!"

As Yoshi had acquired no more than two or three words in basic English, he clearly could do nothing with the text. However, phantoms and sorcerers were part of his everyday world, and a rigorous training in the Noh theater had taught him the vocabulary of the supernatural. When he stood up, even before he moved, his body had a special lightness. Impulses from a source of energy very different from the one we normally recognize sent knees and arms upward as though tapping lightly on the sky. It was an undiscovered bird that now took flight before our eyes, uttering hauntingly rhythmic cries, then suspended in moments of stillness, as though painted on a scroll. None of the other professionals could have created such an image spontaneously, yet it spoke with equal directness to us all. What interested us most was that Yoshi was not presenting a stock figure from the Japanese classical theater—on the contrary, without any preparation but with all the resources of his well-trained body, he had in an instant created a new image that we all could share. This made it clearer to everyone what had brought us together: we were not trying to exchange methods or techniques; we were not pretending that a common language could be invented by adding together bits and pieces from each one's background. The signs and signals from different cultures are not what matters; it is what lies behind the signs that gives them meaning. This is very hard for the twentieth-century mind to accept, as our terror of the indefinable has led us to believe that every aspect of human behavior must come from conditioning—genetic or social. The theater, however, exists to open us to a wider vision.

The French government had lent us a vast stone gallery intended for tapestry exhibitions, inside the Mobilier National—a storehouse out of which the furniture of officialdom comes and goes—and while we were working intensely within its walls, outside the country was preparing to erupt. The first intimation of what later became known as the "events of 1968" or simply "68" came when I went to the airport to fetch an actor who was joining our workshop. Driving back into Paris, the traffic was unusually thick. It grew denser and denser until eventually we came to a complete stop. By chance, we were just in front of a café. Natasha and the newcomer got out, sat at a table, and ordered a coffee, ready to leap back into the car if the traffic began to move. After two coffees, I had only edged forward a few feet, so they ordered a complete breakfast. Since they finished this comfortably in the time it took me to drive past their table, we could not fail to recognize that something unusual was under way. As we reached the city we learned that what had started as a small movement of social unrest was suddenly spreading like a forest fire throughout the country and, with students everywhere in the lead, across the whole of Western Europe. The next day, we were close enough to the events to join an impressively silent march across the city, and soon I was blessing the makers of Volvo for constructing a vehicle so heavy that when all the other cars in our street had been dragged to the barricades, mine was left behind, unharmed.

Our French actors immediately left the workshop to fling themselves into the events, but they came to visit us daily, not only to bring news of the uprising but also, they said, to benefit from the tiny corner of calm that we had preserved. I was less impressed than they were by the sudden discovery that everything needed to be questioned. This was after all what had brought us all together in the first place, and I felt more than ever that we needed to carry on with what we had begun in our own field. Outside, it was often hard to discover what was concrete and what was dream.

There was certainly plenty of excitement, but as the violence was strictly contained in clearly defined areas, it was often sufficient merely to cross the road to be out of the tear gas and in the tranquil world of a Parisian spring. On our day of rest, I sat with a friend in a little Greek restaurant. She had her back to the window. As we chatted, the little street outside was suddenly full of panic-stricken figures running, ducking, trying to avoid the police with their black helmets and shields who were charging and plying their truncheons. Inside the restaurant there was no reaction, no acknowledgment of what was on the other side of the door, so I too curiously accepted this strange unreality, seeing the face of my friend in close-up as in a film, with the dangerous incidents of the street out of focus behind.

During the day, we continued to work peacefully on our experiments, and when evening came we wandered into the streets. Late one night on the first floor of the Café de Flore a white-faced and excitable young man came over to say that his leader, barricaded inside the Théâtre de l'Odéon, which the students had occupied, wanted to see me. I accepted at once and was led through back streets, slipping rapidly between police posts until we came to a side door of the theater. Onstage, a nonstop marathon of speech making, which had begun on the first evening, had now become repetitive and self-indulgent. The hedonistic sex in the corridors was sinking into an apathy of drugs and squalor; dealers, thugs, and operators were taking over the theater, and boredom was overcoming the last handful of listeners still scribbling notes in the stalls.

In a tiny red-plush dressing room I talked for half an hour with a tense and pallid intellectual. Although he was continually interrupted by his lieutenants bursting in with reports of barricades fallen or recaptured and giving his instructions with a great show of efficiency and discipline, all he wanted from me was a serious conversation about the culture of the future. I found him badly informed and unattractive and left by the same surreptitious routes, completely mystified. Some weeks later I learned quite simply that he was a police spy, playing the role of a cultural iconoclast, giving a sordid reality to Genet's image in *The Balcony* of a world made of mirrors.

A beautiful young Vietnamese girl I knew came to see me, very moved, to tell of a good friend of hers who was an old-time Communist of the early incorruptible vintage. He believed deeply in revolution and was convinced by Marxism's human ideal. However, as the years went by, like many Parisian intellectuals, he had settled into a comfortable left-wing Left Bank existence, writing about a transformed society that he knew in his heart he would never see. Then came the sudden and unexpected events of 1968. This changed everything for the grizzled man who now took to the streets like any student, the dreams and convictions of his youth renewed. After dark, the elderly combatant would go to the Sorbonne. Here the streamers boldly proclaimed "L'Imagination au Pouvoir," that imagination had taken over, and it was for him as though barriers were dropping, as though love and joy were the natural breath of a new way of life. Each day, the miracle continued. One night, it would have appeared to an outside observer that the liberation was now at its height; the music, the dancing, the streams of spontaneous poetry still seemed to stem from true euphoria. But the old man was not deceived. His sensitivity took him beyond his wishes; he saw the invisible worm, he sensed the canker as it invaded the bloom. He stood quietly in a corner, watching and listening. Then he went home and took his life.

I remained very troubled by this event. Many years previously, I had been in Cuba just after the revolution. Here too I had experienced the intoxicating marvel of a sudden liberation and had naively believed that this could continue, without understanding the complex processes that develop after every new beginning. The events of 1968 showed acutely how often in any activity, however admirable the aim, something essential is missing because the vision of those taking part is inevitably incomplete. Years later, one of the most impressive people I have ever met in the militant world of political activism, the Gandhi-like leader of the United Farm Workers in California, César Chávez, told me that he always listened to and observed carefully the underlying movements of energy in the progress of a strike. He would wait patiently, he said, never wasting an intervention at the wrong moment, knowing it could prove useless or even counterproductive. He would just watch and listen, remaining ready to leap into action if a natural pressure point appeared. Everything rises and falls, and it is very hard to accept that there are forces we can neither dominate nor deflect. Yet it is this realization that can help us to be part of a social movement without illusory hopes or unfounded recriminations.

The upheaval, however, had put the French government into a state of shock, and in a panic all official buildings were closed. We found ourselves out in the street, and as our team was now more anxious than ever to complete its work, the only viable course was to go back to England. Here, money was needed, and fortunately there were generous individuals who made it possible for us to start again in London. We met in the Round House, an abandoned and impressive Victorian Parthenon for locomotives that the playwright Arnold Wesker had rescued and turned into a vibrant performing space. Now we found we could fulfill our original commitment and show the results of our work in public. I was once more taking the risk of opening up experimental work to the quizzical English, and we spared them nothing. When they arrived they were alarmed to discover that there were no seats; instead they were issued homemade shooting sticks so that they could change positions fast when dangerously mobile scaffolding charged toward them. As these platforms were pushed through the space in random patterns, the performers chanted the fragments of the completely deconstructed *Tempest* that we had developed together. Once again, many eyebrows were raised.

"At a time like this what could possibly interest you in a children's play like A *Midsummer Night's Dream?*" friends would ask. I was surprised because I had never thought of it as a children's play, or even an artificial one; it seemed exclusively to deal with human realities and in particular the reality of love. It is a play that operates on many levels, and the task in performance is to make each level equally real and true. Invariably, the fairy level suffers, as today — unlike in Shakespeare's time — only small children can be asked to believe in spirits. I had a hunch, fed by the work on *The Tempest,* that a way existed of giving the invisible world its own plausible reality, and I had been particularly influenced by a performance of Chinese acrobats I had seen in Paris. Unlike Western circus artists who demonstrate their strength in a coarsely exhibitionist way, the Chinese, who dressed identically in white trousers and shirts, the sleeves concealing their muscles, did astonishing feats with such ease that they vanished into anonymity, leaving in their place an impression of pure speed, of pure lightness, of pure spirit. My conclusion was that it would be interesting to try to stage A *Midsummer Night's Dream* with a mixed group of Shakespearean actors and Chinese acrobats. This never proved to be a practical possibility, but our Paris workshop had showed that such skills were not outside a professional actor's range, so I abandoned what would have been an extravaganza and turned to Trevor Nunn, who as director of the Shakespeare theater at Stratford had skillfully put together a remarkable young company of actors, and I asked him to choose the cast, which he did with great perception.

When we began rehearsals, my aim was to launch all the many different needs of the play simultaneously and include them in a daily kaleidoscope of work based on our past experiments. This led to a jigsaw puzzle that the young group took on trust for several weeks, as it was impossible for anyone to see how the different bits would fit together. Each day started with gymnastic exercises so that the group would be in excellent physical shape; next, we practiced circus tricks, then we did comic improvisations to encourage inventiveness and to taste playing for the sake of playing. Theater becomes a deadly industry if a performer is not there to play. Performing needed to be seen as a joyful sport — this was a central motor in the work — but we also attempted very realistic improvisations to give those who acted the ordinary working men (the "rude mechanicals") in the story an accurately observed, down-to-earth reality. Later in each day we had music, singing, dancing, and eventually the moment would come when the body was so weary that it happily dropped down onto cushions on the floor. Only then would we read the play, and these readings were simply for the purpose of listening to the sound of one another's voices and letting the text seep into us without comment, without analysis. At first everyone read each role in turn so there was no monopoly on the parts; then after the first few days the reading became more precise. With a body well exercised and a group more open to one another, it now became possible to discuss the text and even analyze the special nature of the verse without ever falling into the intellectual approach that is inevitable when rehearsals begin with discussions round a table. If the whole body is not awake and involved, one is doomed to draw ideas from over-familiar and well-used regions of the brain at the expense of more creative levels.

As we were exploring new ways of work, for the first time we brought in children to watch a rehearsal. In a couple of hours, with the kids sometimes puzzled, sometimes restless, but at other moments enthralled, the state of our work was revealed to us like an X ray on a luminous screen. Through the children's reactions, we saw what we could trust, what was self-indulgent and clumsy or repetitive and obscure. This encouraged us a few weeks later to try another experiment. Still in rehearsal, we staged an impromptu version of the play in a Birmingham social club, with local youths sprawling on the floor and Bottom lying among them with the sporting page of a daily newspaper covering his face. We had left behind the props, actions, and inventions we had developed together over weeks, and we re-improvised everything on the spot, taking advantage of all that the new space could offer. As a result, a performance came into being that had true freshness and vitality. As the spectators knew that it was being made up specially for them, they responded to it warmly, and this response infected the actors and added to their inventiveness. When we returned to Stratford, however, and rehearsed for the first time on the big stage, facing the vast, cold auditorium, we discovered to our dismay that we could not use any of these new rough-and-ready inventions. The lesson was important. A large space demands other devices, ones that increase the actors' concentration and help them project across the distance. So it was that the trapezes, the stilts, the runs, the tumbles, the primary colors of the costumes — all the things that pleased audiences later — proved their absolute necessity in a proscenium theater. But the improvised experience in Birmingham had been important as it had released a new energy and freedom in the group, and this eventually gave the show its particular zest.

At its first preview in Stratford the production of A *Midsummer*

Night's Dream seemed a total disaster, and friends who were there clutched my hand at the end with the familiar signs of excessive goodwill and cheeriness that usually precede a flop. If that first performance had been our official first night, this version of *A Midsummer Night's Dream* would have sunk without a trace. Mercifully, we had a series of previews, and our intense work during the day in response to the nightly reactions of the audiences enabled us to make changes—scores of tiny adjustments that cleaned away the blockages that had prevented the work from coming to life at its first showing. This was a reflection of the deep practical wisdom behind the old American system of creating musicals over weeks of trial and error on the road. It showed me that the need to be taught by audiences does not belong only to commercial work. Quite the contrary, it was now clearer than ever that the spectators are inseparable ingredients in the chemistry of the theater process, and I became determined to understand more fully how this occurs.

This experience also taught us that a production has two distinct sides and that if need be, they can be separated from one another. There is the mise-en-scène—the external production—which belongs uniquely to the physical conditions in which the performance takes place; these conditions include the auditorium, the height and width of the stage, the number of spectators, and so on. Then there is the hidden production, which is an invisible network of relationships among the characters and themes that grows up during rehearsals. This has its own existence independent of the external form and can give birth to new and very different stagings whenever the outer conditions change. One day Trevor Nunn, who had directed *Hamlet*, Terry Hands, who had staged *Richard III*, and I agreed to make an exciting experiment. We each took our production from the season's repertoire to London and asked the actors to reimprovise each one in the undefined space of the Round House. Here there was no center, no privileged point of focus. Seven or eight hundred people squatted on different parts of the wide concrete floor, and the actors instant by instant had to find new moves, new actions making fresh images—all that is normally called "the production" had to change. In the case of *Dream*, we left behind all our ropes and trapezes, and since these had seemed to everyone to be the very basis of our work, it was a risky experiment. However, I felt I could trust the energy of the actors and, even more important, the understanding of the play that had now become second nature to them. To express the same thoughts and feelings in these new conditions, they needed to invent new acrobatics and exploit every staircase, pillar, and gallery of the building. It was thrilling to see. Without the long work on improvisation during rehearsals, this would not have been possible, but now the group, on the spur of the moment, was capable of discarding the original pattern of images and replacing them with others without losing any of the essential meaning.

Without the hard period of research that had preceded it, none of this would have been possible. New ways of work were opening and we had hardly scratched the surface. There was no reason at all to sit back. And yet, I could not help feeling that we had come to the end of a certain line. To make matters worse, now that *Dream* was under way, friends and journalists kept asking the same question. It was like a well-meant but maddening refrain: "What next?"

What next? Like all important questions, this one first went underground and lay dormant. A year went by. Then one day, there were three of us, very old friends, two actors and a director, in Denmark to make a film of *King Lear* — out for an early ride before the shooting began. When the pony in front of me lurched, throwing its rider to the ground, I reined in sharply, and in the time it took me to swing to one side, the riderless pony had already sunk up to its neck in the sand. Bob Lloyd clambered to his feet, I dismounted, and Barry Stanton, who was just behind us, slipped cautiously out of his saddle to the ground, which was smooth and firm with nothing to show where the treacherous quicksand patches were hidden. The pony had stopped sinking. Now only its head, its shoulders, its great rump, and its tail showed above the surface of the bare gray Jutland landscape, as lonely as the moon. We wondered where we could turn for help. Barry set off at a hopeful gallop, while Bob and I squatted on either side of the pony, stroking her nose and murmuring quiet sounds of reassurance. She was a stubby white barrel of an animal and like all Norwegian ponies, she was gentle, swift, and sure of foot, never losing her balance even on sheets of ice where other horses slip and slide. The shifting sand had caught her unawares, but her inner balance was nonetheless unshaken, for she seemed, in her present stillness, completely calm. Following her example we waited quietly. An hour went by, and we heard no reassuring sound of hooves, no rattle of a rescuing tractor bearing a providential winch. As there was no wind, the snow settled lightly on our shoulders and on her thick mane.

Suddenly and without any warning, the mass of the pony buckled and heaved, her front legs rose, she doubled forward, and then triumphantly she was out, standing on firm ground, breathing heavily, sending clouds of steam through the cold air. A moment later, a truck drew up with willing farmers, disappointed to be of no use. I rubbed the pony's nose and looked admiringly into her eyes. With ancient Nordic wisdom, she had patiently been gathering her strength, and it was only when she felt completely ready that she made her unique, successful effort. She had known how to bide her time and when to act. She seemed to be speaking to me, and I pondered her lesson. Yes, I concluded, I too must heave and stretch — a big change in life was due.

For years, when asked the inevitable question, "Why did you move to Paris?," I would give the answer that seemed to suit the questioner, and the reporter would scribble it down in delight. Now I realize that the whole of this book is a relatively full answer to that question: Why Paris?

In England artistic experiment is always viewed with suspicion while in France it is a natural part of artistic life, and I knew I would be welcomed back to Paris if the decision to live there was made. Paris has a long tradition of being a melting pot for artists from all over the world, and although I never like to think of myself as an artist, a long thread leading back to my first enjoyable adventures in the boulevard theater gave me enough connections to be reasonably sure that I could find here an area in which to earn my living. The first experiment with an international group in 1968 had allowed me to explore a way of work that now, two years later, I wished to continue, and so in 1970 I formulated a plan to set up an international center in which to practice theater research.

For many years, I had been spared all responsibility for administration; there had always been a parent organization, a producer, a management, or a theater subsidized by the state to give me the elements I needed. Now, at forty-five, I felt I had to assume this grown-up responsibility, so for the first time in my life I entered a field of which I had always been afraid. This meant dealing with money in all its aspects, whether it was money to be collected or money to be redistributed, and discovering the positive and negative aspects of each of these operations. A new game now had to be learned: fund-raising. This led to intriguing experiences, such as sitting at a dinner in New York waiting for the coffee before asking for the dollars and watching the smiling hosts play at cat and mouse as they sadistically dragged out the meal. Rapidly I discovered that seeking out private sponsors was a dreary way of life, for apart from the cocktails and the dinner parties, it involved admiring wealthy people's collections of paintings and sculpture and enduring long gossip-filled phone calls that were mere wastes of time. So I learned the much more agreeable rules of begging from foundations, and I found within them a serious and courteous form of artistic patronage that resembled academic life. So social life gave way to writing countless pages of proposals and reports and accepting lunches in paneled dining rooms, as though back in an Oxford college, discussing the nature of Greek tragedy with enthusiastic, scholarly minds.

All foundations are cautious: by law they have to give away certain vast sums each year, so in one way they are relieved when they meet anyone willing to take these sums off their hands; at the same time, as they are permanently liable to harsh criticism, every grant exposes them to torrents of partisan reproach, and each highly paid executive needs to be constantly on guard. For a request to be accepted, it has to be both foolproof at the time and unassailable later. The Ford Foundation had an officer, MacNeil Lowry, to whose perception and dedication American culture owes a permanent debt. He was very receptive to my proposal, but for reasons incomprehensible to anyone outside the complex web of foundation politics, he could give us 50 percent of our budget but only if other foundations were sufficiently convinced to match his grant. We needed three million dollars over three years and I would have been lost had it not been for a chain of introductions that led me to a marvelous ally and adviser, the composer Nicolas Nabokov. A tall, shuffling figure with a wizened but heroic head, amused and deceived by life, his bitter anger hidden behind a mask of academic culture and wit, he possessed an extraordinary Russian flair for understanding the mysterious maneuvers of fund-raising; in his blood were the intuition and tactical cunning of a nineteenth-century European statesman. In the two-room flat he had in Greenwich Village, we sat side by side on his bed while he worked out his strategy, slapping his knee with anticipated delight before picking up the telephone to make the necessary calls. He arranged an appointment for me with the head of a wealthy foundation based on petroleum, run personally by a Texas multimillionaire named Mr. Anderson. When I arrived at Mr. Anderson's New York office, there *was* no office; this was not a place of business, it was just a Japanese empty space elegantly punctuated by a few cubist tables and chairs. Perched on a block, I was ready for a long wait when a tanned, healthy, and confident Mr. Anderson appeared, shaking me warmly by the hand, only to apologize that he had no time. His diary was produced: no, not tomorrow, nor the next day, but Thursday, would noon on Thursday be all right? Of course, I said. Then as we were shaking hands again, he added as an afterthought, "Not here. I'm leaving New York. Let's make it Aspen."

"Of course you must go," said Nicolas.

"Can I ask his office for the ticket?"

"Ridiculous. Buy it yourself. It's an investment."

Aspen, Colorado, was half a day's flight from New York, and Nicolas, his experienced nose scenting blood, offered to come with me.

At Denver we changed to a small six-passenger plane. It was a bumpy flight through thick clouds between mountain peaks to the high-altitude ski resort called Aspen. Here, the same benefactor had established through his foundation a sort of superuniversity.

In the evening, we had drinks at the house of a resident professor who wished to show me his collection of pop art. As we entered the hall, on a table by the door among the mail that had just arrived was a very small parcel wrapped in brown paper and tied up with string. "A very early Christo," the professor said casually, flicking it as we passed, and we entered a sitting room that was an Aladdin's cave of Warhol, Lichtenstein, and Jasper Johns. A good friend of Nicolas's, Joe Slater, who ran the Aspen Institute and was entirely on the side of our project, was there looking extremely worried. Drink in hand, he took us aside. "Anderson's shares slumped this afternoon. There's been a spectacular drop on Wall Street. I can't imagine him giving out a grant at a time like this." Anyway, he continued, Anderson had not yet arrived; his private plane was bringing him in the following morning just before our noon appointment. The only ray of hope was that he had not yet canceled his trip.

The evening was gloomy, and when I got up the following morning, the mountains had disappeared under a blanket of thick white fog. After breakfast we went over to see Joe. He was even more pessimistic. "The shares are still dropping. And anyway, I don't see how Mr. Anderson can land." At that moment, there was the hum of an engine somewhere in the clouds.

Joe shook his head. "That's the local plane. It always gets through. But Mr. Anderson's got a jet."

Nicolas and I walked around disconsolately, waiting for a miracle. I remembered the infinitely loving and much-loved English actress Sybil Thorndike telling me that when she and her husband Lewis Casson were already very old, they stopped on their way home from Australia to realize a childhood dream and see the sun rise over Everest. They stayed in the special tourist bungalow and rose at 4 A.M., but to their dismay Everest was concealed by a dense mist. "I spoke to God," Sybil told me. "I told him this was our last chance. Don't let Lewis and me down, I said, we will never come again. And the clouds lifted. We saw Everest, we saw the sun rise." Now I also spoke to God, but not having Sybil's immeasurable store of credit, the clouds did not move.

At exactly twelve o'clock, however, Joe came rushing toward us. "It's all settled. It's come through."

"What has?" For a moment we couldn't understand.

"Mr. Anderson was circling in his jet while talking to me by radio. He was appalled at the thought of having made you come all this way for nothing. He asked me to apologize for circumstances quite beyond his control; he is very embarrassed at his lack of hospitality, so he has asked me to put the maximum grant in motion." And Joe added, "Had he been able to land, I know he was going to refuse."

So it was a tiny act of chance that shaped many years of activity. The Ford and Gulbenkian Foundations followed Mr. Anderson's lead, and the International Center of Theater Research was born, thanks to a fog—the perfect symbol for a journey into the unknown.

The day before rehearsals for my first production began, when I was nineteen, I was suddenly seized with panic. "Where am I meant to sit?" I asked myself, because, as a self-appointed director, I had never seen a rehearsal. "In the auditorium or with the actors on the stage?" Sneaking into the Haymarket Theater through a side door, I managed to catch a glimpse of John Gielgud in the middle of the stalls, his long legs bent over the seat in front of him, a trilby hat covering his bald head, calling his instructions to the actors. This reassured me: the director is someone apart who keeps his distance. Later at Covent Garden I would stand on a soapbox to give orders to the chorus, but I constantly felt a need to descend among them to talk, consult, encourage, suggest. To my dismay, they resented this disappearance of authority and forced me to climb back to the high place where a commander is supposed to stay.

In most theaters, the awesome set of tables with stage managers, assistants, and technicians makes a phalanx of shields that similarly expresses the hierarchical nature of rehearsal life, so for many years, following this time-honored tradition, I would assemble the actors on the first day and place them in front of me so as to make a long and didactic opening speech. This was designed to explain my view of the text while at the same time laying down the lines of the work to come, and I was reassured to discover that all the best directors would begin in this way. One day, I was sufficiently free from my own self-involvement to watch the actors while I spoke. In each pair of eyes I saw a glazed and absent look and realized that carefully chosen words were a waste of time; neither a sublime lecture nor a jolly attempt to make everyone laugh had any chance of crossing the first-day barrier of tension and fear.

When we began our first international workshop in 1968, I decided to try a new approach. Encouraged by the spirit of the times, I asked each actor and actress as they arrived to close their eyes. Taking them by the hand, I led each one to where another uneasy figure from some distant country was waiting, eyes already closed, and suggested they both make acquaintance just by touch. When some time later I asked them to open their eyes and take a look at the person with whom they had made contact, the ice was broken, fear had dissolved into companionship, and we could begin.

What one does on a first day is of little importance in itself; what matters is releasing tension, calming fears, and creating a climate in which confidence can develop. Only the means vary, and they must be tailored to suit each project and the people who are there. In Paris, years later, the first rehearsal of *The Cherry Orchard* was a great Russian meal, which my precious assistant Nina prepared with vodka, piroshki, and loving care. When in the afternoon we settled at a large round table with a green baize cloth, we were already like friends and relatives in a country dacha. For the rest of the day, we enjoyed the simple pleasure of reading Chekhov's short stories to one another and chatting about them freely, as though we had no other purpose than to pass the time.

On that first morning in the autumn of 1970 when the new International Center had become a reality, the inevitable question seemed insoluble. Where to start? Gathered together were some twenty actors and actresses with whom I was going to live for the next few years, and again glazed eyes betrayed the expectations and fears that each was concealing in his or her own way. There was so much I wanted to do, so many fields to explore — but what to do in *this* moment? Touching and groping was out of date, and although I had tried many games, tricks, activities, and devices on other occasions, today nothing seemed right. Certainly not explanations — we had little common language, some spoke bad English, some even poorer French, and anyway I was determined to keep our early investigations strictly nonverbal. The Americans were already lying on the floor, stretching and relaxing, but I couldn't see myself starting off with anything as prosaic as gymnastics. I looked round the room. This was even more discouraging; at the time we had no place of our own, and the space we had been lent at the Cité Universitaire was miserably drab. How sad the setting seemed for a new beginning — yet it was this uninspiring bleakness that suddenly inspired its own solution. I called everyone together: "Let's transform this dreary room and start with a celebration." Instantly, the unease and the apprehension vanished; teams were made, cars commandeered, homes ransacked. A few hours later, a brilliantly colored tent filled most of the space; within it were lamps and candles, and on a floor covered with red and green crepe paper, bottles of red and white wine punctuated a splendid array of dishes. Several of the group had brought musical instruments with them, and as we were in no hurry to eat, we closed the flap of the tent, letting the shadows of the trees from outside the windows play on the cotton sheets as though we were already on one of the distant journeys we were hoping to make. Music alternated with stillness, and a quiet sense of confidence was beginning to develop when slowly the flap of the tent was drawn open and very suspiciously a young girl whom we had never seen before peered in. The newly formed group experienced its first shared impulse: one of us rose and, gently taking the girl by the hand, led her to a place of honor on a cushion, while others served her; then we all ate and drank in silence. She asked no questions, and we offered no explanations. When the meal was ended, after music and many songs, she left as simply as she had arrived. Who she was, what she thought of us, we will never know as she never returned, but she was the unconscious guide who led us across the obstacles of the first day. The following morning, everyone was ready and work could begin.

There is a story by Grimm that we later used as a Christmas play. The young hero must rescue a princess, but his own resources are insufficient; he needs unique faculties that only others can bring. So he forms a group. One of them can see an ant at an incredible distance, another can hear the drop of a pin many miles away, a third can drink the entire contents of a lake, still another can be hot when it's cold and cold when it's hot — in the end they are seven who succeed in a task that none could accomplish alone. In isolation, each was insufficient, but together they make a whole. In our new group, we all came from different backgrounds, and while this normally leads to barriers and conflict, our aim was to recognize through working together that each is no more than a fragment of an incomplete jigsaw, in which every oddly shaped piece may have a vital function. Each piece must click into other crooked shapes for a meaningful pattern to emerge.

People often ask how our group was formed. Even today I usually stress chance as an inevitable factor in casting, but at that time I pushed the principle to an extreme, allowing the net to open itself as widely as possible and wishing to be free of judgments that are so often wrong. Bruce Myers roared up to the Riverside Café in Stratford while I was eating a sandwich, got off his motorbike, and, crash helmet under his arm, brushing the dust off his leather coat, explained he'd do anything to get away from this "bloody British theater." "Right," I answered, instantly convinced. Malick Bowens came from Grotowski. Grotowski loves staying up all night alone with each of his students and he told me that Malick had sung with him until the dawn. With the first gray light came an extraordinary transformation in the sounds that Malick made; they seemed to arise from some very deep layer of awareness that fatigue had uncovered. "Take him," he said, and I did so. There was François Marthouret, bringing a quick intelligence, a lightness, and a wit that are essentially French, while an equally French sense of streets and soil was carried by Sylvain Corthay and Claude Confortes. There was João Motta, with the sadness of a Portuguese fado singer; there was an extraordinary giant, Andreas Katsulas, whom Ellen Stewart had sent from La Mama, her experimental theater on Fourth Street in New York—Andreas had her special recommendation because she saw in him a future great tragedian, while our experience was to discover in his darkly humorous and unpredictable mind limitless possibility for comedy. Bob Lloyd had been with me from the very first innocent and exciting days of the Theater of Cruelty, through *Marat/Sade*, *US*, and *The Tempest*; with him was a beautiful girl, Pauline Munro, with Pre-Raphaelite golden hair who had been in *US* and the film *Tell Me Lies*—she could catch everyone's breath with her unexpected improvisations. There were André Serban, whom I met by chance in a New York corridor, fresh from Romania, directing his first American production and giddy with the bewildering freedom of Fourth Street and the Village, and Arby Ovenassian, whose exquisitely refined work at the Shiraz Festival in Iran had made him the youngest and most envied of Persian directors. Others came in more ordinary ways, through working sessions or recommendations, but always chance played the leading role. There was Lou Zeldis, also from New York, the tallest and thinnest of hippies, sensitive to the tips of his fingers and the straggling ends of his long fair hair. He suffered every time we tried to formulate our work, refusing to join in discussions but returning to the joy of pure action, such as peeling an apple with an involvement so tender that the pale green spiral unfolded before us like a story of infinite meaning. He lived in a strange silent limbo that he had created, existing within patterns that only he understood and that he would describe as "my lies for the year"; he brought a close and generously built friend, a Mother Earth from America, Michelle Collison, who could sing splendidly and lead the others into her powerful world of sounds, stretching the voice far beyond its limits and against all the rules yet never doing anyone's vocal cords any harm. There were Natasha, bringing her own exquisite and fragile insistence on truth, and of course Yoshi, treasured since our first meeting in 1968, a living example of what a highly trained instrument can be—a body not rippling with muscles and an outer show of strength but instead a transparent organism in which every fiber was integrated to serve the flickering of each new impulse. And there were still many others at different moments, all good companions, in a group that Mary Evans mothered, shepherded, encouraged, and disciplined with an art for which her years in English stage management had been the finest schooling.

We were installed once again in the Mobilier National, in the vast stone rectangle — the old tapestry gallery — at the top of a long flight of stairs. We were sitting in a circle on a carpet preparing an exercise when suddenly someone noticed the presence of a stranger. We all turned and looked frigidly across at a black girl standing at the top of the stairway. On the few earlier occasions when someone had wandered in, one of the group would go over and firmly ask the person to leave. This time, however, something in the girl's bearing made me say, "What do you want?" without hostility, and she answered, "To work here." Again, to my surprise I heard myself say, "Come and sit down," with the intention of telling her kindly at the end of the session that we had no way of including a further member in the group. She joined us and sat discreetly silent, poised and alert to everything that took place. At the end, as they left, the members of the group one by one murmured to me, "We must have her." In fact, she never left. Miriam Goldschmidt, with a father from Mali, a German mother, and a Jewish upbringing in Berlin — a mixture that corresponded perfectly to our work — stayed with us over many years, never again to be so still and silent, but rebellious, original, and unique, a passionate and untamable searcher for striking and outrageous forms in the service of emotional truth.

In strange contrast to the young French, Portuguese, and American actors and the Africans and the Asiatics sprawling on the floor, there was a splendid classical actress and good friend, Irene Worth, who had been Goneril in *King Lear*, Jocasta in *Oedipus*, and the megalomaniacal doctor in Dürrenmatt's *The Physicists*. She was with us through a deep misunderstanding, and I am afraid she suffered greatly. Having mastered with dazzling authority all the facets of her art, she joined us with the total commitment she always brought to her work, trusting me completely when I had first spoken to her of a Center of Theater Research, as this suggested to her well-trained mind a sort of Princeton Institute for Advanced Studies, which she was eager to serve with all her abilities. I failed to explain that we were attempting to work not forward with the other highly developed talents she expected to meet but backward. We were there not to learn but to unlearn, discarding hard-earned skills so as to discover something from the most innocent of our members. To start at the beginning meant being naive and simple, which bred an equal impatience and frustration in some young directors who had joined us expecting to be initiated into the most subtle and sophisticated tricks of the trade, only to find themselves being asked to make work for small children instead.

For the part of me that had for so long been the director, the new way of life that now unfolded was less enjoyable than I had anticipated. I too had to unlearn, and I was dismayed to discover that pure research had none of the physical excitement of the hectic productions of the past. Previously, I would not merely watch the actors from a distance, I would rush among them, whispering, encouraging, pushing, pulling, stepping back, observing, trying to charge them with my own energy, while now for hours on end I had condemned myself to sitting with them around a carpet, simply attentive. As my mind resolutely refused to make a long-term plan, each day began with the same agonizing question of what to do next. With a play, there is always a new scene to be tackled; in an opera, the music itself carries one along, but experiment over a long period of time can be slow, painful, even boring, and all day I would be looking for different ways of maintaining the interest of the group, as well as my own. After lunch this was particularly difficult, as bodies slumped and yawns were stifled, so changes of pace and gear constantly had to be invented in order to revitalize the day and keep the laboratory alive. I had to recognize that however much actors can be inspired by the idea of exploring their craft, nothing can take away their need for an audience. They have to perform, so for part of each day, we had to play in order to keep one another entertained and to calm my own doubts, at least temporarily.

Bruce Myers enjoys recounting that for the first three years he had not the least idea of what he was doing. The work was indeed bewildering, if only because of the number of doors we were opening at the same time. Nonetheless, a pattern lay behind the confusion. As the first thing we all had in common was the body, the starting point was physical, exploring in each of our cultures the most ordinary gestures, such as shaking hands or putting the hand on the heart. We exchanged dance movements from various traditions; we practiced words and syllables from one another's languages; we let simple cries gradually evolve into rhythmic patterns, then into one-note songs; we let our voices vibrate together harmoniously or in deliberate discord until they became truly disturbing; we used bamboo sticks to make silent geometries in the air. We invited deaf children, then deaf adults to join us, improvising together, as with them the motive for communication comes not from art but from instant need. Outsiders would say we were trying to invent a universal language, a new Esperanto, but this was very far from the aim. There was something inexpressible that I was trying to develop. This was the capacity to listen through the body to codes and impulses that are hidden all the time at the root of cultural forms. I was convinced that if they were brought to the surface, they could be instantly understood.

Indeed, each culture has its own set of clichés, and from the start we tried to explore how to go beyond stereotypes and imitations, how to find the key to actions so transparent that they appeared completely natural, whatever their form. The first step was to free ourselves from the influence of the normally selective brain that had already divided us up into Europeans, Africans, Asians. Whenever we allowed this analyzing mind to relax, we could enter directly into one another's backgrounds and listen to sounds and movements closer to their source, without having to explain to ourselves what they meant.

An early revelation came when Natasha and Bruce improvised on an ancient Greek text, neither of them having the faintest clue to its meaning. As they played together, a stranger entering our space would have been very moved; he would have thought that he was witnessing two performers playing with passion and skill a text whose meanings they had investigated in detail and only mastered after long rehearsals. In fact, they were reading the words for the first time but were giving more attention to listening than to speaking, and in this way it was the echoes that returned from somewhere deep in their consciousness — or perhaps their subconscious — that informed and illuminated their acting. Words and actions were not a "showing" to others of the performer's previously developed understanding; what was projected outward came from what was heard within, and the two were inseparable.

Another early exploration was to study and reproduce the way birds communicate. Each bird cry has a sound and rhythm pattern for which there is no exact equivalent in music, and this frees the listener from any normal associations. Often, when a group tries to make spontaneous musical sounds, the lack of discipline can lead to a shamble of self-indulgent noises. However, when the model is as strict as the signals of birds, where repeated calls, never twice exactly the same, intertwine with one another, then to re-create them with the human voice demands an extraordinarily rigorous and intense listening. This would lead us to a fresh approach to sound, trying to find a form of melody with the intricate simplicity of the music of the Pygmies or the Solomon Islanders, which had become our models. We struggled to abandon — if only provisionally — all intellectual pretension so as to treat every sound as a nugget of "unknowingness" to be felt, sensed, heard, and tasted — to be understood but not analyzed. At once, among those who speculated on what we were doing, suspicious voices were raised, saying that we were trying to deny language, reason, and mind. This was never our aim. We were simply concentrating on one area by eliminating others. We knew we had to return to words and intellectual meanings eventually, but in a new way, on a differently prepared ground.

If I try to explain to people through a simple image what our work was about during this period, I ask them to raise their hand and clench their fist. Then to tighten the fingers and tighten them further. Whether they wish it or not, the hand becomes more and more threatening. Filmed in close-up, it would truly express a threat. Now I ask, "What is the difference between this fist and one that is genuinely raised in anger? Where is the dividing line? Is this a 'real' fist or an 'acted' one?" Is there an emotion charging the muscles, or is the emotion only in the eye of the beholder? Can we eliminate the impression of menace by changing the feeling with which it is charged?

In daily life there are "normal" actions and "bizarre" behaviors. In the theater nothing whatsoever in the entire range of human possibilities need necessarily appear "unnatural." The conviction that everyday movements are "real" leads us inevitably to conclude that "normal" behavior is closer to life. Unusual movements are only accepted on the stage because theater is "artificial." I could never believe in this distinction. "Everyday life" is also an artificial convention, and all schools of "realistic" acting are artificial attempts to capture an ever-evasive reality. In the theater, nothing need be excluded, nothing need be labeled "artificial," "real," or "unreal," for an everyday movement can be hollow and trite while a seemingly bizarre gesture can become the vehicle for a profoundly touching meaning. All that matters is that the action should ring true at the moment of execution. At this instant, it is "right." This is the absolute test. *This* is theatrical reality. But what are its rules? This interrogation, which had been with me for so long, was behind all our first tentative experiments. The simple question of "what is right?" accompanied all our work day after day.

One day, we made an improvisation around blindness. A series of unconvincing attempts produced the various stereotypes of bad acting: groping arms, hesitant steps, unblinking stares. When Malick Bowens, the actor from Mali, stood up, he seemed to make no effort, and suddenly, simply, a blind man was there. Undoubtedly a deep impression from his childhood in an African village had invaded every tiny muscle of his body. He was no longer the person who had been sitting beside the carpet an instant previously; he was "acting," and yet it was of a different nature from the very best professional acting I knew, where the effort and the skill are always visible and in fact applauded. At the same time, the impression of naturalness here was not accidental, nor was he, like a medium, in a trance. Malick knew what he was doing, and when, as he sat down a moment later, he let his assumed identity drop, his acting was over. This incident opened up a new set of values, for the African actor is not artless, any more than is his culture; the highly complex and ancient civilization that feeds him is inscribed in his body as a whole, and when he "impersonates," he "becomes" indivisibly. At other times, in other ways, it was the Japanese, the Persian, the Indian, or the Balinese, those with a traditional culture behind them, who could find the same immediacy. This phenomenon is not an accident, yet in the moment it demands no preparation. There is no buildup, no analysis, no "method"; body, mind, and soul speak as one. An old Indian actor, using the most obscure and ancient stylized gestures, once explained to me that in his mind, there was nothing "artificial" in what he was doing, he was just "playing life." All good actors have had the same experience, although they express themselves in different terms. Alan Howard, who played Oberon in A *Midsummer Night's Dream*, surprised everyone in a discussion on verse speaking by saying that if he were shot during a performance — although why he should be, I cannot imagine — he would like to think that the whole of his past would be present to him, feeding the word that was on his tongue. Such immediacy does not come about easily; it takes in-born talent, relentless work, and a precise craft to make the actor's instrument sharp and sensitive. Then, in the moment of creation, all the circuits of the mind can open and give the word and the action their truth.

On one occasion, I tried an exercise that Grotowski had invented. It seemed quite innocent: each person is invited to imitate the type of person he detests the most. "But there's a catch," said Grotowski. "You will see. The actor will reveal his own deepest nature without knowing it." Andreas Katsulas, half American, half Greek, claimed to have a horror of religion, and he played an invaluable role in the group, for he would puncture any solemnity or pretentiousness with irresistible ridicule. For this exercise, he chose to imitate a pious young monk and walked up and down, pulling his face into a parody of a holy look. Gradually, though, the reality of the image he was illustrating outran his intention, and a deeply hidden contemplative quality in himself transformed his expression, giving to his body a luminous tranquillity that was truly his own. Actors often fear that if they lose the personality that they know, they will become bland and anonymous. This is never the case. Through the grit of hard work, it is the true individuality that appears.

In the beginning, we allowed no one to observe our experiments — and yet we needed spectators. If we were only to be watched by ourselves, we would quickly fall into the narcissism we wished to avoid. However, our experiments were too fragile to bear the blows of harsh criticism. So the first to be invited into our space were children, and they taught us a lot, because their reactions were immediate and penetrating. Initially, we tried to encourage the children to enjoy the freedom of the space, but to our dismay they just ran wild. After a humiliating session when they had seized our bamboo sticks, chased us into corners, and beat us up, we thought again. We had seen the way a false freedom leads to chaos and realized that there was no point in giving children an experience that was no different from running and screaming in their own playground. We could not be casual; they deserved something better, and this compelled us to study the precise conditions that govern focus and concentration. At the next session we began differently. Very quietly, we assembled the children around a platform, and the actors, using very simple improvisations, such as exploring the mysterious and comic possibilities of a cardboard box, had no difficulty in holding their attention and their imagination. Then the actors attempted a very difficult experiment, which was to come down from the platform and walk among the children in order to see if they were still capable of maintaining the same silence and concentration without staying at a point of command. Naturally, once the dominant position was lost, the children's attention went with it.

Then, to our astonishment, Yoshi succeeded without difficulty where the others had failed. By an inexplicable yet precise effort that demanded a subtle mastery of his energies — by "making an emptiness," as he called it — he became so powerful a magnet that even when he descended and walked among the children, at times deliberately disappearing from sight, they all stayed silent and attentive until he regained the platform again. This concrete result was of great importance, opening many experiments to discover more exactly the nature of the process that is normally glossed over with a vague word such as *presence*.

"It's difficult because it's difficult." This became a slogan in our center, and I think it contains the best practical advice that one can give anyone when truly up against a problem. Guilt, frustration, self-accusation, discouragement, and above all disappointment with oneself are all caused by the moralistic idea that "I should have, thus I could have." Once one recognizes the simple truth that it is through no one's fault that something is difficult — that it is difficult simply because it is difficult — one can breathe a sigh of relief and work more freely.

My friend and colleague Micheline Rozan loved difficulties. She responded with all her energy to the crisis of the moment and so terrified some and fascinated others by the passionate intelligence and ruthless perfectionism she brought to her work. With an astonishing grasp of all aspects that went into creating a new organization, she took everything off my hands, so once again I was in the position of being protected while concentrating on other needs.

These had now become clear. I knew that we could only find

something valid by throwing aside every prop that previous structures had given us. In order to explore space, to enter new relationships, to be challenged and put in the wrong, to explore
means of expression, to find the outer form that can reflect the
intangible nature of an impulse, we needed to work without a
theater, without any given words, codes, or techniques, finding
our way outward from nothing. In their place, we had to develop
the ability to improvise, learning that this is excruciatingly difficult because although anything is possible in improvisation, if
everyone does just anything, the result is nothing.

At first, we found that a good improvisation could sustain itself
for no more than one and a half to two minutes. There were
many reasons why it would then fall apart; clumsiness, showing
off, lack of listening, or often blind panic would cause the actors
in desperation to resort to feeble gags, until rapidly the improvisation began to turn in circles. During years of steady practice the
span of our team concentration grew longer and longer, until
once, and once only, an improvisation went on developing in a
flood of shared invention for a full two hours. In this way, a complete, coherent, and entertaining story was created that was the
length of a normal play. But such is the fate of an improvisation;
it gave pleasure to some twenty teenagers in a girls' school and
was never to be seen again. We liked the story so much that we
attempted to repeat it, but however hard we tried, the same sparks
could never be struck a second time. This unfortunately is the
price the improviser has to accept.

We learned a great deal from leaving our own protected base
in the Mobilier National to adventure out into the everyday
world. If one invites an audience into one's own space to witness
an improvisation, the result is almost always strained and artificial, because the mere fact of being invited is in itself a promise
of entertainment, and inevitably one tries to entertain at all costs.
However, if one visits people in their own surroundings — in the
Portuguese hostels in Paris, in hospital wards, or in African villages — the conditions and rules are exactly the same as those that
govern all meetings between strangers. If there is no mutual attraction, nothing will happen, but if a wish for contact is truly
there, then after some hesitant opening gambits, a common territory can always be found. Pleasure brings inspiration, and words,
images, humor, confidences follow naturally. They in turn take
on a rhythm; music creates a field of energy, and the laughter of

the spectator enriches it further until the most barren room is transformed into a glowing space.

Before attempting an improvisation under these conditions, the actors have no sense of superiority; their nervous tension is as great as before a Broadway opening, and if the improvisation has not gone well, the feeling of shame and emptiness is even more acute than in the professional theater because one has clearly seen on the faces of the people around that one has let them down; the audience provides a mirror for one's own inadequacy.

On the other hand, themes almost always arise by themselves. In a hostel for North Africans in Paris, Andreas fiddles with the television set—it has been broken for months—the audience laughs, complicity is established, and immediately a story develops. He pulls some dollar bills from his pocket. "What is this? Real money? Phony money?" The audience picks up the game, and we are away. The American actress Michelle Collison takes a broom and sweeps the floor; her hips undulate, and a catcall from the audience leads to the situation that every North African who sends money home to wife and relatives knows and dreads: a chance meeting with another woman whose existence threatens the stability of his life. Or Miriam Goldschmidt, in a Portuguese hostel, without thinking raises her thumb and suddenly discovers from the audience reaction that she is in fact thumbing a truck, so instantly she plays the role of a hitchhiker, and this naturally develops into a saga of immigration that involves everyone in the room.

The most touching moment came after a performance we had given on the outskirts of Paris. As usual, there was a lot of initial resistance from those responsible for this hostel for migrant workers, who were especially suspicious when they learned that we did not expect to be paid. No one from the outside had ever entered this all-male refuge without a strong motivation, either with something to sell or else to pick up information for the police, yet by waiting patiently outside in the yard we managed to establish our good faith, and the improvisation that followed brought us very close to our audience. When it ended, an old African came up to me. "I have been in France for five years," he said, clasping my hand between his long thin fingers, "and this is the first time I have laughed."

If these experiences were a great opportunity for learning, this came from being completely unprepared. After each session we would analyze in detail what had happened and would discuss in concrete terms what an action is, what a scene is, what a rhythm means, what characterization demands, and above all what can reflect the concerns of the shifting world around us. Such experiences are not only rich for performers; I know of no better way for directors and writers to discover the basis of their craft. When Jean-Claude Carrière joined our team, he had already written countless movie scripts, but by throwing himself courageously into these improvisations, he tasted the freedom of theater. This changed the nature of his writing, and he became an irreplaceable, integral part of all of our activities.

As a child I had always been told, "Never ask anyone to do what you can't do yourself," but as a director I knew that this was untrue, as I could neither act nor sing nor dance and was too afraid to try. Nonetheless, my own understanding as a director was transformed by taking part in the exercises with the others, no matter how badly I did them. It was both a necessity and a blessing for a director to leave his soapbox and take the plunge.

The title of "Center of Theater Research" may suggest something academic, where learned minds, grouped round a table, scan sheaves of paper and exchange information on theater history and techniques. In fact, research means *doing* and, in this case, performing, whether to one another in intense conditions of privacy or in unusual conditions in public, but always performing — a vital necessity for the performers themselves. Over the years we gave a large number of unpaid performances, never in theater buildings or for theater audiences. We needed spectators to test our explorations, spectators who knew nothing about us, who were not conditioned by the title of the play or the name of the author, with whom we shared no easy references, who would take what was offered on its own merit. And so we had to travel. This led us to Iran, to Africa, to the Chicanos of California, to American Indians, even to a park in Brooklyn. We went to wherever there was nothing to rely on, no security, no starting point. In this way we were able to investigate the infinite number of factors that help or hinder performance. We could learn about the difference between big and small audiences, about distances, seating arrangements, about what works better indoors and what is gained by playing outside, what in the experience is changed if the actor is placed higher than the spectator or vice versa, about parts of the body, the place of music, the weight of a word, of a syllable, of a hand or foot, all of which years later would feed our work when inevitably we returned to a theater, tickets, and a paying audience.

An invitation from the Shiraz Festival to work with a group of Persian actors and play in the ruins of Persepolis took us to Iran. On my very first visit to Persepolis, I had sat motionless on a rock for several hours, brought to a stop by the power of the place. It was a reminder that in the past, great sites were chosen because they were on centers of unusual energetic force. Now, when we did our performances — at sunset in the courtyard of a temple, at sunrise in the long valley of royal tombs — this idea was again no mere theory; its reality was experienced by actors and spectators alike. After years of involvement with wood, canvas, paint, spotlights, and flood lamps, here the sun, moon, earth, sand, rock, and fire opened up a new world that would influence our work for years to come.

In Iran a very unusual lady, Mahin Tadjadod, read to us Zoroaster's poems. None of the sounds she made corresponded to any letters or syllables we knew, but we could recognize the power of the words that they formed. As we had spent so many months experimenting with our voices, we were fascinated when she explained that she had studied with a scholar who claimed to have reconstructed the sounds of the very ancient pre-Persian language called Avesta. His theory was that Avesta was a ritual language used only for declamation and that the complex shape of the letters in the written script were precise diagrams indicating the movement of the breath through the larynx, the mouth, and the lips. According to him, the last remnant of this system that has survived to this day is our letter *o*, which is a clear illustration of the movement required to produce the letter's sound. Too intrigued to bother with whether this was true or not, we followed Mrs. Tadjadod, imitating her until our breath could rise from the stomach, enter the head, descend again, modulate with throat and tongue, resonate in the chest, and produce compact words of intense emotional power.

The experience of this language, whether in a vibrant call made by Natasha from a temple roof toward the setting sun or chanted by moonlight from the tops of the cliffs into the chasm between the tombs, opened us all to an awareness of how time-lessness and myth can come into the present and become part of direct experience. The power of Avesta made a deep impression on the English poet Ted Hughes, who had been a good friend ever since he translated Seneca's *Oedipus* for the production with John Gielgud that I had done in London a few years previously. Hughes had been working with us in Paris for several months and was deeply touched by how the seemingly incomprehensible syllables from ancient Greek with which we were experimenting could carry rich layers of meaning simply through the quality of their sound. The play he then wrote for us to perform at Persep-olis, *Orghast*, had fragmentary archetypal situations drawn from ancient myths, but the words were all his own, captured, he would say, in the strata of the brain where deep-rooted semantic forms arise, at the moment when they are becoming coated with shape and sonority but prior to the intervention of the higher lev-els of the cortex where concepts emerge.

These emotional experiences were so strong that they enabled us to accept the climate of deviousness and suspicion with which the shah's land was infused. We were invited by the Shiraz Festi-val with warmth and courtesy, but once installed, our same hosts watched every move with hostility and suspicion, constantly blocking the work they had seemed so anxious to encourage. Gardeners climbed on boxes to spy on us through the windows, extraordinary but untrue rumors were spread about our decadent exercises and nightly orgies, and even the Persian actors working with us found cause for endless confusions and painful layers of misunderstandings. In exchange, we found a number of occa-sions in which we could react with openness and passion against the brutal stupidity of the shah's regime, giving ourselves the comfort — which may not have been completely misplaced — that such outbursts might have been of use, if only for the mo-ment. In all, it was a complex and difficult experience, but one that was full of precious information for our work, especially as the contact with the mythical past was soon balanced by a second aspect that proved of equal value.

In Iran, there are two great theater traditions: the Ta'azieh, which is the only form of religious mystery play that Islam has produced, and the Ru'hozi, a form of commedia dell'arte that is still very much alive, in which simple artisans and shopkeepers — like Bottom and his fellow workmen in *A Midsummer Night's Dream* — band together in little groups and play whenever a wedding or some other event requires an entertainment. These performances are joyfully obscene, charged with physical energy, and very topical, playing directly off the audience's reactions. A very special form of Ru'hozi was housed within the closed quarters of Tehran's brothels, a sort of inner city that could only be reached through a narrow passage that ran through police headquarters. Here there were shops and even a theater where each morning the actors would assemble to hear the manager announce to them the theme he had chosen for the day. Then hour after hour onstage they would improvise, letting the theme evolve, elaborate, and polish itself through the chain of performances, until late at night would come the last show, which would be the most perfect. Then the theme would be dropped, while the next morning brought a fresh start on a new subject. These groups played with dazzling speed and lightning invention, and as we had long experimented with the same form, we were full of admiration. The temptation to try our hand was too great to be resisted, so choosing a remote village we attempted to do our own Ru'hozi, using as our theme something that all cultures have in common — bride, bridegroom, parents, marriage. What resulted was no more than a very crude first attempt, but it gave a start to a way of work that we now wanted to explore in public. For this, we needed a quite different terrain, and after we left Iran, Africa presented itself quite naturally. No sooner were we back home than we began to plan to visit Niger, Nigeria, Dahomey, and Mali. Behind this choice, there were many reasons: our already firmly established respect for the richness of African traditions, the feeling that there was something unique we could learn from the freedom of African performers, and above all the conviction that in Africa we would have no credit to draw on, no easy falling back on the shared references and topical jokes that never fail in a city. We would be out on a limb, and this danger was both stimulating and essential.

It is how you enter a village that counts. When we worked in Africa, we never entered a country through its capital city. On the contrary, we would pass unobtrusively through some minor frontier post and drive into the bush, swinging off the main track until in the distance we would see a conglomeration of huts. Realizing that nothing could inspire greater distrust than the sight of half a dozen Land Rovers roaring toward the village in a great cloud of dust, we would leave the vehicles some distance away and walk. The lessons I had learned years before in Afghanistan were invaluable, for in Africa as in Asia hundreds of eyes register every detail of the stranger's body language, and the interpretation is instantaneous. Does he walk arrogantly as though he possesses the world? Does the rhythm of his steps express the self-importance of the superior person? Does his head swivel from one side to the other with the indiscreet curiosity of the tourist, or even worse, is it full of the benevolent enthusiasm of the do-gooder? We had to master the very first exercise in which theater and life meet: how to walk, being no less and no more than ourselves, just a little more collected, a little more open than usual.

In the village, we would ask to see the chief. We had Africans among us, but as in this vast continent languages change every few miles, they had no better means of communicating with the villagers than did the Europeans. Fortunately, even in the most remote villages, among the children who would at once surround us, chattering, gesticulating, laughing, hiding behind one another, covering their faces with hand and arm, there was always one child who would boldly step forward, a boy who had gone to school, two hours' walk each way every day, and who would confidently offer to put his French or English at our disposal. We would follow him to where the chief would be sitting in his customary place, under a tree; on either side of him would sit a group of ancient, wrinkled, venerable men.

After an exchange of bows and courteous noises, the chief would ask why we were there. His question was the same one I had been asked time and again by journalists, critics, and professors. Back home the answer usually demanded a long stream of words and arguments before the frown of suspicion would begin to relax. In Africa, it took one sentence: "We are trying to see if communication is possible between people from many different parts of the world." This would be translated, the old men would murmur, nod their heads understandingly, and the chief would invariably say, "That is very good. You are welcome here."

Then all that remained was to unroll our carpet, and the entire village would assemble. In this way, we learned that an ideal audience is a natural mixture: squatting on the earth closest to the performers were the most enthusiastic, the children, then the mothers holding the babies, then the old men, then the youths, some of them with bicycles, leaning skeptically on the handlebars. Once, in a Sahara village, the Tuaregs, their faces hidden behind their dark blue veils, rode up on camels and halted behind the back row, watching over all the heads as though in privileged royal boxes. Even before the performance began, we saw the great advantage of sharing the sunlight: there was no artificial pretense; we were there for the spectators, and they were there for us. We saw one another in crystal clarity within the same space.

But how were we to start? Before the journey we had tried to prepare for this moment and had discussed many possible ideas and themes. Once we were in the real situation, we saw how impossible it was to project conclusions onto the unknown.

From the start, our carpet was the unknown. It became the very simple and direct expression of the difference between theater and everyday life. Once on the carpet, a new intensity, a new concentration, a new freedom were required instantly. The actors became more and more vividly aware of this ever-repeated challenge. At the moment they took the first step onto the carpet, they accepted a responsibility that lasted as long as they were in that special zone.

In the first village, we placed the one object we had used again and again, a cardboard box, in the middle of the carpet. For the spectators, for us, it was the same: it was real. An actor got up and went toward it. What was inside? As the actor wanted to know, the audience wanted to know with him, so at once we were on the common ground where the imagination can spring to life. Another time, it was a pair of shoes and a shoeless person who came toward them — again, common ground. A piece of bread, two people eye it, a third approaches — common ground. We tried to be simpler still. One sound on an instrument or one sound from a voice, repeated and repeated. We used no musical idiom, no musical language, just a sound. Anything could be a starting point, provided it was simple enough.

At night when we made a camp, we would always be surrounded by a whole village who would stare at us, fascinated by our strange ethnic rituals such as the brushing of teeth. This led us to see that the simplest way of beginning a performance was to present ourselves as we were, so we now made our first contact just by walking across the carpet, putting ourselves on show. This worked well, but we were ashamed of our clumsy movements in front of the magnificently developed bodies in the audience. One day, after we had improvised a dance, I spoke to one of the elders, apologizing for our physical inadequacies. He reflected for a long while, then he shook his head. "Each tribe has its own small number of movements, which it can do again and again. But we never learn other movements, ones that are not part of our tradition. We do not even know that they exist. To see them now is very important for us."

Seminars thrive on such questions as "Has the theater any function? Is it of any use?" Sometimes, on rare and special occasions, about an hour after we had begun to perform in a village, "something" took place. Through our playing, we were always offering that "something," and on these occasions the village accepted the offering. Had we sat smiling, shaking hands, giving presents, showing goodwill, a year could have gone by and no barrier been broken. But a theater performance is a strong action; it has an effect on all who are present. The image vanishes, but something has been opened.

Beginning with a point of mutual recognition, however, was not enough; a performance needs to develop. It is too easy to stay with a knockabout series of jokes and tumbles just because they always go well, and this was where our first true difficulty arose. We tried to increase the quality and the depth of the improvisations we performed by going toward the more unfamiliar areas we had touched on at home. So we used our chants or the extremely formal movements we had devised with bamboo sticks, and sometimes the timbre of the sounds or the pure geometry of the patterns the sticks made was enough to create a hush of wonder in the audience. But isolated moments were not a whole, and we felt an urgent need to bind them together with a theme. In Paris our work on bird cries had been linked to an old Persian poem, *The Conference of the Birds*, a Sufi allegory, in which a group of birds sets off on a perilous journey in search of a legendary bird, the Simourg, their hidden king. Many of the comic and even painful elements of the story were very close to what we were now living, as the journey was a merciless stripping away of each person's facades and defenses, so we felt we could use this as a starting point for a new series of improvised performances. Fed daily by the astonishing beauty and variety of the birds in the trees round our camps, we would now start with birdsong; this delighted the audience and gave us the common ground we always needed. Then bird characters would establish themselves, and the dramatic story would unfold. Occasionally, when playing at night, the darkness carried us way beyond our normal capacities, as though thanks to the vibrant presences around us we had become the projection of a collective imagination far richer than our own.

Sometimes we would meet anthropologists, and on these occasions we always disagreed, for they would maintain that every gesture, every custom, every form is an expression of a culture, each no more than a codified sign belonging to that culture alone. The theater, we would answer, shows the exact opposite, and our daily experience was proving this. Kissing with lips or rubbing noses may well be conventions rooted in specific environments, but all that matters is the tenderness that they express. "What is love? If it has a substance, show it to me," says the skeptical behaviorist. The actor does not need to reply; invisible feelings are what animate his actions all the time. Muslims put the hand on the heart, Hindus bring the two palms together, we shake hands, others bow or touch the ground — any one of these gestures can express the same meaning provided that the actor is capable of finding the necessary quality within his movement. If that quality is not there, every gesture is hollow and carries no meaning. One can enter an African village and smile automatically — and no one will be fooled. If hostility is concealed behind the smile, it will be sensed at once. But if the actor genuinely wishes to convey a deep feeling, if the truth of this feeling is there, it will be felt and understood by everyone, even if the outward sign chosen to express friendship is as unexpected as a clenched fist.

One day, in a village in northern Nigeria, Helen Mirren, who had joined the group just before we left Paris, decided to accept the ultimate challenge of starting from nothing. Without warning, this beautiful young actress jumped onto the carpet and shrunk her body into a crumpled, limping, twisted hag. At once, several young men sprang forward to help, convinced that she had been suddenly struck down by some alarming disease. So we saw that even the notion "This is make-believe" is not as obvious as we had thought. Nothing can be taken for granted. Even a performance is not automatically a performance. Whatever the game, its rules have to be established again and again.

From then on, walking became the obligatory opening routine; one after the other, this disparate collection of eleven actors would present themselves to the audience, accompanied by a percussion beat onto which each laid his own particular rhythms. Then they would hover, trip, leap, tease, or oppose one another playfully, until the sense of a game would emerge and a situation would start to evolve. How to begin is a lesson that can only be learned by daylight, when there is nothing to hide the performers. On the contrary, it is because the audience sees and begins to trust the actors as ordinary human beings that it opens to their imagination and willingly enters into their play.

"This will be the first time that *Oedipus* has been played in Nigeria," says the local director proudly. "We have adapted it very slightly, the action takes place here in Oshogbo, and Oedipus kills his father at the crossroads you passed a mile from here."

Every surface is crammed with excited bodies, not only the courtyard but the walls, the roofs of the little white buildings, the window ledges are all jam-packed, and children are in the trees or on their fathers' shoulders. Men with long supple branches whip the ground in ritualistic and harmless threats to drive the most eager of the children back from the acting area, and the performance begins. A jovial little tubby man enters speaking volubly in Yoruba. The audience likes him and laughs at his jokes. Who could he be? I wonder, rapidly scanning my memory of the Sophocles text. An impressive figure enters, he is blind, and I now find a point of recognition: the newcomer must be Tiresias. He speaks severely to the fat man. The audience roars with laughter. I whisper to the others; yes, we agree, the little man must be Oedipus. We realize that the audience is not preconditioned by the knowledge that Oedipus is a famous tragedy and that the doomed protagonist will proceed step by step toward catastrophe, so at the start the story has all the natural ingredients of comedy. The endearingly wily Oedipus is a character that can be found in every village; the spectators know in advance that he is going to ask all the wrong questions, which will inevitably land him in trouble, and the audience relishes every false step he takes.

In the same farcical key, Sophocles' scenes with the priest, with the chorus, with the old shepherd unfold, and we join the audience in their delight at the energetic knockabout acting. At the same time, part of my mind is buzzing with critical misgiving. The performancee seems to take the same scoffing approach that has become so common in Western theater today, where the modernizing and "sending up" of great works cheapens them, depriving us of a whole level of emotion that is richer and more precious than all the pleasure that debunking can bring. But even as I voice these reservations to myself, the laughter suddenly ceases. "You have murdered your father!" Oedipus is stopped dead in his tracks; he and the audience are appalled at the same moment and to the same degree. The meaning of family, the sacred nature of family relations, is present to everyone — this likable hero, who could have been part of any African family, has blundered into the most appalling crime of all. The most appalling? The silence seems to say that nothing could be worse, until even that silence grows more intense a few moments later as Oedipus and audience both learn that he has broken the most sacred of all taboos and has taken his mother to his bed. The gravity and the tension remain unchanged to the end of the performance, leaving the audience deeply shaken and us, professional observers, full of questions relating to our own understanding of what tragedy and comedy mean, where they are separate, and where they unite.

It was now the middle of our journey. Night had fallen and we were sitting in a clearing at the edge of the forest, going over the performance we had improvised in a village earlier in the day. Suddenly three young Africans came out of the trees and approached us smiling, talking in their local language and pointing. After a moment, a small boy joined them and as usual proved to be the only possible interpreter. "The village invites you," he said in English. "They want you to sing with them." Without hesitation — this was why we had come to Africa — all of us plunged into the darkness of the forest. There was no moon so the going was hard, and we moved forward cautiously, touching one another, the boys laughing and taking us in turn by the hand. We must have walked for over an hour when the trees thinned out, the blackness became a dark misty gray, and we sensed we were approaching a village. As we came out into the open, we heard murmurs and felt the presence of villagers, but we still could not make out any recognizable shapes. Then the singing began, a singing so quiet, so grave it gave us the impression that we were out of place. As our eyes grew accustomed to the dim light, we made out a central mass, and then we understood it was a funeral pyre and that they were mourning a death. We stayed by the trees, not moving, both touched and confused. Why had we been brought here? we asked ourselves. The night wore on, the singing renewed itself again and again, and we stayed on, silent witnesses. After a few more hours, a shadowlike figure came toward us and spoke. "Now you must sing," said the small boy.

Where did our sound come from? What was its starting point? Were we singing, or were we being sung? There was no way of knowing. For a year we had many times attempted to improvise a chant together, and now for the first time something happened that was totally new: a strange and beautiful chorale came into being, not from us but through us. It was created by the night, the forest, and the occasion. We became one with the village, we knew about death, we shared their grief. When we had finished there was complete silence. We left again in the dark, never having seen a single face, never to know why we had been invited to share this moment nor what quality had led us so far above ourselves.

Ifé is the city the Yoruba consider the navel of the universe, where the first man descended from the sky on a chain and where, according to a primordial pact, life is re-created and maintained anew each day. Here there is a goat market. In the center of the uneven expanse of dry ground is a place, hardly noticeable, where there are a handful of stones. During the day traders from other cities walk across these stones, children play, and goats urinate and defecate. When it grows dark, the strangers leave and the market is reserved for the evening ritual. The people who come do nothing to clean up the spot, to make it more beautiful, more respectable to the pious eye. Quite simply, their attitude has made the stones sacred, and in this way they have immediately transformed the ordinary without changing its outer shape.

This has always seemed to me to be one of the essential ele-

ments of theater. We do not need to do what is so hideously unconvincing in bad opera, to make fake jewels and fake golden
goblets. We can take any stone, any mug, and if in playing with
it we can bring the necessary quality and intensity, we can temporarily transform it into gold. For this reason I have always admired the traditional storyteller's art. In India, there are story-
tellers who tell the whole of the *Mahabharata* using one single
stringed instrument that their imagination transforms: as they
speak or sing, it changes from an instrument to a sword, to a
lance, to a spear, to a club, to a monkey's tail, to an elephant's
trunk, to the horizon, to armies, to thunderbolts, to waves, to
corpses, to gods.

During the time we were in Nigeria we witnessed many states
of "possession." I had seen people in states of trance in Haiti and
Iran, and at first this was very striking. Gradually, one realizes
that there is only a limited series of hysterical, spasmodic movements that are roughly the same all over the world. There is no
real transformation, no opening on an unknown world, so the
phenomenon of "being possessed" becomes disappointing and
uninteresting. In Nigeria, however, I encountered the unique-
ness of the Yoruba tradition of possession, which is the direct
opposite of all other possessed states. Here, the dancer who is
possessed by a god does not lose himself in a hypnotic condition
that extinguishes his awareness; even while he is possessed, he
remains fully conscious. So although it is the god and not the
dancer who takes charge of the body, the dancer's movements
are totally dependent on his own understanding of the nature of
the god, or in theater language, on his understanding of his role.
When a young novice in the cult begins a dance with the aim of
calling down a god, his intellectual and emotional understanding
of the god is very elementary, and so it is naturally a beginner's
god that appears. As year after year his understanding deepens,
this is reflected in the richness of his interpretation. When with
age he is initiated into priesthood and becomes a master, his performance too becomes masterly. The process through which this
imitation deepens is very noble; it involves all of life and relates
to what is implied when a Christian talks of the "Imitation of
Christ." All too often an actor or actress can live one life onstage
and another quite separate one in the world outside. Often over
the years the stage experiences may grow finer while those at
home remain banal, and an old actor may retain in himself no

residue from the riches he has portrayed. Gradually I became convinced that this need not be inevitable. The two areas of personal development can be linked; then and only then can each feed the other. Once again, an intellectual conclusion is easy to reach. When one sees how far away one is from turning this into a living experience, the journey starts again, though not necessarily on the familiar road.

We went to the United States to work with a remarkable Chicano group called El Teatro Campesino and its equally remarkable director, Luis Valdez. At first there were many surprises — we had been invited to their "village," only to find that in present-day California a village has nothing to do with what the word suggested to us in Africa. Nor did the vast and highly organized acres of crops correspond to the English image of "a farm." The Chicanos, we came to understand, are unwilling parts of an industrial process. Many of them had come across the Mexican border illegally, and whole families were living in battered Chevrolets that had become their mobile homes, trying in some way to remain in touch with the ancient traditions that were in their blood. They had learned their first lessons of theater in the thick of life. The idea of performing had grown out of necessity, within the urgency of the *huelga*, the farmworkers' strike. The militant strikers in the fields stood to one side of the picket lines, calling to the reluctant workers on the other side to join the movement. When arguments and exhortations failed, they made lightning improvisations with brutal caricatures and hard-hitting images. Humor and anger transformed their untrained bodies into highly professional instruments. And such was the force of their conviction that they succeeded beyond their expectations in drawing the workers across to their side.

This baptism by fire had created an unusual theater group that had rapidly found its way to a precise and practical understanding of the theater process. "When we sit together in a circle," said Luis Valdez to us on the first morning, "time goes by in the usual way. But the moment someone gets up and enters the action, time changes. The first step is like a birth and the end is a form of death. In performance, intensity comes from sensing the precarious nature of time."

This sensibility was very different from those of the many political groups we had come across in the sixties. Here, there was no division at all between the group's daily life and its performances. Yet its preoccupations went beyond fair play and social justice. Even as they boycotted the supermarkets, the campesinos were concerned with the Mexican-Indian heritage pulsing in their veins, reminding them of the living nature of the earth, of the rhythms of the seasons, of the cosmos. "When we explain that we try to make our work 'universal,'" Luis said, "this often leads to a misunderstanding. 'Universal' does not mean pretending to be like everyone else. 'Universal' simply means related to the universe." So we spoke of our interest in *The Conference of the Birds*, improvised fragments we had developed, and found that the theme of a group of birds searching for a mythical king was as close to them as it was to us.

The period we spent together was rich and joyous: days were full, love was made and couples formed, friendships and emotional bonds were tied. We performed together and met in other towns with other groups. One joint performance was memorable because no one came to it at all. When the time to begin was past and we stood in the carefully prepared space, looking dismally at the empty benches, our group suggested the old ploy we had used in Africa of going into the streets with drums to call people in. The others smilingly agreed, leaving us to discover that in California there are no passersby. So we banged our drums at the windows of cars when they stopped at traffic lights. The drivers were friendly and seemed pleased to be invited to our show, but as the lights changed they slipped into gear and we realized that Africa was very far away.

Everywhere we looked, the spaces were wide and open, but this was still an urban scene. The Teatro Campesino had been invited to perform at a huge political rally, and naturally we went with them, as by now we were familiar with the issues that animated the farmworkers' strike. Nonetheless, we were no more than well-meaning and sympathetic outsiders. Once we were within the throbbing turmoil of the meeting, however, listening to the passionate eloquence of the speakers and caught up in the cries and the applause, a phenomenon occurred that was very close to our experience at the strange funeral in the darkness of the African night. Without warning, our group was called upon to play. The actors could not refuse, and although they had no idea of what to do, the crowd acted for and through them. In a whirl of high-speed comic improvisations, our actors found themselves exteriorizing the images that the spectators needed to see. With a new level of skill and humor that was suddenly granted to them through the energy of the meeting, they impersonated to the life heroes and villains they had never seen, but at whom the crowd needed to cheer or hiss.

It was a crowded year and experiences began to accumulate so fast that the group could no longer tell whether it was being nourished or overfed. When the time came for us to leave San Juan Bautista, there was no pause for breath — we went to work in new conditions with an American Indian group in Minnesota, and then on to Connecticut to pick up a relationship that had begun in Paris with the National Theater of the Deaf, whose talented actors used every possibility their bodies offered so as to be able to communicate. This taught us a lot, because the eloquence of speech was there in their movements, perhaps even more so because words were lacking.

In Brooklyn I had a very special friendship with Harvey Lichtenstein that went back to the days of *A Midsummer Night's Dream*. After *Dream* had finished its Broadway run, Harvey had insisted on our staying a little longer to play in his theater, the Brooklyn Academy of Music. The idea of relating to a very different audience attracted me; with Harvey's enthusiastic support we proposed reversing the normal seating pattern. For a dollar, one could sit on a cushion, on the stage, which enabled us to put closest to the actors those who had paid least. For a long while, I had been obsessed with the fact that in our theaters those who enjoy involvement most are always the farthest away. The reluctance of the occupants of the expensive front rows to enter into the life of the stage had been particularly confirmed in the New York production of *King Lear* when the angry knights overturned the banquet tables, sending knives and tankards flying into the stalls. The mutters of disapproval we heard were nothing compared with the fury at a performance of *Marat/Sade* from the head of a film studio, accustomed to the safety of a screening room, who received a gob of spit in his eye from the foaming mouth of an asylum inmate. He had come to offer us a deal to film the show, but after he got up noisily and left, we never heard from him again.

In Brooklyn we could at last change the relationship between audience and stage, and this proved its merit. Harvey and I found we shared many of the same values, and he became a devoted and invaluable partner in all our American activities. Many years later, he made the extraordinary gesture of rebuilding an abandoned movie house, the Majestic, so as to give us a space in which we could play the *Mahabharata*, *The Cherry Orchard*, and eventually *The Man Who*.

However, at the end of 1973, a space on this scale was not yet necessary. We had no new production and could not bring to Harvey a finished performance. Instead, we were happy to be offered the old vamped-up BAM ballroom, and so the International Center made its first appearance in Brooklyn with what we called "Theater Days." These were daylong open work sessions that included demonstrations, discussions, and fragments of work in progress. *The Conference of the Birds* was the subject to which we kept returning, for we were searching for a form that always eluded our grasp. On our last night in Brooklyn we divided into three teams, each of which improvised its own version of the poem. In the early evening, Yoshi and Michelle Collison launched a performance that was rough and joyful, carrying the audience along with its exuberant energy. At midnight, Natasha and Bruce Myers lit candles, produced a dove, and guided the spectators into a delicate and grave reading of the same theme. At four in the morning, many of the faithful audience that had left for a couple of hours of sleep returned across the dark and silent city to be with us again, and Andreas Katsulas and Liz Swados led a cantata that grew as the light of dawn came through the windows and filled the space with light. The singing died away and there was a long moment of silence. Then we got up and left. Our American journey was over.

After three years of wandering together, the time now came for the group to settle. Nearly all of us, by birth or by circumstance, were or had become people of the city, drawn into the Western-influenced twentieth-century world. We possessed a craft, and we had a responsibility to the theatergoing audience that had kept us in work during most of our lives. So we now had to take our multitude of experiences and see how we could link them to the primary obligation of playing to a paying audience in an indoor space.

It was at this point that the Bouffes du Nord rose miraculously from its ashes, just when it was needed. Micheline Rozan had heard rumors of its existence, so one day she and I crawled through a hoarding on hands and knees, and when we stood up, we found ourselves contemplating a forgotten, battered shell within which was a space that fulfilled all the requirements that we had discovered during our travels. It is an intimate space, so the audience has the impression that it shares the same life as the actors; it is a chameleon space, for it allows the imagination to wander freely. It can become a street corner for rough performances or a shrine for ceremonies. It is like an indoor and outdoor space all in one. Its ground plan, we have since discovered, is very close to that of the Elizabethan theater, the Rose, and its very intimacy tolerates no underplaying; it demands from the actors the energy that will fill a courtyard, coupled with the naturalness of playing in a small room.

We could never discover more about the architect than that he had studied in Russia, but this does not explain why at the end of the nineteenth century, behind a railway station, in a zone for prostitutes, cutthroats, and apaches, he conceived a playhouse with the flying arches, the rhythms, and the proportions of a mosque. The theater had had a checkered career. It had opened originally with a musical show called *Ta Da Da*. Then came another musical, *Tiens, v'la le train qui passe*, inspired no doubt by noises of the Gare du Nord that still penetrate the theater walls. Soon the manager went bankrupt, and as this happened again and again as each new director went in search of audiences, the programs swung from crude variety to high art and back again. Once in desperation, the name was changed to Théâtre Molière, but as this had no effect, it mercifully became the Bouffes du Nord once more. The great French director Lugné-Poë did the first performance of Ibsen's *Enemy of the People* here, and on opening night the audience was infiltrated with plainclothes policemen sent by an anxious cabinet minister seeking to identify enemies of the state. The whore with the heart of gold whom Simone Signoret made famous in the film *Casque d'Or* was a real-life character who worked in the nearby bars. After her lover had been guillotined, posters went up saying that Casque d'Or would play her own story in person at the Bouffes du Nord. Such was the outcry of the respectable neighbors that this bold attempt at realistic theater was instantly abandoned. Adaptations of Zola, along with bourgeois dramas, Scandinavian epics, burlesques, and more bankruptcies, followed one another, leading to a grimly political period when only Soviet plays were shown, including the revolutionary classic *The Armored Train*. The audiences continued to dwindle. After the war, a last manager tried his luck with a play by Simone de Beauvoir, and when this failed, the theater finally gave up.

The building we crawled into had been abandoned for more than twenty years, only used from time to time by homeless people in search of shelter. They didn't hesitate to burn whatever they could find, making fires that were only extinguished when the rain poured in through the holes in the roof. The stalls vanished, the stage collapsed, the floor became a dangerous series of craters.

When we rediscovered the Bouffes, the minister of culture at the time told us it would take two years and a vast budget to reopen it. "Very well," said Micheline, "we will do the minimum in three months for a quarter of the sum."

Let me pause here to evoke this unusual person. Micheline lives and functions game by game. Impatient and sharply intelligent, she is bored by long-term planning, and even success is not particularly rewarding. But she is like a general: give her a crisis or even a disaster and at once her very best qualities come into play. Whether the problem comes from human friction, lack of funding, or illness, a simple phone call and she is on the spot, mobilized, mobilizing, finding solutions, with a mind that is pitiless in its logic. She would have been a brilliant businesswoman, the feared head of a multinational corporation, and indeed she began in show business as the dynamic newcomer in the oldest established acting agency. Curiously, however, neither a sense of money nor a need for power led to any ambition to dominate a large organization. More than most people, she is an unfathomable compound of contradictions. Impulsive and deeply emotional, she has never been interested in watching over more than a handful of people at a time, whose interests she could guide and serve down to the last detail of their lives. For a while, this constant attention was mostly given to Jeanne Moreau. Then to my good fortune, it was turned to me and especially to my work just at the time when it was most needed. Without her, neither the center, the Bouffes du Nord, nor the long series of experiments could ever have taken place. She maneuvered us through the complex web of French politics so that our work was always independent, never connected with any social or political group, free from all pressures, from any obligation from the need to haunt ministerial corridors more than absolutely necessary, from the need to attend Parisian dinners or in any way to play the expected games in order to receive the subsidies that were vital to us. In Europe this was no mean achievement. Quite often she was secretly not in sympathy with the nature of my work, distrusting the experimental and metaphysical, but not only was this of no importance, far more than that, no one could express and defend these aims more compellingly than she.

The opening of the Bouffes advanced on us with alarming speed, mistakes and delays were inevitable, Micheline's impatience grew daily, and one day I saw her hurl a plank across the scarred concrete floor of the theater in anger and frustration over some postponement. But she kept her promise, and right on the dot this theater that would become renowned for its uncomfortable seats but loved for its ruined splendor was ready to open with *Timon of Athens.* The play was topical, even though it was by Shakespeare, because it concerned themes that seemed to the French closer than ever: money, ingratitude, and bitterness. Also, the play was virtually unknown and as surprising to the audience as the theater's battered walls.

There are many approaches to the relation between stage and audience. For Artaud, the actor is the victim at the stake desperately signaling through the flames. For Grotowski, the actor is a martyr with whom the spectator cannot presume to identify; he can only witness in awe a hero's courage and the sacrifice that is offered to him as a gift. Samuel Beckett once confided to me that for him a play was a ship sinking not far from the coast while the audience watches helplessly from the cliffs as the gesticulating passengers drown. But our three years of wandering had suggested a different approach. We had become used to meeting the spectator on his own ground, taking him by the hand and setting out on an exploration together. For this reason, our image of theater was that of telling a story, and the group itself represented a storyteller with many heads.

We gradually found we could apply much of what we had

learned in our travels. There was, above all, a need for transparency, contact, and clarity in our work that derived in part from our direct and shared experiences. We gravitated between works from the past, respecting what is unquestionably greater than anything we can achieve today, and material from the present day. And we kept our seat prices as low as possible so that the audience could continue to be the rich mixture we had found so rewarding.

The hardest problem that confronted us lay between what I had labeled in *The Empty Space* the Rough and the Holy. How could we combine crude humor with the mysterious quality of silence we had encountered at certain moments in our travels? Nothing is more precious than laughter, but it can cheapen and confuse as often as it liberates. Over the years, as we went from serious themes to comic ones, we tried to discover how to pass across this barrier, to capture the deceptive innocence of a fable, for in a fable the deeper the meaning, the lighter the way in which it is told.

A Balinese dancer once visited us at the Bouffes, showing us something we had never encountered before. At first what he did seemed familiar to the culturally hard-bitten travelers we had become, for as he danced, he would appear to be possessed, his breathing would change, his body would be transformed, and he seemed inhabited by a strange demonic power. This was no surprise. The revelation came an instant later when he advanced toward the audience with the easy familiarity of a clown, exchanging crude jokes, topical references, and lewd innuendos. At one moment he would be a villager among villagers, yet in the next breath, he would withdraw again into the trancelike state of total and frightening possession. To find the secret of this seamless transition became our aim.

One day I was driving through New York with Madame de Salzmann when she turned to me and said very lightly, "Why don't we make a film of *Meetings with Remarkable Men?*" These few words changed the pattern of my life for several years, weaving a thread through our first period in the Bouffes. I had not an instant of doubt; her proposition to film Gurdjieff's autobiographical book took precedence over every other plan and project. This was no act of sacrifice; it was simply a moment when all the options fell into place in an unmistakable scale of values. Once again, I could see that decisions are not made; they arise when something more essential than our own ideas breaks through the clouds of our wishes. Then one neither counts the cost nor determines the result. In this case, the reward lay in the intimate, daily work with Madame de Salzmann. Hour after hour we would sit together, she a motionless center of collected energy, and as we went over each detail of the script, I could feel my own thinking lifted to a previously unknown level of intensity through her presence, through the challenge of her demand.

My first reaction had been to imagine the dynamic, colorful film we could make, reflecting the extravagant and provocative sides of Gurdjieff, who during his lifetime acquired a rich coating of lurid and fantastic myths. This seemed admirable material for an exciting picture, but I soon discovered that it was of no interest at all to Madame de Salzmann. Her aim was not to make an "interesting" film for its own sake nor to pay homage to the man she had known so well. Her purpose was to give to the spectator a direct taste of that "something else" she had experienced with Gurdjieff over the years.

The first scene of the film is entirely her own creation, for it is hardly indicated in the book. Whenever we met to work on the script, we would go over and over this opening sequence, and as we always began again at the very beginning, we found we could seldom proceed any further. Apart from the dances at the end, the opening remains for me the most successful part of the film, as the meaning of the whole story is caught here with hardly any words, just through images and sound.

The sequence presents an ancient competition, held at rare intervals in a remote and mountainous part of the Caucasus. To win the competition, a number of musicians must improvise "freely," and it is the special meaning of freedom that this scene dramatically throws into relief. The condition given to the participants is merciless in its precision. Each note must lead out of the previous note with an absolute and logical inevitability, yet at the same time it must be melodious. If the phrase is predictable, there is no true melody, and if it is too ornamental, then the clarity of its progression is lost. The line of melody once launched must never be broken; it must continue to develop until it reaches a particular intensity that can make the rocks vibrate.

This one tone is very hard to find, but once it is there, the whole mountain will respond with an echo that is the proof that the contest has been won.

This image comes from the depths of a mythic imagination, but in a film it had to have its own reality, its flesh and blood, and for this we needed the help of traditional musicians. Many were heard, and gradually a group was assembled. Then the difficulties become clear.

As each one began to play, he would attack the opening phrases with his usual confidence and skill. But invariably Madame de Salzmann would draw his attention to the moment when this initial intention would go astray. Maybe the musician had permitted himself just a slight slackening of attentiveness or a little moment of self-indulgence, maybe no more than the pleasurable repetition of a phrase he enjoyed or even the elongation of a note with a touch of sentimentality—and then the melody's natural flow would be blocked. It was poignant to witness in rehearsals how each musician would recognize and acknowledge that there was a point where the acuity of his listening had slipped away. For this reason, the scene of the musicians is like a blueprint of the whole film. It puts under a microscope the difficulties of every searcher, whatever his field, and shows how it is that so many searchers, however ardent and sincere, drop by the way. Very exact conditions govern the evolution of intentions within each human being, and this scene gives a vivid expression to a vast idea.

"The highest energy is always there," Madame de Salzmann would say, "ready to act if we are there to receive it." As she spoke, it sounded so simple, but working with her revealed how far we are from understanding what this subtle link may be.

Everything to do with cinema interested her. We went constantly to films as she wanted to see every new picture. But as soon as she had grasped the essential, she became impatient with the story, and we would get up and leave, generally at moments when the rest of the audience was most enthralled. Everything in the universe is in movement, she would say, and for her the cinema was yet another form of movement. In this way her understanding of its requirements was immediate and professional, for action, dialogue, composition, color, sound, montage were all manifestations of the fundamental dynamic processes that she had studied all her life.

She had no knowledge of the camera or of dramatic construction, but here too her unerring sense of movement made it possible for her to detect immediately what rhythm, what tempo, what distance, even what close-up was required. The entire unit, both technicians and actors, were touched by this, and each one strove to become the instrument through which her vision could be realized. Naturally, it was seldom possible, and when things went wrong, many scapegoats were found, but Madame de Salzmann herself was always respected. Her quiet authority was absolute, even when it could not easily be obeyed.

One of our greatest difficulties lay in the film medium itself. The cinema is by its very nature overwhelming; its images and sound invade every corner of the brain, washing away all sense of distance, making our identification with the action complete and irresistible. In the theater, a line of verse, a song, a dance, even a leap in the air are often all that is needed for the most secret of meanings to appear. With the camera, however, the obstacle is far greater, for to try to film the invisible seems to deny the very nature of photography. In this film, the evocative power of Gurdjieff's words had to be replaced by images, by an exact rightness in the choice of people and of the natural backgrounds to which they relate. Only if these elements were found could photography make each scene a living document and not just a fiction.

The search for locations took us to remote parts of Turkey, to the real backgrounds of much of the story, to the transparent beauty of Lake Van, to Kars, where Gurdjieff was born, to the ruins of Ani, the city of a thousand shrines, where a vital part of the story was to occur. But after many long months of waiting and negotiating, Turkish bureaucracy proved even more byzantine than the ruins, so we moved farther afield. We crossed the border to Iran and then to Egypt, only to find that thousands of years of subtle experience in handling foreigners had made the country ruinous for filmmakers; and so on to Ladakh, the land of monasteries, magnificent in their isolation, luminous in the rareness of the air, but too inaccessible for practical work. Finally, in Afghanistan, we found the people and the conditions that we required.

Now the same problem presented itself in different form. Beyond the fine faces we could pick up in every bazaar, we needed professional actors. We had a story to tell, and these actors could not be found on the spot. We had to return to the parts of the world where performers are trained, recognizing that what we needed in this case was not within an actor's normal range, especially when he has trained in the midst of twentieth-century urban life. Gradually, we put together a most interesting group of performers from many countries and backgrounds, each of whom was in some way touched by the theme.

The role of Gurdjieff was the most difficult to cast, as the actor had to be convincing for those who had never seen him and not offensive to those who had known him well. As we needed to find someone whose physical type would immediately suggest Gurdjieff's Greek and Armenian origins, we investigated the vast pool of actors in the United States who had Middle Eastern backgrounds. To our disappointment, we found that the acquired mannerisms of American culture, the way of holding the body, the slouch, the laid-back walk, the nodding head had completely obliterated all traditional characteristics. We auditioned in London, in Paris, in Athens, in Cairo — to no avail. Then it was suggested that perhaps in Yugoslavia, which had a very rich and interesting film and theater activity, we might find the person we needed. I saw many actors in Belgrade and was immediately struck by their powerful physiques, their strong personalities, and their fine acting skills still linked to deep ethnic roots. But none of them spoke a word of English and they had no interest whatsoever in working abroad. Then a young man from Montenegro, Dragan Maxsimovic, entered the room. The way he walked, the expression in his eyes told us that we were at the end of our search. Having established through an interpreter — he knew no English — that he was willing to leave the country, we invited him to Paris to meet Madame de Salzmann, and we set up an audition in a friend's garden. While waiting for the camera to be ready, he sat patiently on a stool. Then, at one moment, he crossed his legs, and leaning forward, he clasped his hands together on a stick he had picked up off the ground, his body relaxed yet poised and alert. Madame de Salzmann was delighted, recognizing a characteristic attitude of Gurdjieff that Dragan had unwittingly assumed, simply through the power of essential roots and type.

Of course, Dragan knew nothing of the man he was asked to play, but what he had gathered had fired his imagination, and he was prepared to commit himself to everything that was needed. His first challenge was to learn English, so we enrolled him in a school in London, where during very long hours, day after day, he worked with passionate dedication in an austere self-imposed solitude until the time came when he could both understand and speak an English that was fluent and free. As an actor he recognized that there was nothing in the film for him to act in the usual sense of the word. This was a daunting task, but he was undaunted; each painful difficulty that he encountered helped him to discover what a searcher can be, even though at times the demand to go way beyond himself made every fiber in his body cry out in despair.

When we moved the production to Afghanistan, Madame de Salzmann was well over eighty. We set up a little booth for her on every location where she could watch on a television screen what the camera was recording. After every rehearsal and each take she would send a messenger to me with some criticism or suggestion. Often, to the bafflement of the professional technicians who resent changes of plan, I would run back to her tent and then emerge to change everything we had set up with hours of care.

One day we were working on a high mountain ridge, very hard to reach, where the equipment had to be hoisted up with ropes and winches. We took a minimum crew, leaving Madame de Salzmann with the others at the base camp. But in the middle of the afternoon, she arrived, rapidly making her way up the fragmentary track with only the help of her walking stick. The first sight of her calmly and determinedly coming over the skyline crystallized the deep respect that the crew had already begun to form, and for the rest of the shooting they followed her with unbounded admiration.

When it was time to edit the film, she was again with us every day, judging the passage from one shot to another in terms of the succession of patterns of energy. When the highly experienced English editor, John Jympson, would present a finished, fine-cut sequence that he had polished to the last frame, she was never satisfied, proposing new corrections. He would then leave the projection room, muttering under his breath yet secretly impressed.

Natasha and I shared a house in Kabul with Madame de Salzmann. A noisy projector in a large square metal box had been set up in the entrance hall, and on this day we were screening our first rushes, which had only just arrived from the laboratory in London after several weeks of shooting. We had begun our filming with the first sequence, and for well over an hour we watched the fragments of this opening scene: the horsemen and the crowd gathering in the valley and swarming down the hillside to listen to the musicians. The sequence had been well prepared, and as we watched it we were all relieved and pleased. It had come out as we had hoped, and it seemed an encouraging basis for the rest of the shooting. Only Madame de Salzmann was silent. Knowing her, we did not expect her to be even remotely satisfied, least of all to express simple praise, but we were troubled when she left the room deep in her own private thoughts.

That evening at dinner she spoke little, and we still did not discuss the rushes. It was only at the end of the following day that she expressed what had gradually formed itself through her ruminating. "Something is lacking," she said, picking up a phrase she would use again and again: "Il y a quelque chose qui manque."

"In the scene, there are the musicians, the crowd, there are the judges," she continued, "and yet something is missing, something to link them to a level that cannot be shown. It's not an idea, it has to be represented by someone, someone who carries within himself the strength of a real tradition. Our judges are fine-looking old men with white beards, but that's not enough. They haven't the necessary weight. We need someone of real presence. In fact, one man is not enough, there should be three men to lead such a ceremony, and they must be believable. Without them, something will always be missing. We must put them in."

As often happened, I tried in vain to explain to her the reality of filmmaking. We had shot the scene five weeks earlier in a remote mountain valley. We were now nearing the end of our stay in Afghanistan. Neither our schedule nor our tight budget would permit us to reshoot this, the most expensive of all the scenes. And in any event the material we had was good.

"Just put in the extra men," she said.

I explained that this was technically impossible, three important characters cannot be pushed into the frame once it is shot. "Besides," I added, "we know all the good faces from the bazaar by now. Where can we find someone new?"

I saw from her expression it was no use arguing; she knew what was necessary, and it was up to us to find a solution. Of course, after discussions with the editor and the cameraman and after reexamining the scene shot by shot, we saw that technical solutions could be found. We did not need to reassemble the whole crowd; simply rebuilding a platform and putting some twenty extras in strategic positions would give us material that would cut imperceptibly into the film. But where were we to find these three men with spiritual presence?

The following day was our rest day. I was sitting on the terrace of our house when I saw three men in white robes approach. They were not old, they were upright and noble, and they came to visit, explaining that they were the elders of a *khanakar*. They had heard about our activity and said they wished to pay their respects. Looking at them, I realized that I was looking at the faces we needed and ran to fetch Madame de Salzmann, although I was suspicious of extraordinary coincidences and could not believe that they would ever consent to appear in a film. We sat and talked together, and after a while I felt we had nothing to lose, so I made the proposition. "I have never seen a film," answered one of them. "But my son who lives in America has told me what it is. I think what you intend to do could be useful to other people. We would be happy to follow your wishes if we can help." So, a few days later, they were there on the set, doing all that they were asked in an impeccably professional way and giving to the scene the authoritative presence that had been lacking.

When the film was shown, some people were disappointed, finding it too simplistic as cinema, too exotic in its imagery, too naive in its narrative. Certainly, when at last the distant monastery is reached, the dancers assembled there in white are unmistakably European, and this is hard to swallow from the point of view of normal storytelling logic. But the unique and unknown dances themselves are what matter. They have never been shown before, and these movements are authentic, re-created from the complex principles that Gurdjieff discovered during his journeys and had transmitted directly to Madame de Salzmann, who in turn had taught them to her pupils. It is interesting to see that when the film is shown, most spectators are deeply touched by these dances and exercises and are totally unconcerned by their lack of verisimilitude in the story.

I know that Madame de Salzmann herself was not fully satisfied with the film, although she never said so to me. I feel she needed to be confronted by a thinking even stronger than her own, to which she would have been ready to yield, but without that friction, which I certainly could not bring, what she truly had in mind could not find its expression. Nonetheless, I think that anyone who watches and listens to the film in the way that it proposes can experience a purity, a special quality that is entirely her own and that can give one a direct taste of what a search is, of what another level of awareness can mean, in a way that no words can equal.

When Madame de Salzmann died at the age of 101, she seemed to be taking the center of life with her. Now, after a long and ashen period of grief, the reality of the present has re-emerged, a present that is waiting to be served in a new way through those who had the fortune of sharing what her influence transmitted. Life continues, a new generation arises, and the world's need for a living body of understanding is more vital than ever. The enigma of tradition and the mystery of transmission cannot change, but the great set of keys is always there.

The deep conviction that had led me to Matila Ghika, to the harmonic proportions of the Golden Section, and then to the teachings of Gurdjieff was that part of our mind relates to an order that no other animal can perceive but to which a human brain can have access through mathematics, geometry, art, and silence. No other animal conceives numbers; however, when the right conditions are there, part of the human brain can open itself to oscillations that touch us deeply, that seem full of meaning and yet are without imagery or content. In the Bouffes du Nord, I could not avoid touching on these mysteries in the daily practical work.

I had always avoided great symbolic themes, seeing how easily one can ride on their back as on an elephant, giving oneself a feeling of importance because one is lifted so high. Every time someone labels me a guru I wince, as many actors are only too ready to dream that they have become part of an esoteric group, and so they look for spiritual advancement in a field where it is necessary to keep one's feet firmly on the ground. Now I began cautiously to believe that the years of experiment had made it possible to confront the challenge of a work as dense in levels of meaning as the *Mahabharata*, in which each member of an international group could find his or her place.

For many years the hope of finding a theatrical form for this work had been a distant aim, and when we tackled *The Conference of the Birds*, it seemed like a halfway house. When we passed from the rough anarchy of *Ubu* with new improvisations in every performance to the documentary precision that was essential to portraying a starving African tribe in the *Ik*, from the joy of uncluttered acting in *The Cherry Orchard* to the exorcising of the operatic phantoms of the past in *The Tragedy of Carmen*, each of these served a definite purpose; together, they consolidated our position in the theater world so that we would be able to command the support needed for a major undertaking, and they offered the opportunity to experiment with different approaches. For *The Conference of the Birds*, the need to meet any audience on simple unpretentious terms led us into playing a very down-to-earth African village farce, *L'Os*, to start the evening. It helped establish a climate of simplicity and confidence that made it then possible to lead the audience into the more rarefied poetry of a Sufi work without them feeling that the esoteric was portentous or forbidding. When the *Mahabharata* took shape, we felt it would at last be possible to let lightness and humor be part of the passage into the difficult labyrinths of the work, and for this it was clear that we would need all that an international group could draw from its mixture of traditions and resources.

Perhaps India is the last place where every period of history can still coexist, where the ugliness of neon lighting can illuminate ceremonies that have not changed in ritual form nor in outer clothing since the origin of the Hindu faith.

In Madurai, there is a huge temple, a sort of city where a single step takes one into another world. Time is not abolished — it does not seem to exist at all in these great dark inner passages, where a dense mass of plump men, all naked but for a strip of twisted cloth round the waist, make eddies and whirls in a river of humanity. Light leads to darkness, darkness to shadowy limbs, to oil lamps. Sudden cries from voices fight with calls from long shining horns; on walls striped alternately black and white, devotees hurl fistfuls of powder against pillars, streaking them red, or else rub colored earth on the trunks of carved elephants, caking the stone. Every child dreams of a time machine for exploring the past. It exists: an Indian temple is such a machine. Step into it and ancient Babylon is at your feet.

One night in Benares, a waving banner of lights came slowly out of the darkness, accompanied by the powerful trumpeting of musicians. As it approached, the lights took on the triple pattern of Shiva's emblem, in the form of a series of neon tubes strapped like tridents to the heads of naked men. It seemed to be a procession of penitent slaves linked together by long and dusty serpents, a strange bondage that finally revealed itself to be a fat cable leading to a bicycle, on which a figure in cotton trousers dripping with perspiration was forcing down the reluctant pedals to drive a rusty dynamo on wheels. The time machine brings you back to today.

A temple in India is a marketplace in no way separate from the street; it is a place for families and a noisy kitchen where priests rush from one boiling cauldron to another to stoke fires, stir liquids, or anoint sacrificial rocks with milk. There is no silence, only activity, as the gods feed indiscriminately on the energy of elephants, beggars, and Brahmans, all of whom bear the same sacred symbols streaked across face, body, or trunk in yellow paste; it is only on the steps that lead down to the vast tanks of slightly stagnant water that there is a slackening of the fever, for here the women slip into the cool wetness until their saris stick to their flesh like patterned skin. The ground teems with insects and rats, and even the air is incessantly alive, with monkeys swinging along telegraph wires or hiding behind elaborately carved figures on the temple walls. There is no simplicity of form — how could there be? — for here the sacred art is a reflection of the secular life, and this life has no simplicity, only an inexhaustible variety that is always in movement.

Yet there is a supreme, unattainable, ultimate deity of formless stillness, Brahma, who encompasses all movement and rules beyond the heavens, beyond God, beyond human understanding. The phenomenal universe demands a division into three: Brahma, Shiva, and Vishnu, whose forms are complex and interchanging, and as they too are still unattainable to human understanding, they are compelled to subdivide again, so that only through an exact genealogy of intricate family relationships between great-aunt goddesses and third-cousin gods can we glimpse an explanation of the diversity of our daily experience.

Accordingly, a temple is not a static object to be contemplated; it is a journey to be undertaken, a story to be visited, a theology to be understood. Each carved figure, dancing, offering, and coupling, is like a word or sentence within the syntax of a text. For a Brahman, the act of walking through one courtyard after another to reach the sacred flame is like a passage through pages of script; this is not far removed from the experience of the Australian Aborigine moving through his landscape, where the rocks and mounds are "songlines," the words of unwritten myths.

It had all begun with the young Indian who, during the rehearsals of our play about Vietnam, *US*, had first mentioned the strange word *Mahabharata* to me. The image he evoked had haunted my mind. Two great armies face one another, straining at the leash. In between them stands a prince, who asks, "Why must we fight?"

Again and again, I returned to this picture. One day I told Jean-Claude Carrière about the battle, about the warrior's questions. He wanted to know more, and we went to call on Philippe Lavastine, the scholar friend who had dedicated his life to Sanskrit studies. We asked him to explain to us the situation of the two armies, and who was the prince and why does he question the meaning of war? Philippe began by telling us the name of the prince — Arjuna. Then he said that we needed to understand why his chariot was being driven by Krishna, a god. But to understand this, he continued, we needed to know all about Arjuna's brothers and his cousins, why they were in conflict and how they were born, and for this we had to go back to a long time before they were even conceived, to the creation of the world. Darkness fell, and when we left late in the evening, the tiny apartment crammed with books and papers seemed to glow with the great epic that was just beginning to unroll. The next day we returned. Now one breathless and amazing session followed another as the story continued, not in a logical order, but as Philippe remembered it, in all its intricate criss-crossing complexity. Then, one night, the story was finished. We had received it as a child does in India, orally, from a storyteller. Leaving in silence, we found ourselves in the dark, deserted rue Saint André des Arts. We paused. We knew we shared the same decision. We could not keep what we had heard to ourselves. We had to pass it on to others through our special field, the theater.

For ten years Jean-Claude read, wrote, and struggled. Version after version of the story came and went. Workshops with different groups of actors were started and left incomplete. It was as though the *Mahabharata*, which had lain asleep for so many centuries, suddenly awoke. It had needed to come out and cross the world. Luckily for us, we were there to help it on its way.

More and more journeys now became necessary and we returned to India many times over the years to prepare the *Mahabharata*. We — the word arises constantly, because for years "we" had become a changing, evolving team. "We" in India were sometimes Maurice Benichou and Alain Maratrat, two actors who had been with the French ensemble and had joined us to become part of *Timon of Athens*; they were to stay on, year after year, invaluable companions through many adventures and an indivisible part of the preparation of others. Alain loves all forms of movement; he is always close to the experience of his body, and for the *Mahabharata* he plunged into learning all he could about the martial arts from tradition to tradition. Maurice had already played the mysterious Hoopoe in *The Conference of the Birds*, which had opened a whole new area in his sensibility, and now he was facing the daunting challenge of the role of Krishna.

There was also Jean-Claude Carrière, in the tenth year of his patient and sensitive search for the heart of the *Mahabharata*, never satisfied, always open to criticism, untiring, never short of ideas, writing all the time. He would read new scenes to us as they came off his pen in taxis, hotel rooms, and airport lounges where the planes were reliably late, giving us plenty of time to work. For Jean-Claude, this was the climax not only of all we had done together but of his film scripts, his literary experiments, his wide reading, and his philosophical reflections. Suddenly, the *Mahabharata* was there to call on his thinking and bring together the wide range of his experiences. I cannot imagine a better collaborator. I know that without him the project could never have come into being.

Equally central to our work was Chloé Obolensky, proving again the inestimable value of the mutual understanding that comes from affection, respect, and trust, built on challenges lived through together. Chloé had joined us at the Bouffes to design *The Cherry Orchard*. Now she would listen to the readings and then vanish, indefatigably searching for objects and textures in every bazaar.

Meanwhile, watching and noting, serving as eye and ear for us all, was Marie-Hélène Estienne. Many years before, Micheline Rozan had first spoken of Marie-Hélène as a young person who she felt had very unusual talents, although she could not tell what form they would eventually take. When I met Marie-Hélène at dinner in Micheline's flat, my first impression was of a tense, silent figure refusing to be drawn into the chatter and the laughter. The next day we met again and rapidly discovered we shared the same birthday — the first day of spring, though the years are far apart. Gradually a deep and close relationship came into being, and she entered into every facet of our work, until her talent and intuition became a vital part of each new experience. With lightning rapidity, she would plan our activities in precise detail; when we needed new actors, she would discover them in odd corners of the world through some astonishing and unpredictable process of her own; when not working on texts, she would maintain the cast members' peace of mind with sorely tried affection and hardly concealed impatience. To this day, she changes her mind as often as I do, if not more, as the only way to reach a firm decision.

When we began to rehearse for the *Mahabharata*, we tried to share our impressions of India with the large group of actors, but we soon saw that this was impossible, so we scooped up our company and flew them to India. Jean-Claude, Marie-Hélène, and I had picked an itinerary in which every significant place we had visited over the years was now crammed together into ten days of breathless travel. This proved a very good method: a surfeit of indigestible impressions is part of the Indian experience and is a reminder that the conclusions one draws can never be complete; whenever one dreams that the outlines of India are beginning to become clear, a sudden new impression tips the previous structure on its head.

In the *Mahabharata*, the most commonly repeated metaphor is that of a river. The battlefield is a river, the severed limbs are rocks, the amputated fingers are little fish, the torrent is blood. India is such a river. As soon as we arrived, we thrust the actors into the vast dark whirlpool of the great temple of Udipi, eating off palm leaves, squatting on the stone floor like the hundreds of thousands of pilgrims who are fed there each year. We quickly found old Brahmans who were ready to talk about the *Mahabh-arata*, and after this first introduction, we led the group to our favorite among all the holy spots we knew, a tiny temple called Parasinikadavu by a river deep in the Kerala countryside. Here the most ancient of rituals takes place, not at a special season but twice each day, and nowhere is the sense of ancientness more powerful. Within a small, crowded stone circle, enclosed in iron bars, six near-naked drummers pound on long drums, while in the flickering oil light a small, brisk man caked in yellow paste, with ornate half-moon-shaped plates extending his lips, leaps and dances, aiming an arrow at each cardinal corner with a tiny silver bow. In this minuscule vault we felt in direct contact with the Vedic world in which the intricate actions of the *Mahabharata* had taken shape. The dichotomy between past and present was dissolved.

We journeyed with the actors in a circle, down through Kerala, across Tamil Nadu, up to Madras, over to Calcutta, by train to Benares, then to Delhi, giving each of us a store of vital images and the group as a whole an enormous spool of impressions to be edited in rehearsal when we returned. At the same time, holding us firmly in reality was the India of today: swarming and limping, shoving and struggling in its misery, immobile in beggary, or huddled in sidewalk sleep. This washes the brain of any vestiges of romanticism, any lingering dreams of an East veiled in mystery. India was the night train, the stifling hot metal cylinder with tarnished metal bunks and barred windows through which thin hands would grope at each station for any watch left carelessly under a pillow. It was godheads whose divinity is outlined with colored electric bulbs. It was the reality of starvation, the reality of violence, the reality of the irresistible cascade of life enveloping both shape and time.

Giddy and surfeited by the impressions we were receiving, about halfway through the journey, in Madurai, I felt we had to make a stop. We talked together at breakfast, and everyone agreed that we needed to rehearse. Our journey had a strict aim, and the pressing needs of the coming performance meant that our experiences needed to be related to our work. We left the city and walked to a nearby forest where, finding a clearing, we gave ourselves as the beginning of an exercise the task of selecting one natural object from among the trees and collecting them at the clearing's edge. We had hardly finished doing so when, as if out of nowhere, an old lady appeared and quietly prostrated herself before our homemade pile. After a while she rose, stepped backward, and was gone, leaving us to recognize with astonishment that we had added one more to India's shrines.

I then proposed another exercise: "Very rapidly, going round the circle, let each person produce one word, one word only, to pinpoint his most vivid impression of India." There was no hesitation; like a swift percussion, beat upon beat, adjective or noun followed like the many facets of a rotating crystal: "frenzy," "color," "tranquillity," "age," "vulgarity," "hunger," "faith," "splendor," "misery," "matriarchy" — thirty people, thirty different words that seemed so inadequate that at once we made another round, thirty more words after which we left off, accepting that the list could never be complete. It now seemed an interesting moment to rehearse one of the scenes we had evolved in the Bouffes du Nord, to see what the influences of the journey could bring to it. We had hardly begun when we saw that the forest was full of hidden human life. An audience had assembled and was watching us intently through the leaves. "What can they make of all this?" I wondered as Jean-Claude's French text unrolled. An actor sprang out from the bushes. "Shiva!" came an immediate cry of recognition from our very first spectators. We were overwhelmed. Our sounds and gestures made sense in India. This, more than anything else, gave us the courage to pursue what up to then had been completely untested work.

Near Madras there is a holy place, Kanchipuram, a sacred center, a city of temples. It is one of the four great shrines making a square across the subcontinent that are devoted to the tradition of Shankaracharya, a fourth-century saint and teacher. Here, in the busy cluster of buildings in his name, there are three Shankaracharyas. There is an old master, who has withdrawn from the world; he no longer speaks, but he can be seen from the courtyard once or twice a day, in silence, behind a face-sized shutter that is momentarily opened and closed. There is also another occasion when the people who wish to participate in his charismatic aura gather on a balcony, on seats, and wait patiently as in a theater in front of a curtain. Sometimes it is never drawn back. But if they are fortunate, it will part without warning. Then, on a slightly lower level to the terrace, lying on the floor in a narrow cubicle can be seen a motionless huddle, for which no words are more apt than the phrase in the *Bhagavad-Gita*, "Time grown old." If the ancient figure can be persuaded to rise, the crowd presses forward, and some may even be allowed to come down a few steps as far as an iron railing. The old man's eyes will now scan the expectant faces, and if this glance is met even for an instant, the observer receives the moment of contact physically, like a shock.

There is a second Shankaracharya, in the thick of life, who has all the energy necessary to serve a leader's practical obligations and is responsible for the running of the temple. One day, the old man will die, and then the second Shankaracharya will take the old man's place behind the shutter, while the third Shankaracharya, now still a young boy being rigorously prepared by daily duties, will step into the second position, and a new boy will be chosen to enter the chain.

The active Shankaracharya, a quick-faced man always ready to switch from laughter to seriousness, eyes alert and dark, stripes of paste on his forehead, a chest bare but for the Brahman's diagonal ritual thread, a staff in his hand, welcomed us warmly. On a previous visit, I had asked him a question about Krishna. Krishna is god incarnate; he descended to live as a man, taking on the suffering of humanity, but unlike Christ he also took on man's activities and pleasures: in the old stories he was a tremendous and cunning warrior and an irresistible lover with twenty thousand wives. He thus reflects the generous Hindu capacity to encompass every aspect of living experience without moral judgment. Does this make him perfect or imperfect? Is imperfection beyond perfection? "If Krishna has all the aspects of a man," I asked, "has he therefore man's natural ability to be wrong, to make errors?" I truly needed to hear his answer, hoping perhaps to find my own weaknesses condoned or at least to understand better the *Mahabharata*. Shankaracharya smiled. "You put this question from a man's point of view," he answered. "A man's mind is forced to make such distinctions. From Krishna's point of view, the question cannot arise." Like a Zen riddle, these words shocked my understanding and showed how much more is revealed by the way of bafflement than by the deceptive ways of reason.

This time Shankaracharya welcomed those of us who had been there before as old friends. We sat on the ground, and I explained that we had brought with us the group of actors who were working on the play. He pointed to them one by one and laughingly identified the characters. Elsewhere, India had often been racist, and repellent questions would be put again and again such as "Why a black man?" "Why black?" Here there was no barrier; to our delight and relief he immediately saw a Hindu hero or deity—a Bhishma, a Drona, a Shiva, or a Krishna—in the African, Japanese, Balinese, or French face turned expectantly toward him. He blessed our undertaking, advised us not to eat meat on the day of the first performance, and asked if we could send him a videotape when the play was ready.

For once, this was a traveler's promise that would not be forgotten, and when five years later we made a film of the play we sent him a copy. Shortly after that, some of us returned to India. As we entered Kanchipuram a crowd of young people collected excitedly, recognizing the actors. "We saw the film!" "Where?" "At the temple." "Very nice movie!" We visited Shankaracharya, who was as active, humorous, and practical as before, and he told us he approved of our version. He was for us our ultimate critic, whom we both trusted and feared.

The more we entered into the *Mahabharata*, the more we came to recognize the richness and generosity of the original Hindu thought. One single untranslatable word, *dharma*, is sufficient to link the universal with the uniquely personal. The cosmos has its Dharma, and each individual has his or her own dharma; our obligation is to discover this, understand it, and make its realization our constant aim. The word is often feebly translated as "duty"; in fact, it implies living in accordance with an imperative that goes beyond all simple moral laws. Dharma respects each person's inborn limits, so each has his or her own starting point, and within the span of one life each man or woman can only go just so far. We each have our destiny, but few of us actually allow our destiny to appear. Dharma cannot be reduced to any code, but it can be reawakened in the puzzled seeker by the whole mythic action of the *Mahabharata*, which shows how an individual's dharma is related to the great Dharma, to the constant rebalancing of the scales of existence. In the *Mahabharata*, Krishna shows that to preserve the balance of the universe, everything must have its place. Sexuality, duplicity, violence—each has a meaning. Thus his unexpected and apparently immoral actions are a constant confrontation with rigid thinking and can even shock true Hindu believers. At a social gathering in Delhi, a distinguished lady burst into tears. "I can't bear the Krishna of the *Mahabharata*," she said to me. "He behaves so badly."

Such misinterpretations are part of the all-embracing nature of the *Mahabharata*, and in our rehearsals we were continually provoked by the contradictions that are part of this work. We often called it Shakespearean, because every schematic idea is blown open by the true humanity of the characters. This sets them beyond easy moralizing and facile judgments.

The journey with the actors to India was perhaps the most important part of our rehearsal process, not so much as a way of putting everyone "in the mood" but as a way of eliminating clichés about the East and about myths in general. Every moment brought a new surprise, a new contradiction, and although we traveled light, we returned to Paris with an excess of intellectual and emotional baggage.

Now the practical task was to find theatrical forms that would be suitable carriers for this load. More than ever in our work, it was clear that forms had to come last, that the true character of the performance would only emerge when a hodgepodge of styles had passed through a filter to eliminate the superfluous. Our only principle was first to discover meaning for ourselves, then find the action that makes it meaningful to others. So in this process nothing could be refused, everything had to be explored. We imitated ancient techniques, knowing that we would never be able to do them well. We fought, chanted, improvised, told stories, or we introduced fragments from each of the group's widely different traditions. The path passed through chaos and muddle toward order and coherence. But time worked for us. Suddenly the day came when the whole group found that it was telling the same story. The different races, the different traditions working together had become a single mirror for a multiplicity of themes.

A century ago the vision of history that ancient Hinduism proposed was quite unacceptable to the West, but its imagery and symbols are becoming more and more confirmed in the present-day world. The Hindu believes that, in the endless cycles of creation and annihilation, human beings rapidly reached the Golden Age, the first and highest Yuga from which the subsequent ones descend. The lowest, the fourth and last period, is the one in which we live today: Kali Yuga, the Black Age. This is not pessimism; reality can be neither optimistic nor pessimistic, it is as it is, and this is exactly why this myth is so relevant. All the stress and anguish, the violent misery and despair of contemporary life are reflected in the complex events of the great epic. Our world is sliding deeper and deeper into the bitter abominations that the *Mahabharata* predicted; the age of darkness is all around us, and with it we seem to reach the ultimate degradation of the human creature — far beyond all that the ancient authors could foresee.

Today, we have many astonishing films, plays, and novels on the horrors of war, but unlike them, the *Mahabharata* is not negative. It leads one into the basic meaning of conflict. It shows that the movements of history are inevitable, that great miseries and disasters may be unavoidable, but within each passing moment a new possibility can open, and life can still be lived in all its fullness. This can help us understand how to live. It can help us cross the darkest age. This alone was reason enough for staging the work. This is why, in French, then in English, touring across the world, and then on tape and on film, it seems to have touched a common human chord. How to survive is an urgent contemporary question, but it can easily cover up a far greater question, which the *Mahabharata* places firmly in its rightful place — not only how to survive, but why?

I had always rigorously avoided philosophical discussions within our group. In any event, the group was never permanent; people came and went, spending shorter or longer times together, each following his or her path. But for many, the accumulation of strange experiences made the question of the relationship between everyday life and work more and more acute. For Natasha, the African journey was the start of a process through which her fears gradually turned into a positive strength. The same fine sensibility that she brought to her daily activities became the firm center of her acting, leading from *The Cherry Orchard* to *Oh, Les Beaux Jours* — or *Happy Days*, as it is known in English — where she could fuse her private search for meaning with the painful self-questioning of Samuel Beckett, whom she so loved and admired. As for myself, I gradually moved from two rooms to one, from stage and auditorium to a shared experience. In the same way, the empty spaces within and without have taken on new meanings, and with each change I have seen that something has to be discarded. When the *Mahabharata* ended, I felt an intense need to move away from myths of the past, from historical subjects, from period costumes, from worlds of the imagination. Above all, I wanted to unload the cultural trappings that had gradually accumulated over so many years. Clearly, the present must always contain the past, and a great myth is a very precise way of expressing through symbolic language deeply hidden truths about the human condition. At the same time, a truth is merely a fantasy if it cannot be rediscovered and experienced directly within the ordinary actions of the present day.

Yet I clearly could not just choose any contemporary theme that preoccupied me, as the situations that we encounter all the time rarely contain dimensions that go beyond their familiar limits. Today, however, we have a new mythology. Science explores the same eternal mysteries with a new symbolic language, so I plunged into the fascinating world of quantum physics. The quantum world seemed at first to be as rich and as disturbing as mythic India, but I soon was forced to recognize that physicists themselves are very rarely as unusual as their discoveries, and charts, diagrams, calculations, and computers are hardly the human material that theater demands.

The contradiction was resolved when Natasha gave me for Christmas Oliver Sacks's book *The Man Who Mistook His Wife for a Hat*. Shortly afterward, Sacks took me to visit the neurological wards of his New York hospital. Here I was amazed to find, in the field of neurology, a legitimate basis for theater work. I began to sense why the great Russian neurologist Alexander Romanovitch Luria had called neurology a "romantic science." Throughout a long and active life in the dangerously shifting conditions of Soviet Russia, Luria had maintained that a human science that was coldly factual was incomplete. Indeed, he was passionately involved in examining every verifiable detail of how the body and brain operate, yet this was not enough. The human element only appeared when each individual was accepted as unique. Seen in this way, science certainly becomes "romantic," and the inner landscapes of the brain do indeed suggest what in another mythology — the Persian poem *The Conference of the Birds* — is called "the Valley of Astonishment." But if neurology is romantic, it is also very exact. As a science, it is far from the diffuse and unverifiable field of so-called madness we had explored in *Marat/Sade*. A neurological patient has a specific lesion in a precise place, and as a result his behavior changes. The neurologist has to develop to the finest degree his power of observation, as every tiny movement can be a clue to what is occurring somewhere, out of sight, in the brain. In the theater as well, behavior is our raw material, so as the basis of our new work, we could at last return to everyday life, distilling ordinary, recognizable movements down to their essence and observing the irregularities that show a hidden tremor in the brain.

We named the new project *The Man Who* and began in our usual way, improvising with Sacks's book in hand. To our dismay, we realized that none of our well-tried methods seemed to work. Our improvisations were empty, and even Jean-Claude found he could not keep from writing fiction. It became clear to us that the specific and frightening consequences of brain lesions cannot be discovered within even the most inventive imagination. We needed personal firsthand experiences to draw on, and as they were lacking, we grew discouraged and put the project aside.

Then suddenly Marie-Hélène Estienne fell ill, and her misfortune, gratefully short and not serious, proved to be our salvation. Finding herself in the great Paris hospital La Salpêtrière where in the nineteenth century Charcot had established a legendary neurological school, she preferred to talk to the professors about our difficulties rather than about her own ailments. As a result, she made many good friends among the medical staff, and soon we were being warmly received in the wards, given white gowns, and allowed to observe and question as much as we chose.

Now that we could make a fresh start, we reduced the group to the smallest possible team. The play thus became a truly collaborative creation among four dedicated actors—Yoshi Oida, Sotegui Kouyaté, Maurice Benichou, and David Bennent— along with the musician who had been especially close to us over the years, Mahmoud Tabrizi-Zadeh, as well as Marie-Hélène and myself. A new rhythm of work arose: we would spend part of the day in the hospital and then would come together in our rehearsal space to share our impressions with one another by acting them out. In this way, we were able to understand something of the conditions we witnessed by reliving them directly through our bodies.

We had returned to a principle that had guided us years before when we had studied forms of acute starvation, which none of us could ever have experienced, in order to make *The Ik*, a play about famine in Africa. Usually, actors speak of working "from the inside out," meaning that they dig for understanding in themselves before trying to project this outward in their acting. But understanding such starvation could only be achieved from the outside in. For a long period we had pored over photographs and fragments of film of the Ik people, paying great attention to every external detail, such as how the shriveled body manages to propel itself forward or what muscle enables a near-atrophied arm to lift a cupped hand filled with water to the lips. Now, for *The Man Who*, the process was similar.

In the hospital, we met patients whose disorders resembled nothing we had seen before, and we found ourselves once again in the valley of astonishment. We saw the mind painfully losing its faculties and then losing the memory of what it had lost or else compensating for the deficit with a sudden and unpredictable burst of excess. We followed the complex systems of adaptation through which an apparently diminished mind reconstructs a world in which it then lives to the full. The patients in many cases became our best allies, helping and correcting with interest and humor our imitations so that what we did became more and more faithful to their state. In this way, the outside form became increasingly real for the actors, and the more they entered it, the more their own imagination came to life and began to play a role. The patients were no longer "cases"; we could now feel the full and often rich human being within the restricted range of movements that we had first witnessed with such distress.

Then a more familiar work could begin, with Marie-Hélène writing and adapting the words we had heard spoken and the actors using their personal techniques to project convincingly to an outside observer the mysterious areas into which we had been led. As I watched our first run-through in front of an audience, there came a moment when I felt we had found a link with what we had attempted in Africa when we had first put a pair of shoes on the carpet in front of the audience in order to establish a common ground. In *The Man Who*, the pair of shoes was replaced by a table, a candle, and a box of matches. Yoshi Oida came to the table, lit the candle with special concentration, and then for a long time gazed intently at the flame. Then he blew it out, took another match, lit the candle, and blew it out again. As he started once more, I could feel the tension in the audience increasing. The audience could read into the simple actions far more than they apparently expressed; for this, the audience needed no preparation, no education, no reference, and above all no culture. It understood directly what was going on. We seemed at last to be approaching the transparency that for so long had been our aim.

Once in Italy I sat with a group of fellow directors in the canteen of a factory where a fine liqueur was being distilled. We agreed that our professional function was badly described in our various languages. I disliked the bosslike overtones of the English word *director*, the Frenchman felt the term *metteur-en-scène* was inadequate because it feebly suggested nothing more than a "putting on," the Swede found the Scandinavian term *instruktor* unhappily close to spartan physical training, while the German found *regisseur* merely evocative of a bookkeeper on a country estate. I suggested the French word *animateur* because calling on the "animus" would be a fine occupation, but the Frenchman shook his head; today this noble word has been downgraded to become simply the label for a youth-club leader. Then Ermanno Olmi, an Italian director whom I greatly admire, raised his finger, and as we listened to the throb and gurgle of the liqueur being squeezed from the grapes on the other side of the wall, he said, "I propose we call ourselves *distillatori!*" Distillers. We all agreed, awed by the challenge that the name implied.

An autobiography is like the life that furnishes its raw material. Both have to come to an end. But while life is just like crossing a river on a log—clutching a leaf, never knowing when one is going to fall—in a book one can choose the right moment to stop.

As I move toward a conclusion, I try to understand why I have come back to the theater so often, and the reason is simple. Theater is not just a place, not simply a profession. It is a metaphor. It helps to make the process of life more clear.

It is said that at its origin, theater was an act of healing, of healing the city. According to the action of fundamental, entropic forces, no city can avoid an inevitable process of fragmentation. But when the population assembles in a special place under special conditions to partake in a mystery, the scattered limbs are drawn together, and a momentary healing reunites the larger body, in which each member, re-membered, finds its place.

Hunger, violence, gratuitous cruelty, rape, crime—these are constant companions in the present time. Theater can penetrate into the darkest zones of terror and despair for one reason only: to be able to affirm, neither before nor after but at the very same moment, that light is present in darkness. Progress may have become an empty concept, but evolution is not, and although evolution can take millions of years, the theater can free us from this time frame. As the old saying goes, "If not now, when?"

Through the remarkable people I have met, I have reached only one luminous certitude. Quality is real and has a source. At every moment a new and unexpected quality can arise within a human action — and just as quickly it can be lost, found, and lost again. This unnameable value can be betrayed by religion and by philosophy; churches and temples can betray it; the faithful and the unfaithful betray it all the time. Still, the hidden source remains. Quality is sacred, but it is always in danger.

I have witnessed no miracles, but I have seen that remarkable men and women do exist, remarkable because of the degree to which they have worked on themselves in their lives. This is my only certainty, and it has been the quest for this "something" elusive that has guided me, however often it has been forgotten or ignored. When I was small, nothing enraged me more than to hear grown-ups say that with age they understood less and less. Now I look at my own experience and feel the intimate rightness of Lear's words: "I have taken too little care of this." As I grew older, I hated above all else piety and head-bowed humility, yet today it is clear that one's isolated efforts are straws in the wind, and we can do nothing alone — we need others, all the time. When I first became articulate, I felt that everything could be explained; now I see what a disservice I would commit if I attempted to explain here in a few neat phrases what has guided me over the years, because I do not even know. Not knowing is not resignation; it is an opening to amazement. Joyfully, I have tried to lead others or have tried to do things alone, and inevitably this attitude has had to bow before the always uncomfortable truth that we only begin to exist when we are serving an aim beyond our own likes and aversions.

Nothing changes. Life is not a straight line, and the material in the pages of this book recurs all the time; only the order is shuffled and the balance shifts. There will always be new projects, new directions, new enthusiasms. I will still cling uselessly to a leaf, my horses will continue to gallop in opposite directions, leaping and falling, a glittering piece of red tin will be as seductive as something of infinite value, and a voice will often murmur, "If you let this moment pass, it will never come again."

When I was young I used to think, "It's possible to 'get there' spiritually within one's lifetime"; in fact, I felt a moral obligation to accomplish an inner "getting there" before it was too late. Then as the nature of our human condition became clearer, this was replaced by the more realistic thought that "it would need several lifetimes." But bit by bit, common sense has prevailed and shows that one is no more than a fleeting particle within a humanity that is struggling, groping, rising, and falling endlessly, searching for a "there" that in the whole future course of human history it may never know.

Yet at any moment, we can find a new beginning. A beginning has the purity of innocence and the unqualified freedom of the beginner's mind. Development is more difficult, for the parasites, the confusions, the complications, and the excesses of the world swarm in when innocence gives way to experience. Ending is hardest of all, yet letting go gives the only true taste of freedom. Then the end becomes a beginning once more, and life has the last word.

In an African village, when a storyteller comes to the end of his tale, he places the palm of his hand on the ground and says, "I put down my story here." Then he adds, "So that someone else may take it up another day."

Index

Index

Index